Control Your Retirement Destiny

Second Edition

Achieving Financial Security Before the Big Transition

By Dana Anspach

aBM

Published by:

A Book's Mind
PO Box 272847
Fort Collins, CO 80527

www.abooksmind.com

Copyright © 2016 Dana Anspach

ISBN: 978-1-944255-23-7

Library of Congress Control Number: 2017936252

Printed in the United States of America

"If you don't design your own life plan, chances are you'll fall into someone else's plan. And guess what they have planned for you? Not much."

-Jim Rohn

Contents

Disclosures

Dedication

To Francois Gadenne, and The View Across the Silos

About the Author

Since 2008, Dana Anspach has been writing for About.com as their Money-Over55 Expert. The MoneyOver55 content can now be found on The Balance (www.thebalance.com), where Dana writes as their Expert on Retirement Decisions. She also contributes to MarketWatch as one of their RetireMentors.

Anspach has been practicing as a financial planner since 1995, and founded Sensible Money, LLC (www.sensiblemoney.com) in 2011. Sensible Money is a registered investment advisory firm in Scottsdale, Arizona, with a developed specialty in the area of retirement income planning.

Dana is a Certified Financial Planner, Retirement Management Analyst, a Kolbe Certified Consultant, and a member of NAPFA (National Association of Personal Financial Advisors), FPA (Financial Planning Association), and RIIA (Retirement Income Industry Association).

As an expert in her field, she has spoken for numerous organizations, associations, and conferences on the topic of retirement planning and interacts regularly with readers and clients on these topics. Anspach believes the retirement income planning process is not static; it is alive with choices and variables. To make the best decisions, consumers need a way to understand the interactions of the choices they make and the corresponding impact on their future. To trust the information they see, they need an independent voice that provides information free of the influence of politics, financial products, or media articles that are advertising in disguise. As her clients can tell you, Dana Anspach is that independent voice.

Note From the Author

Some of you have been following my work for years. Thank you for all your kind words. And thank you to those of you who take the time to send corrections. If you spot a potential error, feel free to email me at <u>moneyover55@</u> <u>gmail.com</u> with the subject line "CYRD2 correction".

It takes an entire team of people to proof a book that has technical information. We have done our best to make sure everything is accurate, but there can be no guarantee that we have not made errors. And of course the laws and rules can change at any time.

This second edition has been updated with 2016 tax rules, easier-to-read examples, new content in many chapters, and an entirely new chapter on estate planning. I think you'll find it a valuable resource that you turn to many times.

Acknowledgements

To my first financial planner, Les Zetmeir. You started it all. You showed me what financial planning is really all about.

Francois Gadenne, this project would never have come about if it weren't for RIIA and the RMA® designation. Thank you for all the work you do for our industry, and for truly offering a View Across the Silos.

To my team at Sensible Money; Jody Hulsey, Brian Duvall, Kathy Mealey, Chuck Robinson, and Suzanne Nagel - I could not have completed this without you. Thank you for your support, hard work, and your amazing dedication to our clients. Brian, thank you for your detailed review of my examples.

Wade Pfau, Moshe Milevsky, Michael Kitces, Carl Richards, Mike Piper, and Dirk Cotton - thank you for being an inspiration to me, each in a different way.

Joe Elsasser, thank you for always answering my Social Security questions so thoroughly and promptly.

Stephen Huxley, thank you for your comments and review of Chapter 5.

Jeff Carman, thank you for always answering my life insurance questions so thoroughly and promptly and for your review of Chapter 6.

Scott Stolz, thank you for your review and comments on the use of annuities in Chapter 8.

Dan McGrath and Hank Segal, thank you for your insights and comments on Chapter 10.

Nicole Gurley, thank you for your input, review, quotes, contributions, and incredible thoroughness in regards to the long-term care section in Chapter 10.

Larry Kotlikoff, thank you for all of our conversations, for allowing me to run scenarios using your software, and most of all for encouraging me to continue my work.

Darra Rayndon, thank you for taking the time to read and send me your comments on Chapter 13. Your time was most appreciated.

Preface

This book is not about saving money. It's about saving the right way. It's about doing more with what you already have. And it's about aligning your financial decisions toward a common goal; creating reliable life-long income.

You'll read stories about people just like you. You'll see examples—with numbers—explaining why something works, or perhaps doesn't work. You'll learn how to create a plan and use it to compare various financial scenarios.

You'll learn which factors you can control, and which ones you can't, so you can focus on what matters. And when you're done, you won't be done. You'll be beginning a journey—a journey of using your money as the valued resource that it is; a resource that can allow you to pursue those things that are nearest and dearest to your heart, whatever they may be.

I'd recommend you start at the beginning, and for the most part, read in order—with one exception. If you're still many, many years away from your earliest Social Security claiming age (which is 62 for most people and 60 for widow/widowers), then you may want to simply scan Chapter 3 and keep going. It gets kind of technical, and the techie stuff won't apply to you till you're older. But that's the only break you get! The rest of the chapters are appropriate for all, and you're bound to learn something that is going to be valuable for you. (And even with the Social Security chapter, you may learn something that can help out a neighbor, friend or co-worker.)

So, no time to waste. Let's get started. It is time to take control of your retirement destiny.

Chapter 1

Your Finances

Why It's Different Over 50

"The question isn't at what age I want to retire, it's at what income."

—*George Foreman*

There I was sitting across the table from Jay. He and his wife Sally were wondering if they could go from full-time to part-time work, or perhaps leave the workforce altogether.

Jay said to me, "You realize if I do this, I can't go back? I won't be working anymore. We'll be living off our acorns. This has to work. It's different than when I was 40 and I had my career ahead of me. Do you understand that?"

Whenever someone says such things in my office, which is relatively often, I am amused. For the last 20 years, I have spent nearly every day helping people align their financial decisions around the goal of allowing them a smooth transition out of the workforce. The people who come to see me know this is what I do. Yet they still feel compelled to remind me that if they retire they will be living off their savings.

I understand. You save money, and then save more money. And then one day you are faced with the prospect of having to start withdrawing some of those savings each and every year. It's scary.

I try to address this scariness: "Jay, I know the transition is scary. You've saved this money your whole life. Starting to spend that savings brings up a whole slew of emotions, and it is normal to wonder how—and if—this is all going to work. I can assure you that it will, if you follow the plan we develop."

As you'll see, having a plan is the key to a successful transition out of the workforce. Your plan must encompass far more than how much you have saved and what types of investments you own. All of your financial decisions must be aligned to work together.

Note   Having a plan is the key to a successful transition out of the work force.

This means considering taxes, Social Security, health care expenses, pensions, lifestyle decisions, home ownership, investment risks, age differences between spouses, and more. You must consider all these items in context. It makes no sense to look at them in isolation. You have to look at how they can work together to deliver a secure outcome.

The planning needs to be different when you reach 50 and beyond. You face a new set of challenges, and traditional planning often neglects to address them in a meaningful way. These challenges are:

- Longevity risk

- Sequence risk

- Inflation risk

- Overspending risk

Let's look at each of these in detail.

Challenge One: Longevity—An Unknown Time Horizon

Have you ever planned a road trip? It's fairly easy math to determine that if you are going 300 miles, your gas tank holds 15 gallons, and your vehicle averages about 20 miles per gallon, that you can get to your destination on one tank.

Yet you may want some wiggle room. Most vehicles get better mileage on the highway than in the city. If you know part of your trip will be city driving, maybe you'll want to fill up the tank halfway through the trip, just to be sure.

Now suppose you don't know how far away your destination is or how much of the driving will be city driving verses highway driving. The only thing you know is there won't be any gas stations along the way. How much gas do you take then? Do you stock up on gas or get a more fuel-efficient car? Or both?

This is the challenge you face as you plan a transition into retirement. Do you need income for 20 years or 30? What about your spouse? Is he or she significantly younger or older than you? What investment returns and savings rates will you experience along the way?

When making the transition to retirement, you are headed out on a road trip. You don't know how long the trip will be, nor can you predict the conditions you will encounter. It sounds scary, but really, is it all that different than it was when you turned 18? Or when you started your first job? Or had your first child?

I would argue you have an advantage now. You have years of experience to draw from and the ability to lay out a plan that leaves wiggle room for life's unknowns. It starts by creating a model, or projection, of what the future may bring.

When I do financial modeling for people, I start with a series of default assumptions. In my initial scenario I have males living to 85 and females to 90. Without fail, about once a week someone looks at me with big eyes and says, "Well, I'll never live that long."

I look back and say, "What if you do?" It is my job to think about the future you.

Note	What might the 84-year-old you wish the 52-year-old you had done? What decisions might the 92-year-old you wish the 63-year-old you had made?

These are the questions a good planning process must ask and answer.

Longevity risk is the technical term for the challenge of charting a path into a trip of unknown duration. It is a fancy way of saying that you have a finite set of resources that must last for an unknown amount of time.

As with other forms of risk, you have your own tolerance of longevity risk. Some will want to diligently plan so the 92-year-old you will be in great shape. Others will prefer to let the 63-year-old you have a little more play money.

The choice is a personal one. To choose in a personal way, you have to explore what your road trip might look like from many angles.

There are some decisions you can make that can help protect the 92-year-old you while allowing the 63-year-old you to continue to have fun. Making these decisions appropriately takes analysis.

Many decisions can improve your ability to spend today while also increasing the likelihood that your future income remains sufficient. You must approach these decisions with an open mind.

Learning to Use the Right Tool

You must also be willing to let go of any misinformation you may have accumulated.

For example, suppose I told you that you will need a Phillips head screwdriver to accomplish your goals. In response, you exclaim, "I've heard Phillips head screwdrivers are terrible. No way would I use one." Sounds silly, right? Yet every day I propose solutions that will work, and I get such responses, most frequently around the topics of Social Security, reverse mortgages, annuities, and stocks. These are tools too, just like a Phillips head screwdriver.

You have likely heard stories or read inaccurate information that has affected your opinion about one or more of the tools I discuss in this book. A tool is neither good nor bad. It has a function. Once you understand the function, you know when the tool is appropriate for the job at hand.

When it comes to longevity risk, there are tools that can help you achieve the dual goals of spending today while protecting the ability to continue spending later. Such tools include:

- Delaying the start date of your Social Security benefits
- Working longer
- Buying an annuity
- Using a reverse mortgage
- Choosing investments that offer inflation protection

How do you employ these planning tools in an appropriate way? By the end of this book, you'll know.

REAL LIFE: TOM AND TARA

Tom came to see me at age 55. He was a successful attorney. His practice was being sold to a larger firm, and he would be continuing on in a salaried position. He had some retirement savings and a lump sum coming in from the sale of his practice.

As a high income earner, he thought it would be relatively easy to save sufficient assets for retirement over the next ten years. There was only one catch: his wife Tara was 40, and they had a two-year-old son. His income and savings needed to provide for a much longer time span than it would for a couple closer in age.

In their case, the solution was the appropriate use of life insurance along with some revised spending habits. They were used to traveling, eating out, and maintaining homes in two locations. As we developed their plan, they realized they both wanted to enjoy some retirement years together. In order to do so, they committed to making substantial changes to their current spending habits in order to save more.

Couples with such a big age difference may be rare, but it is common to see couples with a spouse three to ten years younger. Women live longer than men, so longevity risk takes on increased importance for couples where the wife is younger by several years.

What Do the Odds Tell You?

Figure 1-1 is a graph of life expectancy probabilities.[1] Based on a male and female each age 62 today, it shows their respective probabilities of living to a particular age. Age is the horizontal axis. Couples should focus on the Either line. You can see that, at any age, there is a higher probability that either of you will live to a particular age, which means your resources have a potentially longer time horizon when planning for two.

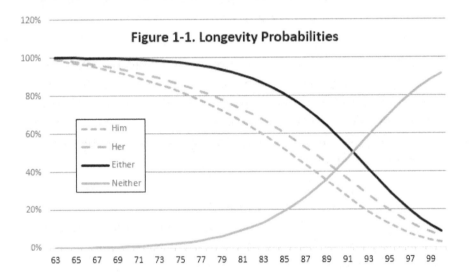

Figure 1-1. Longevity Probabilities

The crossover point—where the odds that neither of you is alive exceed the odds that one of you is alive—occurs at age 92. Planning for the possibility that you, or if married, one of you, will live past 90 is important,

Suppose you were the betting type. You have a decision to make, such as when to begin Social Security or whether to buy an income annuity. You want to look at the odds to see which way you should bet your money.

- The odds tell you that if you and your spouse are both 62 today, there is an 81% chance that one or the other of you will still be going strong at 85.

---

1   Figure 1-1 derived from a spreadsheet developed by David E. Hultstrom of Financial Archi-
tects, LLC, using RP 2014 Mortality tables. David provides financial planning in Woodstock,
Georgia.

- The odds tell you there is a 2% probability that neither of you will still be here at 75.

You would think you would make the decision that would put you in a more secure position 81% of the time, but many people do not look at it this way. We have a tendency to place more value on a dollar of spending today than a dollar of spending in the future. That can hurt you in the long run. When it comes to retirement planning, it's good to play the odds.

Playing the odds means you can't look at each decision in terms of an expected rate of return. Instead you have to determine which type of risk each decision protects against. I've watched many people struggle with this concept as they enter retirement. Some people are so focused on achieving a rate of return objective that they make decisions that put their retirement security at significant risk.

Challenge Two: Sequence Risk—The Gas Mileage Question

In addition to an unknown time horizon, you face unknown "driving" conditions. You don't know how many miles per gallon you're going to get along the way. In other words, you don't know what rate of return your savings and investments will earn.

Will you enjoy a long period of highway driving, as we saw in the 1980s and 1990s, with decent savings rates and strong returns on invested assets like stocks and bonds? Or will you suffer the inefficiency of city driving—a decade or two of low interest rates and mediocre returns?

You might have a period of great returns followed by a period of poor returns, or vice versa. The order in which your returns occur has a big impact on your future standard of living. This is called *sequence risk*, and there is no effective way to explain it without looking at the math.

History provides great examples of sequence risk. The average annualized return of the S&P 500 Index from 1973–1982 was 6.7%.[2] A software program using this average return would show funds growing, as you see in the second column of Table 1-1. Actual results are reflected in the third column.

2 Returns from Dimensional Fund Advisors, *DFA Matrix Book 2012* (Austin, TX: Dimensional Fund Advisors, 2012).

Table 1-1. Year-end balances for growth of $100,000 initial investment based on 6.7% annualized returns and real historical returns

Calendar Year	End of Year Balance @ 6.7%	End of Year Balance Actual	S&P 500 Return (%)
1973	$106,700	$85,300	−14.7
1974	$113,849	$62,696	−26.5
1975	$121,477	$86,018	37.2
1976	$129,616	$106,491	23.8
1977	$138,300	$98,823	−7.2
1978	$147,566	$105,346	6.6
1979	$157,453	$124,729	18.4
1980	$168,002	$165,141	32.4
1981	$179,258	$157,049	−4.9
1982	$191,269	$190,658	21.4

Table 1-2. Year-end balances after a year-end withdrawal of $6,000, based on $100,000 initial investment at 6.7% annualized returns and real historical returns

Calendar Year	Annual Income Withdrawn	End of Year Balance @ 6.7%	End of Year Balance Actual	Difference
1973	$6,000	$100,700	$79,300	($21,400)
1974	$6,000	$101,447	$52,286	($49,161)
1975	$6,000	$102,244	$65,736	($36,508)
1976	$6,000	$103,094	$75,381	($27,713)
1977	$6,000	$104,001	$63,953	($40,048)
1978	$6,000	$104,970	$62,174	($42,796)
1979	$6,000	$106,003	$67,614	($38,389)
1980	$6,000	$107,105	$83,521	($23,584)
1981	$6,000	$108,281	$73,429	($34,852)
1982	$6,000	$109,536	$83,143	($26,393)

Whether using average returns or actual returns, you ended up with around $190,000.

But remember, you'll be withdrawing income. Table 1-2 shows the results after taking out $6,000 per year.

In the example in Table 1-2, the difference in ending account value based on averages verses actual market returns is $26,000. The sequence, or order in which the returns occurred, left you with 24% less money than a projection based on averages said you would have. Now you know why it's called sequence risk!

Average returns can provide a misleading picture of what might happen. Yet financial-planning software and online calculators often run scenarios using average returns.

A series of poor returns early in your retirement years, once you start taking income, can have an exponential effect. If you have a sequence of bad returns early on, and you are withdrawing income each year, your future portfolio will look far different than if you had a sequence of good returns early on—even if, over time, the average annualized returns for both time periods are identical.

This example illustrates the effect the order of annual returns can have, and for simplicity's sake I am basing it on one stock market index. No prudent person would invest their retirement savings in just one stock market index.

CD (certificate of deposit) investors could have experienced a poor outcome for different reasons. Table 1-3 shows three-month CD rates[3] from 2000–2015.

---

3   Data from the Certificate of Deposit Index (CODI) which is the 12 month average of nationally published 3-Month Certificate of Deposit rates. Data downloaded from http://mortgage-x.com/general/indexes/.

Table 1-3. Average three-month CD rates, 2000–2015

Calendar Year	Average 3 month CD rates (%)	Annual Income per $100,000
2000	5.23	$5,230
2001	6.09	$6,090
2002	5.10	$5,100
2003	2.18	$2,180
2004	1.35	$1,350
2005	1.27	$1,270
2006	2.75	$2,750
2007	4.63	$4,630
2008	5.30	$5,300
2009	3.85	$3,850
2010	1.52	$1,520
2011	0.31	$310
2012	0.30	$300
2013	0.32	$320
2014	0.15	$150
2015	0.07	$70

As you can see, planning for a stable income can be difficult when the annual interest you might earn per $100,000 of savings can vary from $6,090 to $70.

An unfortunate order of returns occurs for reasons outside your control. These can include poor economic conditions or lower interest rates. But you sometimes play a part as well, by making poor investment choices. Whatever the reason, the effect is the same.

To minimize the effect of sequence risk, you must invest differently. You have several choices:

- Take no market risk and choose only safe, guaranteed investments, which may require saving more to reach your goal.

- Segment your investments into what is needed for different legs of your trip: short, medium, and long term.

- Create a reserve account that can be used in low-return years.

- Use a disciplined rebalancing process.

All of these choices involve creating and sticking to an investment plan that is designed to reduce your exposure to sequence risk. Chapter 5 is devoted to exploring these various approaches.

Challenge Three: Inflation

There is no question prices will increase. As a result, everyone understands *inflation risk*. There is a question as to how much of an effect inflation will have on you once you are retired. You have your own unique spending patterns, and a one-size-fits-all rule won't work.

The standard rule of thumb is to assume a 3% inflation rate. In Table 1-4, you see $10,000 in 1990, steadily increasing at 3% per year. In the next column you see that $10,000 increasing at the actual rate of inflation as measured by the Consumer Price Index.[4] The numbers show that in 2015 it took about $18,768 to buy what $10,000 could buy in 1990. Notice that over these 26 years, real inflation has been less than a 3% annual increase.

---

4   CPI rates from DFA's *Matrix Book 2016*, p. 53.

Table 1-4. Twenty-six years of inflation data

Calendar Year	$10,000 inflated at steady 3%	$10,000 inflated at real inflation rates	Real inflation rates (%)
1990	$10,300	$10,610	6.1
1991	$10,609	$10,939	3.1
1992	$10,927	$11,256	2.9
1993	$11,255	$11,560	2.7
1994	$11,593	$11,872	2.7
1995	$11,941	$12,169	2.5
1996	$12,299	$12,571	3.3
1997	$12,668	$12,784	1.7
1998	$13,048	$12,989	1.6
1999	$13,439	$13,340	2.7
2000	$13,842	$13,793	3.4
2001	$14,258	$14,014	1.6
2002	$14,685	$14,350	2.4
2003	$15,126	$14,623	1.9
2004	$15,580	$15,105	3.3
2005	$16,047	$15,619	3.4
2006	$16,528	$16,009	2.5
2007	$17,024	$16,666	4.1
2008	$17,535	$16,682	0.1
2009	$18,061	$17,133	2.7
2010	$18,603	$17,390	1.5
2011	$19,161	$17,911	3.0
2012	$19,736	$18,216	1.7
2013	$20,328	$18,489	1.5
2014	$20,938	$18,637	0.8
2015	$21,566	$18,768	0.7

If prices have almost doubled over the last 26 years, do retirees in their 80s spend twice as much as they did in their 60s? The answer seems to be no.

Ty Bernicke looked at U.S. Bureau of Labor's consumer expenditure data and concluded, "Traditional retirement planning assumes that a household's expenditures will increase a certain amount each year throughout retirement. Yet data from the U.S. Bureau of Labor's Consumer Expenditure Survey show that household expenditures actually decline as retirees age."[5]

The decrease in spending that occurs as one moves into later decades was observed across all major categories, with the exception of health care. Health care expenditures increased as one aged, but spending in other areas declined enough to more than offset the increase in health care expenses.

Some might say this decline in spending occurs out of necessity, because retirees who have less are forced to spend less. This does not seem to be the case, however, as total spending was observed to decline even while net worth was increasing.

Similar research was conducted by David Blanchett, head of retirement research for Morningstar, and published in a 2013 paper titled *Estimating the True Cost of Retirement.*[6] David found consumption to exhibit a pattern where it decreases in mid retirement, then increases in later-life years due to health care costs. He also found that retiree expenditures do not, on average, increase each year by inflation and that lower income/lower net worth retirees have a far greater need for their spending to keep up with inflation than do higher income/higher net worth retirees.

The conclusion: although prices on individual items will increase, retirees who spend on average $50,000 per year or more in retirement are not likely to need their income to increase each year at the same rate as inflation. Planning for a steady 3%-per-year increase in total spending needs may result in over-saving for retirement.

---

5   Ty Bernicke, "Reality Retirement Planning: A New Paradigm for an Old Science," *Journal of Financial Planning* vol. 18-6 (2005): 56.
6   https://corporate.morningstar.com/ib/documents/methodologydocuments/research papers/blanchett_true-cost-of-retirement.pdf

Note	Inflation has a bigger negative impact on low-income households than on high-income households.

Like other aspects of your plan, you need to look at inflation needs on a personal basis. If your income amply covers the basics and leaves you with spending money to spare, when prices rise you'll have room in your budget to cut back on discretionary spending items (although you may not want to).

If you live on a tight budget, mild price increases on necessities such as food, household items, and health care may have a bigger impact on you.

Factoring the effects of inflation into your planning decisions is important. Here are some options that can improve your ability to adjust to rising prices:

- Delay the start date of your Social Security benefits.

- Grow your own food.

- Choose an energy-efficient lifestyle.

- Use savings vehicles that have an interest rate that adjusts with inflation, such as I-Bonds or TIPS (Treasury Inflation-Protected Securities).

With a rapidly growing global population, you may see prices rise more quickly on food and energy items than on consumer durable items like furniture and electronics. In your post-work years, you are less likely to spend as much on furniture, electronics, and clothing; but you will most certainly be consuming food and energy.

If your financial resources are limited, you may want to focus your efforts around finding a home that is energy efficient, has access to public transportation, and has a yard conducive to growing basic food items. The time invested in such planning is likely to deliver a far higher return than trying to find the best mutual fund.

Challenge Four: Overspending Risk

There are things you can control, and things you can't. One of my frustrations with the media—and with the financial services industry—is that they are so good at getting you to focus your efforts and energy on the wrong things.

Look at Figure 1-2, which I call the *control box*. The bottom right-hand corner represents the things that you have the least control over and that have the lowest impact on your long-term success.

Figure 1-2. The control box helps you see where to focus your financial-planning efforts.

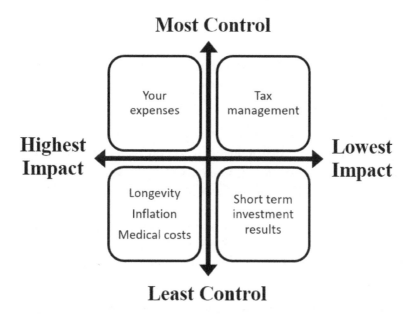

Most Control

Your expenses

Tax management

Highest Impact

Lowest Impact

Longevity
Inflation
Medical costs

Short term investment results

Least Control

The top left-hand corner is where you have both control and impact: your expenses. It's also where a lurking problem resides for many: *overspending risk*.

Accounting for future spending is a challenge. Twenty years ago, could you have told me what you would spend each year going forward?

You may spend more in your first few years out of the work force, perhaps traveling and diving into new hobbies. Others may spend less than they did while working, perhaps by downsizing and enjoying a simpler, less-demanding lifestyle.

Estimating post-work spending is most certainly a case where a one-size-fits-all rule doesn't work. Your expenses will vary depending on your chosen lifestyle. Your choices will vary depending on your values.

Suppose after analysis you discover you can retire five years earlier if you are willing to spend $10,000 a year less? You may willingly find a way to downsize your lifestyle in order to exit the work force early. Or you may look at this trade-off and choose to work longer to insure a continued higher standard of living well into your later years.

Health care spending is another unknown. If you want to exit the work force before age 65 (when Medicare coverage begins), you must accurately estimate and account for the cost of insurance, which can be hefty.

After Medicare begins, you still have Medicare Part B premiums and Medicare Part D drug coverage premiums, and if you want to be fully insured you'll also be paying premiums for a Medicare Supplement or a Medicare Advantage plan, as well as long-term care insurance.

When you create a model that determines how successfully your finances can meet your future needs, that model is based on a specific amount of annual spending. At some income levels, spending $5,000 a year more than what is projected in your model means your plan may not work, and the 78-year-old or 82-year-old you may be in trouble.

Overspending doesn't always come from spending too much on extras like travel, hobbies, eating out, and such. It can come from inaccurately projecting what you will need.

A successful spending plan needs flexibility built in. Just like now, in retirement you will not spend exactly the same amount each and every year. You need some wiggle room.

These action items can help you avoid overspending in retirement:

- Estimate current spending and compare that to a post-work spending projection that includes changes based on planned lifestyle decisions
- Build in estimates for health care costs
- Track spending in relation to your long-term plan
- Take corrective measures when overspending occurs
- Accurately project taxes in retirement

In Chapter 2, you'll begin to incorporate these actions into your plan.

A Note on Estimating Taxes

A spending plan is incomplete until it incorporates taxes. Tax management is another area in which you have some control, but accurately estimating taxes in retirement can be tricky. Many people make mistakes in this area when they run financial projections.

Here are a few areas where taxes get overlooked:

- When using a popular rule-of-thumb called the 4% *rule* to gauge how much cash flow you'll have available. The 4% rule would lead you to believe you can safely withdraw $4,000 per $100,000 of capital. However, if this $100,000 is in an IRA, 401(k), 403(b) or other tax-deferred retirement plan, then after taxes you may only get to keep $2,000 - $3,500 of each $4,000 withdrawal.

- Each withdrawal from a Traditional IRA, 401(k), or other tax-deferred account[7] is taxed at your ordinary income tax rate. These withdrawals may make more of your Social Security income taxable, causing your marginal tax rate to be higher than what a glance at the tax tables would lead you to think.

- At age 70½, you are required to take withdrawals from retirement accounts like IRAs and 401(k)s. This requirement—called a *required minimum distribution*—creates an increase in taxable income and may cause other sources of income you have to be taxed at a higher rate.

- Upon the death of a spouse, your tax filing status changes from married to single, leaving many spouses with less after-tax income because of the change in filing status.

- If you have money in after-tax savings and in pre-tax retirement accounts, the decision about when to withdraw money from which type of account will affect the amount of taxes you pay each year.

---

7 Roth IRA withdrawals are generally tax-free if you follow the rules, and they are not included in the formula that determines the amount of your Social Security that will be subject to income taxes.

As things stand today, many financial services companies and advisors do not incorporate tax planning into their processes. How can you deliver appropriate advice without looking at someone's entire household financial situation, including taxes? I don't think you can.

Although you can't control taxes, you can manage taxes in a way that may deliver more after-tax income.

In Chapter 4, I will teach you how to take taxes into consideration as you go forward into your transitional years and which factors play a role in reducing taxes and maximizing your after-tax income. I'm also going to encourage you to use software or seek professional advice to make sure your numbers are accurate.

Summary

Your financial planning should be noticeably different as you move into your 50s and beyond. A well-designed scenario accounts for all of the following:

- *Longevity risk:* The potential for a long-lived you and/or a long-lived spouse

- *Sequence risk:* The unknown order of investment returns and interest rates

- *Inflation risk:* Increases in prices, particularly on necessities such as food, energy, and health care

- *Overspending risk:* Miscalculating what you may need to spend and thus spending down savings too quickly in retirement

To appropriately align your finances for a transition out of the work force, and to account for these new challenges, you need to look at the financial resources of your entire household. This is the only approach that makes sense.

You'll learn how to do this in Chapter 2.

Chapter 2

Starting With Planning Basics

The Balance Sheet, Income Timeline, and Spending Plan

"If you don't design your own life plan, chances are you'll fall into someone else's plan. And guess what they have planned for you? Not much."

—Jim Rohn

I worked in a CPA firm for several years. One year, one of the managing partners announced he was leaving. Knowing I was responsible for financial services at the firm, and thinking I might be interested, he stopped by a few days after the announcement to tell me his story.

He said his success story began five years prior when he put together his first personal balance sheet. A simple list of everything he owned, minus everything he owed. After adding it all up, he saw he was in a hole. He earned an attractive salary, but he wasn't using the money wisely.

He started tracking his net worth diligently. He watched as he paid down debts and accumulated savings. He then started looking for investment opportunities. He was lucky enough to catch the real estate market on its upswing (yes, before 2007), and in five years his net worth went from negative to over $10 million.

We can't all get to $10 million in five years. But we can all use a personal balance sheet to improve where we're going.

Tip   Use a personal balance sheet to get to an improved place. When you focus on your numbers on a regular basis, reaching financial goals becomes much easier.

On a smaller scale, I used the same concept to dig myself out of a hole. I had taken a 100% commission job that wasn't working out so well. I had moved across the country, depleted my savings, and was rapidly racking up debt. I thought about the CPA's story.

I started adding up my debts. I had over $25,000 in credit card debt and no savings. I remember feeling physical pain as I looked at the situation. I began to diligently track my spending and pay down more debt. Each month when the credit card statements came in, I dutifully recorded the new lower balance. Sometimes it seemed as if the debt was only inching down. At other times seeing the progress that was being made motivated me to pay down debt faster.

Today the credit card debt is gone, and in place of tracking debt, I track my net worth. Updating it is a simple process of recording account balances at the end of each quarter.

Sometimes getting started is painful. If you are not where you want to be at this point in your life it can be difficult to sit down and take a detailed look at your finances. If you are reluctant, work through it, and do it anyway. It's worth it.

It is also easy to get sidetracked by questions and want quick, easy answers. I receive weekly e-mail inquiries from people who want my opinion on an investment they own or an annuity they are considering. Sometimes they want to know if they should buy long-term care insurance or when they should begin their Social Security benefits.

Would you think of e-mailing a doctor you don't know and saying, "Hey doc, what medicine should I be taking?"

That's how these questions sound to me—completely out of place.

I am always tempted to respond with something along the lines of, "How the heck should I know? I don't know you." I don't like to make recommendations without a comprehensive plan.

Your money has a job to do for you. To pick an investment effectively, you must define that job and the future role that money needs to fulfill. To define the job your money has, you must start with an accurate picture of the whole spectrum of financial resources you have.

Tracking your net worth is the starting point for getting a handle on your entire household financial situation. You have to take stock of what you have to work with.

Throughout this chapter and book, you'll find exercises and examples to help you do that. You may find it beneficial to read through them without stopping to complete the worksheets and, after you have finished the book, circle back and go through the exercises one by one. Or you may feel compelled to complete the exercises as you go along. There is no right or wrong way to do it.

Whether you do the exercises now or later—and whether you use online tools, an Excel spreadsheet, Quicken or other software programs, or professional advisors—the basics matter, and this chapter is about the basics. In addition to covering the basics, this chapter briefly introduces you to many topics that will be covered in additional depth later. When aligning your financial decisions toward a common goal, a decision in one area affects the results in another. By starting with the basics, you will begin to see how it all works. Once you have the big picture in place, you can dive into the details and complexities of individual decisions.

Your Personal Balance Sheet

A company must keep a balance sheet, a complete list of its assets and liabilities. Financial planning starts the same way, by creating a personal balance sheet. It is a snapshot of your financial situation at a given point in time.

Take a look at Figure 2-1, a personal balance sheet for Wally and Sally. Keep in mind that net worth is simply all your assets (investment accounts, house, and so on) minus all your liabilities (mortgage, credit card debt, car loan, and so forth).

Once you have a personal balance sheet, you can use it to track and monitor your progress toward a goal.

To prepare your personal balance sheet, gather the following documents, or have your logins and passwords available to access the information online:

- Bank statements
- Investment account statements
- Mortgage statements
- Retirement account statements

Figure 2-1
Wally & Sally's Personal Balance Sheet as of January 1, 2016

	Asset	Liability	Net Worth
A. ACCESSIBLE SAVINGS/INVESTMENTS			
Bank Accounts			
Checking	$7,500	0	$7,500
Savings/Credit Unions	20,000	0	20,000
Certificates of Deposit	0	0	0
Consumer Debt			
Credit card	0	0	0
Other Non-Retirement Savings			
Money Market accounts	48,000	0	48,000
Gov't Bonds (I, EE, H bonds)	0	0	0
Stocks	0	0	0
Brokerage accounts	0	0	0
Mutual fund accounts	246,000	0	246,000
Life Insurance Cash Value	0	0	0
A. TOTAL	**$321,500**	**$0**	**$321,500**
B. RETIREMENT ACCOUNTS			
Retirement Accounts 1:			
401k - Wally	0	0	0
IRA - Wally	365,000	0	365,000
Retirement Accounts 2:			
403(b) - Sally	546,000	0	546,000
B. TOTAL RETIREMENT	**$911,000**	**$0**	**$911,000**
C. REAL ESTATE & OTHER			
Residence	295,000	0	295,000
C. TOTAL REAL ESTATE & OTHER	**$295,000**	**$0**	**$295,000**
TOTAL ASSETS (A+B+C)	**$1,527,500**	**$0**	**$1,527,500**

Use the following guidelines to list your financial resources in order of how easily accessible they are:

1. *Accessible Savings/Investments*: Start with accounts that are most accessible at the top and work your way down to accounts that are less accessible. (By *accessible* I mean accounts that do not have surrender charges or large tax liabilities associated with withdrawals.) The sample statement in Figure 2-1 lists easily accessible funds at the top, like savings, money market accounts, and mutual funds that are not inside retirement accounts. If you own Series I, H, HH, E, or EE bonds, these belong in section A also.

2. *Retirement Accounts*: Next, list retirement accounts and other tax-deferred accounts such as fixed or variable annuities. Retirement accounts are not considered as accessible because withdrawing the money may trigger taxes and penalties. Annuities may also assess penalties on accessing funds before age 59½, which is why they belong in this section.

3. *Real Estate and Other*: When deciding what to put on your list, determine whether it is an asset that can be used to provide future cash flow. For Wally and Sally, I included the net value of the home under Real Estate and Other, as this equity may be used later in the form of a reverse mortgage, or the home may be sold. "Other" assets that may someday be used for cash flow could include gold, silver, or collectibles. One of my clients had a large gun collection, which his wife sold after his death.

4. *Liabilities*: Now add in any debts you have in the Liability column.

5. *Total Assets*: In the far right column at the bottom of your sheet, tally up what you own minus what you owe. This is your net worth.

Your goal in this exercise is not to list everything you own that has value. I noticeably left personal property off the list. The goal is to be prudent about which things you own that could reasonably be converted into cash flow sources at some point in the future.

Sometimes determining where some items fit and whether they even belong on your personal balance sheet can be challenging. Here are a few examples:

- *Cash value life insurance*: If you plan on keeping the policy until death then all the cash is not available for income purposes, but a portion of it may be.

- *Automobiles*: A paid-off auto you're using does not likely belong on the list. However, a collectible that may be sold one day might.

- *Automobile loans*: You can include this liability on the personal balance sheet, but typically I do not. Instead I include ongoing transportation expenses in the Spending Plan, which you'll create later.

- *Your home*: Your home equity, or a portion thereof, can be used for future cash flow if needed. For this reason I typically *do* include homes on the personal balance sheet.

During your high earning years, your goal is to work toward increasing your net worth. Once you have transitioned to retirement, this goal may change.

It is not uncommon for a client to tell me that their goal is to "die with a dollar in the bank." They want to spend as much as they can without running out. They are okay with a controlled and gradual decline in their net worth.

Others would rather spend less and focus on leaving funds to future generations. Wally and Sally's net worth is $1,527,500. To determine if this number is sufficient to provide their desired standard of living once they are no longer working, they have to develop an income & expense timeline.

MAKING THE JOB EASIER ONLINE

There are some great online resources you can use to gauge your financial well-being. Some of them are limited in scope, and some are more comprehensive. This sidebar provides a few suggestions for trusted resources.

E$Planner® Basic - This is a free financial-planning software program designed by Larry Kotlikoff. You can upgrade to an advanced version to run more detailed scenarios. The advantage to this type of program is that it runs detailed tax calculations behind the scenes, resulting in a more accurate forecast. You can learn more at www.basic.esplanner.com.

Retire Logix for iPhone and Android - For a fun way to get a general idea of how well prepared you are for a transition out of the workforce, try Retire Logix on your iPhone or Android smartphone. It's a cool app that allows you to adjust all your numbers with slide bars. You can learn more at www. retirelogix.com.

Budgeting/Spending Plan Software - Online software is great for those who like tracking and categorizing spending. Here are a few resources you can try:

- You Need a Budget: www.youneedabudget.com

- Mint.com: www.mint.com

- Quicken: www.quicken.intuit.com

Your Income Timeline

As mentioned, a balance sheet is a snapshot in time. An income timeline is more like a movie, fluid and moving. As a result, it provides more information than the balance sheet can.

Unlike the income statement common in the business world, which focuses on a single year, an income timeline looks at what will happen over multiple years. Think about it this way: to project how your personal balance sheet may change over time, you will need to look at when you can add to savings and when you need to take withdrawals.

Eventually, you'll do this most effectively with math formulas in an Excel spreadsheet or by using other software. I suggest laying it out on paper or in a simple Excel spreadsheet first.

You'll use your income timeline for several purposes:

- To provide an estimate of the total amount of fixed income you will have from guaranteed sources and to see how the amount of guaranteed income will change from year-to-year

- You'll then be able to identify the gaps – meaning the amount needed from savings on a year-by-year basis once you, your spouse, or both of you are no longer in the workforce

Let's see how it's done.

Drawing Your Timeline

Figure 2-2 shows Wally and Sally's income timeline. Use this figure and the instructions that follow as guidelines to create your own timeline. Across the top you'll put your column headings for various income sources. Down the side you'll put the number of years, calendar year and your ages.

Figure 2-2
Income Timeline Taking Early Social Security

| | | | | Fixed Sources Of Income | | | | |
| | | | | Wally | | Sally | | A |
# of Years	Calendar Year	Wally (age)	Sally (age)	Take Home Pay	Social Security	Take Home Pay	Social Security	Total Fixed Income
1	2016	64	62	$19,452	$0	$67,485	$0	$86,937
2	2017	65	63	0	18,890	0	19,756	38,646
3	2018	66	64	0	23,121	0	21,983	45,104
4	2019	67	65	0	23,584	0	22,423	46,006
5	2020	68	66	0	24,055	0	22,871	46,927
6	2021	69	67	0	24,537	0	23,329	47,865
7	2022	70	68	0	25,027	0	23,795	48,822
8	2023	71	69	0	25,528	0	24,271	49,799
9	2024	72	70	0	26,038	0	24,756	50,795
10	2025	73	71	0	26,559	0	25,252	51,811
11	2026	74	72	0	27,090	0	25,757	52,847
12	2027	75	73	0	27,632	0	26,272	53,904
13	2028	76	74	0	28,185	0	26,797	54,982
14	2029	77	75	0	28,749	0	27,333	56,082
15	2030	78	76	0	29,323	0	27,880	57,203
16	2031	79	77	0	29,910	0	28,437	58,347
17	2032	80	78	0	30,508	0	29,006	59,514
18	2033	81	79	0	31,118	0	29,586	60,705
19	2034	82	80	0	31,741	0	30,178	61,919
20	2035	83	81	0	32,375	0	30,782	63,157
21	2036	84	82	0	33,023	0	31,397	64,420
22	2037	85	83	0	33,683	0	32,025	65,709
23	2038	86	84	0	0	0	34,357	34,357
24	2039	87	85	0	0	0	35,044	35,044
25	2040	88	86	0	0	0	35,745	35,745
26	2041	89	87	0	0	0	36,460	36,460
27	2042	90	88	0	0	0	37,189	37,189
28	2043	91	89	0	0	0	37,933	37,933
29	2044	92	90	0	0	0	38,692	38,692
			Totals:		$580,678		$809,307	$1,476,922

- *Fixed Sources of Income*: This will include income that does not come from your savings and investments, such as earned income from work, Social Security, pensions, and guaranteed annuity income.

- *Separate by Spouse*: If married or planning with a significant other, you'll want to break out income sources separately for each of you. Each source of income should have its own column so you can adjust amounts and when they may start or stop.

- *Take Home Pay*: For earned income Wally and Sally used their take home pay. For Wally this started as gross income of $55,000 less a $24,000 401(k) contribution less $11,548 of taxes (his share of payroll, federal and state taxes). The result is the $19,452 you see in Figure 2.2. For Sally this started as gross income of $118,000 less a $24,000 403(b) contribution, less $1,740 of payroll deductions for health insurance, less $24,775 of taxes (her share of payroll, federal and state taxes), which results in the $67,485 you see in Figure 2.2.

- *Social Security*: If eligible for benefits, you can collect Social Security at any age between 62 and 70. Your benefit goes up for each month past 62 that you wait. Wally assumed he would begin benefits on his 65th birthday and would receive $1,889 a month, which would increase each year at 2%. Sally would claim at her age 63, and receive $1,796 per month which would increase each year at 2%.[8]

Investment income, such as dividends, interest, capital gains or withdrawals from savings, does not belong on the income timeline. However, if you have an annuity that pays you guaranteed income, that does belong on your timeline.

In Figure 2-2, you see that Wally and Sally plan to continue working for only one year, and then they each plan to take Social Security soon after retiring. During 2017, Wally's timeline shows a partial year (10 months) of Social Security as he starts his benefits at his age 65 and his birthday is in March. Sally

---

8   This Social Security claiming choice is not intended to be representative of the way Wally and Sally should claim. It is a starting place for a projection. Other claiming options and additional details on Social Security are covered in Chapter 3.

receives almost a full year (11 months) of Social Security if she starts her benefits at 63, because her birthday is in February.

In Figure 2-2 under Sally's section in the row for year 2038 her Social Security benefit amount has a box around it to show a change in calculation. Upon the death of a spouse the surviving spouse continues to receive the larger of what their spouse was getting or what they get. Wally's benefit amount is slightly larger than Sally's so she continues to receive the larger amount from that point on – but her own benefit amount goes away.

One thing that many folks are surprised by is what their projected Social Security totals up to be. In Wally and Sally's case, those amounts add up to $1,389,985. Not small change. And in Chapter 3, you'll learn ways you can get even more.

You'll total all sources of fixed income as you see in column A. At the bottom of column A you see a sum showing that over 29 years they expect to receive a cumulative $1,476,922 from their joint last year of take home pay and many years of Social Security.

Once you outline your sources of guaranteed income, move on to drawing your expense timeline.

Your Expense Timeline

You can start your expense timeline with a rough estimate of total annual spending. See Figure 2-3 for an example.

Then you can fine-tune it by adding specifics as you continue gathering information for your plan. (I provide examples of more detailed budgets later in this chapter.)

Wally and Sally started by looking at the total amount they spent last year from their checking account. They did not include amounts allocated to savings or any expenses or taxes that were withheld directly from their paychecks. Instead they looked at what they spent from the take home pay that they received.

They estimated their living expenses at about $62,000 a year. They applied an annual inflation increase to their spending, assuming each year starting in

2017 they would need to spend 3% more than the year before to maintain their lifestyle.

They weren't sure how to estimate taxes after retirement so they asked their tax preparer. Their tax preparer explained that their taxes in retirement would depend on where they pulled their money from. The more they withdrew from their IRAs the more taxes they would pay. She did an estimate assuming they had:

- $40,000 in Social Security income

- $5,000 in investment income (interest, dividends and capital gains that show up on a 1099 each year)

- $30,000 withdrawal from their IRA

This would result in about $8,000 in federal taxes and $1,500 in state taxes. (Detailed tax calculations are shown in Chapter 4.) Wally and Sally used these numbers in their expense timeline and inflated them each year at 3%.

They also knew they needed to account for health care costs, so they estimated about $6,000 a year each ($500 a month) once they retired and were no longer covered under Sally's employer plan. They heard health care costs rise more quickly than general inflation, so they increased health care costs at 5% each year. (You'll see more details on their health care spending later in this chapter and in Chapter 10.)

In Figure 2-3 in the column labeled "B" you see their annual total outgoing expenses, and the sum at the bottom shows that over 29 years they would spend $3,915,243.

At this point I am not going to comment as to whether I think these assumptions are realistic. I am using them as a starting place. I will refine them and show alternate projections throughout the book.

Figure 2-3
Expense Timeline

								B
					Expenses			
# of Years	Calendar Year	Wally (age)	Sally (age)	Desired Annual Spending	Estimated Federal Taxes	Estimated State Taxes	Estimated Health Care Costs	Total Expenses
1	2016	64	62	$62,000	N/A	N/A	$3,000	$65,000
2	2017	65	63	63,860	8,000	1,500	12,000	85,360
3	2018	66	64	65,776	8,240	1,545	12,600	88,161
4	2019	67	65	67,749	8,487	1,591	13,230	91,058
5	2020	68	66	69,782	8,742	1,639	13,892	94,054
6	2021	69	67	71,875	9,004	1,688	14,586	97,153
7	2022	70	68	74,031	9,274	1,739	15,315	100,360
8	2023	71	69	76,252	9,552	1,791	16,081	103,677
9	2024	72	70	78,540	9,839	1,845	16,885	107,109
10	2025	73	71	80,896	10,134	1,900	17,729	110,660
11	2026	74	72	83,323	10,438	1,957	18,616	114,334
12	2027	75	73	85,822	10,751	2,016	19,547	118,136
13	2028	76	74	88,397	11,074	2,076	20,524	122,071
14	2029	77	75	91,049	11,406	2,139	21,550	126,144
15	2030	78	76	93,781	11,748	2,203	22,628	130,359
16	2031	79	77	96,594	12,101	2,269	23,759	134,723
17	2032	80	78	99,492	12,464	2,337	24,947	139,240
18	2033	81	79	102,477	12,838	2,407	26,194	143,916
19	2034	82	80	105,551	13,223	2,479	27,504	148,757
20	2035	83	81	108,717	13,619	2,554	28,879	153,770
21	2036	84	82	111,979	14,028	2,630	30,323	158,961
22	2037	85	83	115,338	14,449	2,709	31,840	164,336
23	2038	86	84	118,798	14,882	2,790	33,432	169,903
24	2039	87	85	122,362	15,329	2,874	35,103	175,668
25	2040	88	86	126,033	15,789	2,960	36,858	181,641
26	2041	89	87	129,814	16,262	3,049	38,701	187,827
27	2042	90	88	133,709	16,750	3,141	40,636	194,236
28	2043	91	89	137,720	17,253	3,235	42,668	200,876
29	2044	92	90	141,852	17,770	3,332	44,801	207,755
		Totals:		$2,803,569	$343,447	$64,396	$703,831	$3,915,243

Solving for the Gap

To solve for the total deposits that can be made, or withdrawals that need to be taken, Wally and Sally need to calculate the difference between column A in Figure 2-2 and column B in Figure 2-3. The results are shown in Figure 2-4, their deposit/withdrawal timeline, as follows:

- *$ To/From Savings*: In Figure 2-4 column "C" shows the annual difference between Wally and Sally's sources of fixed income (A) and their estimated expenses (B).

By viewing column C of Figure 2-4 you see that during their last year of work, Wally and Sally should have $21,937 to add to savings. Since they used take home pay in their income timeline, this $21,937 to be added to savings is in addition to the combined $48,000 they contribute to their 401(k) and 403(b) plans.

Starting in 2017 they will need to begin withdrawals from savings to meet their desired spending estimates. This analysis shows they will need to withdraw $46,714 in 2017. The withdrawal needed goes down the following year because during 2018 they are both receiving Social Security all year long.

To get an estimate of their total financial capital needed, sum line C from now through life expectancy. At the bottom of column C you see the sum of $2,438,322.

I show this simple sum because you can do this at home on paper without any formulas. However, a simple sum is misleading. Here's why: Your savings will earn something. Simply adding up the amounts needed will overstate the amount of money you need today to meet your future cash flow goals. The $2,438,322 number assumes you earn nothing on your savings and investments. The higher the rate of return you earn, the less you need to have in the bank today to cover your future desired withdrawals.

Figure 2-4
Deposit/Withdrawal Timeline

				Income	−	Spending	=	Deposit or Withdrawal	
				A		B		C	D
# of Years	Calendar Year	Wally (age)	Sally (age)	Total Fixed Income		Total Expenses		$ To/ From Savings	Cumulative $ Needed
1	2016	64	62	$86,937		$65,000		$21,937	$21,937
2	2017	65	63	38,646		85,360		(46,714)	(24,777)
3	2018	66	64	45,104		88,161		(43,056)	(67,833)
4	2019	67	65	46,006		91,058		(45,051)	(112,885)
5	2020	68	66	46,927		94,054		(47,127)	(160,012)
6	2021	69	67	47,865		97,153		(49,288)	(209,300)
7	2022	70	68	48,822		100,360		(51,537)	(260,837)
8	2023	71	69	49,799		103,677		(53,878)	(314,715)
9	2024	72	70	50,795		107,109		(56,314)	(371,029)
10	2025	73	71	51,811		110,660		(58,849)	(429,878)
11	2026	74	72	52,847		114,334		(61,487)	(491,365)
12	2027	75	73	53,904		118,136		(64,233)	(555,598)
13	2028	76	74	54,982		122,071		(67,089)	(622,687)
14	2029	77	75	56,082		126,144		(70,062)	(692,750)
15	2030	78	76	57,203		130,359		(73,156)	(765,906)
16	2031	79	77	58,347		134,723		(76,375)	(842,281)
17	2032	80	78	59,514		139,240		(79,725)	(922,007)
18	2033	81	79	60,705		143,916		(83,211)	(1,005,218)
19	2034	82	80	61,919		148,757		(86,838)	(1,092,056)
20	2035	83	81	63,157		153,770		(90,613)	(1,182,669)
21	2036	84	82	64,420		158,961		(94,540)	(1,277,209)
22	2037	85	83	65,709		164,336		(98,627)	(1,375,837)
23	2038	86	84	34,357		169,903		(135,546)	(1,511,382)
24	2039	87	85	35,044		175,668		(140,624)	(1,652,007)
25	2040	88	86	35,745		181,641		(145,895)	(1,797,902)
26	2041	89	87	36,460		187,827		(151,367)	(1,949,269)
27	2042	90	88	37,189		194,236		(157,047)	(2,106,315)
28	2043	91	89	37,933		200,876		(162,943)	(2,269,258)
29	2044	92	90	38,692		207,755		(169,064)	(2,438,322)
	Totals:			$1,476,922		$3,915,243		($2,438,322)	

When you factor in the potential for various rates of return you realize the amount of money needed to cover a lifetime of withdrawals will vary depending on the return you think is realistic. For Wally and Sally this is shown in Table 2-1.

In technical terms Table 2-1 is discounting a future stream of cash flows back to today, so the "return" used is called the *discount rate*, and the dollar amount calculated is called the *present value*.

Table 2-1. Present Value of 29 Years of Withdrawals

Discount Rate	Present Value
0%	$2,438,322
1%	$2,021,409
2%	$1,688,862
3%	$1,421,992
4%	$1,206,509
5%	$1,031,440
6%	$888,316

You can compare this present value to Wally and Sally's net worth to get a rough estimate of how well prepared they are for a transition out of work.

Their net worth from their personal balance sheet (Figure 2-1) is $1,527,500. After discussion, they decide not to include their home value as being available for future cash flow, so that leaves them with $1,232,500 ($1,527,500 minus the $295,000 home value). They also exclude checking and savings balances as those numbers fluctuate based on current year expense items. That leaves them with $1,205,000 of financial capital that is allocated toward delivering retirement cash flow.

Assuming their savings and investments earn 5% or more, their current financial capital is greater than the amount of $1,031,440 shown in the 5% row of

Table 2-1. If their savings and investments earn 4% or less, the $1,205,000 falls short of what they may need.

Another factor to consider is longevity. What if Sally lives to 95? Or what if they both pass by her age 85? Table 2-2 shows how the amount needed changes based on longevity assumptions, and how a simple sum calculation shows substantially more needed than a present value calculation.

Table 2-2. Present Value vs. Simple Sum Shown over Various Longevity Assumptions

Age of Sally as Survivor	$ Needed Assuming 5% Return	Simple Sum
85	$821,082	$1,652,007
90	$1,031,440	$2,438,322
95	$1,226,625	$3,369,032

Based on Table 2-2, if savings and investments earn 5% and Sally lives to 85, their current financial capital is sufficient, but if Sally lives longer, or if investments earn less, it may fall short of what she would need.

A Word of Caution

The basics are just that: basic. In Wally and Sally's analysis, I have not accurately accounted for taxes or future changes in their spending needs. As you learn how to account for these items, the numbers will change.

You'll learn how to further refine these numbers by:

- Adding a detailed spending analysis that breaks spending into fixed and flex (flexible) components.

- Determining how you want to account for inflation.

- Adjusting how and when you claim your Social Security benefits.

- Estimating a realistic growth rate for savings and investments.

- Accounting for taxes in a more accurate way.

The advantage of drawing out a basic scenario on paper, or in a spreadsheet, is that you gain a better understanding of what is happening. It also gives you a first draft estimate of how well prepared you may be.

If you tally up your numbers through the longest life expectancy you think reasonable, and your current net worth is more than your total cash flow needed from savings, it is likely you are adequately prepared.

If your current net worth doesn't come close to the total cash flow needed from savings, it may be that you will need to adjust your expectations, work longer, spend less, or do a combination of these things.

As you move through this book, you will use your timeline to visually see what decisions can improve your outcome.

If You're Close to Leaving the Workforce: Adjusting Your Timeline for What-ifs

If you want to transition out of work sooner rather than later, use your income timeline to see how your fixed sources of income will change based on the choices you make.

For example, you could draw out a timeline that shows what happens if you delay the start date of your Social Security benefits. You'll see what this looks like in the next chapter.

If married, you may want a timeline that shows what happens if one of you has a shorter than expected life. (Hint: At the death of the first spouse, the surviving spouse continues to receive only the larger Social Security amount; the smaller amount goes away and is no longer included in the timeline.) If you have a pension option and are considering whether to take a single life option or an option that provides income for a surviving spouse, you could create a timeline showing both choices.

This may sound like a lot of work. But remember, retiring is something you'll (probably) only do once. Many of the decisions you'll need to make are irrevocable. Getting a solid plan in place is well worth the investment of time.

If You're Still Planning on Working for Quite Some Time

If you still have many years of contributing to savings ahead of you, the income timeline can help you see what your money can do for you in the future.

You will want to focus on saving in a tax-efficient way, increasing your earning power, and carefully choosing investments that have the best likelihood of accomplishing your goals. I cover those things in later chapters.

Regardless of your proximity to transitioning out of the workforce, accurately accounting for spending needs is critical to your success.

Your Spending Plan

My third year in college, I asked my dad for money. I can't remember what for. He asked me for a budget in return. I was mad. I didn't want to do a budget. Who wants to track where their money goes? Ugh.

In hindsight, dad taught me a valuable lesson. Banks don't hand out money without documentation, and perhaps parents shouldn't either.

I revved up both the determined and the playful side of my personality. If I was going to make a budget, by golly, it was going to be colorful. Armed with an array of multi-colored highlighters, I started going through my checkbook and bank statements. Every expense for the past six months got slotted into color-coded categories. I tallied up each category and divided by six to get a monthly average.

Budgeting has been part of my life since.

You don't have to budget to save money. Some people are naturals at spending less than they make. They don't need to track anything.

You do need a budget to make a successful transition out of the workforce. You need to know about how much you'll need to withdraw, and from where, and you can't determine that without an estimate of your spending needs.

Note   You must have a budget to make a successful transition out of the workforce.

Personally, I don't like the word *budget*. It sounds restrictive. So, I am going to call it a *spending plan* instead. A spending plan helps you make trade-offs that matter to you. For example, perhaps you think you don't have money to travel. As you begin to look at how you spend your money and create a plan, you realize you might be able to travel more by shopping less or downsizing your home or car.

There isn't a right or wrong way to spend your money. It is a matter of choosing to spend it on the things you most want to do. Many people unconsciously spend money on things that aren't that important to them. Once you create a spending plan, you can see if this is happening, and if it is, you can decide how to change it. Your spending plan is then used to adjust your expense timeline as needed.

There are several ways to make a spending plan, and the same way is not going to work for everyone. I prefer a bottom line approach rather than specific categories. I am going to show you both options.

Bottom Line Spending Plan

My own spending plan is broken out into monthly or other fixed expenses that come out of my checking account - and everything else. For me "everything else" gets charged on a credit card which I pay off each month.

My everything else includes groceries, gas, medical expenses, shopping, travel, etc. Anything that comes up, I put on the credit card – and always pay it off each month. I like to do this to accumulate credit card points that I can use for travel. I allocate $2,000 a month as my average credit card spending.

In one month if I go over by $500, the next month I cut back so I come in under by $500. During the month I know about where I am by viewing my credit card activity each week through an app on my phone and seeing what the current month-to-date charges are.

If it is part way through the month and I'm nearing my limit, I cut back my spending for the remainder of the month to the essentials; gas and groceries. This means sometimes I put off extras for a few weeks until a new billing cycle begins.

When the inevitable home repairs or health care costs occur, I cover them out of my $2,000 a month. That means sometimes there are months where I have to cut back on eating out, new clothing, home décor, travel or anything else extra.

Figure 2-5 shows a sample bottom line spending plan for Wally and Sally, done in a similar way as how I do mine. Their spending is broken into three categories:

1. Checking/Bill Pay

2. Credit Card

3. Cash

The *Checking/Bill Pay* category includes things that are automatically deducted or paid from the checking account each month such as utilities set up to debit each month, checks that go out through a bill pay service, and anything else that regularly comes out of the checking account, but is not typically charged on a credit card.

The *Credit Card* category includes everything else except cash. In Figure 2-6 you see details of what might be included in their average monthly credit card balance. Some of these expenses, such as cable, internet and cell phone are regularly occurring items, but as they are billed to the credit card and paid off with the balance each month they are listed as part of the credit card category rather than in the checking category.

The *Cash* category is easy – it comes from their average monthly ATM withdrawals. Most bank account statements itemize these for you separately.

These items total to $5,152 a month or $61,824 a year. In Wally and Sally's expense timeline they rounded up to get to the $62,000 of living expenses used.

Figure 2-5
Bottom Line Monthly Spending Plan

	Checks/ Bill Pay	Credit Card	Cash
Fixed Payments from Checking			
Mortgage(Principal & Int.) or Rent			
2nd mortgage /Home equity line			
Real Estate taxes	195		
Homeowner's insurance	92		
Electric	175		
Water/Sewer/Trash	45		
Auto Payment	400		
Lawn care	140		
Auto Insurance	75		
Auto Insurance	75		
LTC Insurance	350		
Credit Card		3,305	
Cash			300
	$1,547	$3,305	$300

Figure 2-6
Credit Card Details

Home repairs	250
Cable TV	109
Internet	42
Groceries	500
Eating out	400
Gas	150
Maintenance	50
Annual Registration	33
Doctor's visits (if not included above)	80
Dental	100
Prescriptions	50
Eye care	20
Clothing	200
Cell phone	150
Gym membership	60
Monthly subscriptions	20
Haircare/haircuts	100
Pets	75
Gifts (birthday/wedding/shower)	75
Walmart/Target/Costco	100
Travel/Cruises	417
Airline tickets	125
Hotel	200
	$3,305

By accounting for spending in terms of how you spend (payments from checking, credit card or cash), you can more easily check your monthly statements to see if you are about where you should be, without having to check individual categories of spending. A spending plan that uses broad categories is great, and as I mentioned, is my preferred approach - but at least once, and especially as you near retirement - you'll want to take the time to break spending into more detailed categories.

Honing Your Spending Plan

Adding detailed categories allows you to see what items may change once you are retired. It also helps you figure out which items are essential and which aren't. To do this, itemize your expenses into sub-categories, and then determine which items are fixed and which can "flex". Some categories, such as food, may have a portion that is fixed (we all need to eat) and a portion that is flex (we don't need to eat out five times a week, although we may like to).

- *Fixed* expenses are necessities, such as food, health care, housing, and transportation.

- *Flex* expenses are extras, such as travel, eating out, entertainment, hobbies, and so on.

Later, when you match your fixed expenses with your fixed sources of income, you will learn how this can help you best select investments that are most appropriate for you.

When starting your spending plan, initially I suggest you guess what you think you spend in each category. Then create a second spending plan by tracking your actual spending habits. Seeing what you think you spend versus what you actually spend can be insightful.

To track actual spending habits, gather the following documents:

- One year's worth of statements from the primary checking account that you use to pay bills.

- One year's worth of statements from any credit or debit cards that you use.

If you use budgeting software, this information should be available and categorized within the software.

The sample spending plan in Figures 2-7 through 2-9 shows Wally and Sally's spending plan with detailed categories.

Figure 2-7
Detailed Spending Plan

	Monthly	Annual	Fixed	Flex
HOME				
Mortgage(Principal & Int.) or Rent				
2nd mortgage /Home equity line				
Real Estate taxes	195	2,340	2,340	
Homeowner's insurance	92	1,104	1,104	
Home repairs	250	3,000	3,000	
Other:				
UTILITIES				
Electric	175	2,100	2,100	
Gas				
Water/Sewer/Trash	45	540	540	
Phone (Home)				
HOA:				
Other:				
HOME MAINTENANCE/UPKEEP & SERVICES				
Cable TV	109	1,308	1,308	
Internet	42	504	504	
Lawn care	140	1,680	1,680	
Pool/Garden				
House Cleaning				
Appliances (small & large)				
Other:				
FOOD				
Groceries	500	6,000	6,000	
Eating out	400	4,800	2,400	2,400
Drinks/parties				
TRANSPORTATION/VEHICLES				
Auto Payment	400	4,800	4,800	
Auto Payment				
Auto Insurance	75	900	900	
Auto Insurance	75	900	900	
Gas	150	1,800	1,800	
Maintenance	50	600	600	
Annual Registration	33	390	390	
Other:				

Figure 2-8 - Detailed Spending Plan Continued

	Monthly	Annual	Fixed	Flex
MEDICAL				
Health insurance premiums 1				
Health insurance premiums 2				
Health insurance (out of pocket)				
Doctor's visits	80	960	960	
Medicare Part B premiums				
Medicare Part D premiums				
Medicare Supplement/Advantage:				
Dental	100	1,200	1,200	
Prescriptions	50	600	600	
Eye care	20	240	240	
Chiropractic				
Other:				
OTHER INSURANCE				
Life Insurance				
LTC Insurance	350	4,200	4,200	
Disability Insurance				
APPAREL				
Clothing	200	2,400	2,400	
Shoes				
CHILDREN/GRANDCHILDREN				
Day care				
Babysitting				
Camps/Events				
Allowance				
Lessons				
Clothing				
Current Tuition				
College Savings				
Other:				
PERSONAL DEBT: List monthly payment				
Credit card 1				
Credit card 2				
Personal loan				
Student loan				
Other:				

Figure 2-9 - Detailed Spending Plan Continued

	Monthly	Annual	Fixed	Flex
OTHER EXPENSES				
Cell phone	150	1,800	1,800	
Gym membership	60	720	720	
Monthly subscriptions	20	240	240	
Tobacco				
ATM/Cash purchases	300	3,600	3,600	
Massage				
Haircare/haircuts	100	1,200	1,200	
Manicure/pedicure				
Drugstore/cosmetics				
Pets	75	900	900	
Storage Units				
Gifts (birthday/wedding/shower)	75	900	900	
Catalog/Ebay/Craigslist purchases				
Walmart/Target/Costco	100	1,200	1,200	
Home Depot				
Charity				
Personal Education/Union Dues				
Hobbies				
Antiquing/Photography				
Golf/Jewelry				
Season Tickets				
Cooking				
Books/Movies				
Travel/Cruises	417	5,000	2,500	2,500
Tickets/events				
Airline tickets	125	1,500	750	750
Hotel	200	2,400	1,200	1,200
	Monthly	Annual	Fixed	Flex
Grand Total:	5,152	61,826	54,976	6,850

What to Watch Out For

There are certain items in your spending plan that need to be accounted for in a particular way. The suggestions I give in this section pertain to your mortgage and health care expenses.

Mortgage

If you have a mortgage, notice on the worksheet there are separate line items for principal and interest payments, real estate taxes, and homeowner's insurance. This is intentional.

Many mortgages wrap your real estate taxes and home owner's insurance into the payment. This is fine, but when your mortgage is paid off, the principal and interest payments go away, whereas the real estate taxes and homeowner's insurance expenses continue. That's an important distinction to make in a pre- and post-work spending plan.

In addition, mortgage interest is a tax-deductible item. If you have a large mortgage, as you pay it down, your taxes may go up. This is one of many reasons why projections that don't account for taxes are inaccurate.

Health Care Expenses

While working, your employer may be subsidizing the cost of your health insurance. Once you transition out of work, your premiums may be higher. In addition, you will likely choose a health care insurance plan that provides benefits that extend beyond basic Medicare coverage (Medicare is the mandatory U.S. medical coverage that begins at age 65).

In the Wally and Sally example, neither is yet 65. They are currently covered under Sally's workplace insurance plan. Workplace coverage will end when Sally retires and they will each purchase a plan from the Marketplace at healthcare.gov. Then when each reaches age 65, they will go on Medicare and purchase a Medicare supplement policy. A five year timeline of their projected health care expense is shown in Figure 2-10.

It is not uncommon for a fully insured retiree to spend 20–30% of monthly expenses on health care.

Figure 2-10
Five Year Timeline of Health Care Costs

	2016	2017	2018	2019	2020
Wally's age at year-end	64	65	66	67	68
Sally's age at year-end	62	63	64	65	66
WALLY - HEALTH CARE					
Marketplace Plan	-	1,754	-	-	-
Medicare Supplement-Policy "F"	-	1,440	1,812	1,903	1,998
Health Care OOP*	1,500	1,575	1,654	1,736	1,823
Medicare Part B	-	1,279	1,611	1,692	1,777
	$1,500	$6,048	$5,077	$5,332	$5,598
SALLY - HEALTH CARE					
Marketplace Plan	-	10,401	10,921	956	-
Medicare Supplement-Policy "F"	-	-	-	1,749	1,998
Health Care OOP	1,500	1,575	1,654	1,736	1,823
Medicare Part B	-	-	-	1,551	1,777
	$1,500	$11,976	$12,575	$5,992	$5,598

Totals: $3,000 $18,024 $17,652 $11,324 $11,196

*OOP stands for "out-of-pocket" health care costs

You can use the online health care calculator by HVS Financial (https://hvsweb1. hvsfinancial.com/hvadvisor/) to estimate your own post- age 65 health care costs.

To estimate pre- 65 health care costs go to healthcare.gov and find their "see plans & prices" section.

Caution In retirement, a full 20–30% of your spending may go toward health care, another reason to plan well.

Many health insurance policies specify a $2,500 - $6,000 maximum out-of-pocket amount you have to pay in any given year, with the insurance company covering expenses that exceed that amount. If an ongoing health event occurs, you may be incurring this expense each and every year.

If you have not yet reached age 59½ you need *liquid* savings (meaning not in a retirement account) to cover your deductible or out-of-pocket costs when they occur. At some point, those expenses will be incurred, and you will need to replenish the savings used. To be ultra-conservative, you could budget the entire max out-of-pocket amount as if this expense will be incurred each and every year. As an alternative you could budget 25–50% of the amount and deposit it to a savings account (or a Health Savings Account if you are eligible) so you are ready when expenses arise.

THE FALLACY OF ONE-TIME EXPENSES

Businesses must budget too. In a former partnership, my business partner and I updated our business budget quarterly. In our first year of business, our actual expenditures always seemed higher than we had projected. There were things that would come up that we had deemed "one-time expenses," and so we didn't build them into our projections. After that first year, we put a permanent line item in our budget labeled "one-time expenses".

The one-time expenses that get left out of personal budgets are not all that different than those that get left out of business budgets. Maybe the hot water heater had to be replaced last year. This year it might be the dishwasher, a termite problem, or an adult child who needs financial assistance. Make sure you include room for those one-time expenses that have a strange way of recurring every year.

Monthly, Annual, and Fixed vs. Flex

It is important to calculate each expense on a monthly and annual basis. If you don't do this it can be all-too-easy to miss expenses that may occur only once a year, such as your auto registration, or an insurance premium that you pay annually.

- When managing cash flow, think in terms of monthly expenses.

- For planning timelines, turn your monthly numbers into annual numbers for use in worksheets, spreadsheets, or software programs.

It is also helpful to take each annual expense and estimate what portion of it belongs in the fixed column verses the flex column. If you live in a modest house and plan to live there the rest of your life, the mortgage payment and associated expenses likely belong in the fixed column. If you live in a super-sized house and plan to downsize later, the portion of your mortgage and home maintenance that would be attributable to a smaller residence would belong in the fixed column, with the excess in the flex column.

Dividing expenses this way will help you evaluate trade-offs later. Some people will choose to reduce fixed expenses so they can have more flex, which for them may involve travel and hobbies. Others may choose to work longer so they can maintain both their fixed and flex expenses at their current levels.

Items That Conspicuously Go Missing

I never used to ask for detailed budgets from my clients. I mistakenly assumed that if they had been decent savers, they would have a handle on how much they spent. If they told me that in addition to mortgage and taxes, they spent about $50,000 a year, then I would use that number in their projections. Not anymore.

For some income levels, an increase of $3,000 a year in spending can mean the difference between having sufficient resources until the end of your life and not having enough.

Now I ask my clients to provide detailed information on spending. And I scour it for missing items.

Here are a few things that conspicuously go missing:

- Premiums for Medicare Parts B and D and Medicare supplement policies.

- New car purchases. If you own your car free and clear, that's great. At some point, you'll still need to replace it. That must be factored into your post-work budget.

- Replacement costs. If you own a home, at some point you'll need to replace furniture, the water heater, the roof, and so on. You must have a line item in your budget for these types of expenses.

- Annual expenses like property taxes and insurance premiums can easily be forgotten.

- Health insurance premiums for those who plan to leave the workforce before age 65. (The price tag for private health insurance between ages 55 and 65 can cause sticker shock. If you want to leave the workforce early, get quotes and factor this expense into your plan before you leave employment that subsidizes this expense for you.)

Gathering information on spending is tedious. The good news: once you spend the time creating a spending plan, updating it becomes quick and easy.

The purpose of gathering spending information is not to render judgment. We all place different values on how we spend our time and money. The purpose is to use this information to help you make trade-offs that are based on what is important to you.

Exiting the traditional workforce early might be worth a downsized lifestyle to you. Or it might not. Once you see your options, you can decide.

Pre- and Post-Work Spending

This is the time to think about how to spend your money on things that matter the most to you. Do you want to travel more? Would you be willing to lower your fixed expenses by moving to a less expensive home?

What items in your spending plan might decrease post-work? Dry cleaning, transportation, and parking costs will decrease substantially for some.

What items in your spending plan might increase? If you plan on more airline travel to see family, account for this expense in your post-work spending plan.

You may find that your pre- and post-work spending plans total up to about the same amount, but that funds get spent on different things.

If you aren't sure what you will be doing with your time once retired, I'd suggest budgeting extra for entertainment. You'll also want to do some soul searching - those who know what they want to do with their time seem to enjoy retirement more.

Entertaining Yourself Can Be Expensive

One of my clients came in six months after retirement finding that she missed work. Although she enjoyed not having to be "on the clock", she missed contributing to a project and the sense of accomplishment that gave her. In retirement she was discovering she had too much time on her hands and it was costing more than she had thought. She commented, "Entertaining myself for an extra 40 hours a week is expensive." This is something to keep in mind as you plan for how you will use your time and money.

This is not an exercise where you simply fill in the blanks. Give thought to your lifestyle and to how a change in it will affect each item.

Revising Your Expense Timeline

After Wally and Sally saw how their health care costs would change, and spent more time thinking about what they wanted to do in their first few years of retirement, they decided to make a revised expense timeline.

In their revised timeline they assumed an extra $10,000 a year on travel during their first five years of retirement. They also projected health care expenses more accurately in their early years of retirement, but later in life they assumed this expense would drop by 50% after Wally's assumed life expectancy of 85. You see this change emphasized in Figure 2-11 with a box around projected health care costs in year 23.

Notice with their revisions their total life-time expenses shown at the bottom of column B went from $3,915,243 in Figure 2-3 to the $3,736,084 show in Figure 2-11.

Again, this is a "rough cut". It doesn't do an annual tax calculation based on withdrawals. It does provide an outline, or starting place, of how the financials may look.

Figure 2-11
Revised Expense Timeline

| | | | | | Expenses | | | |
| | | | | | | | | B |
# of Years	Calendar Year	Wally /	Sally Ages	Desired Annual Spending	Extra Travel	Estimated Federal Taxes	Estimated State Taxes	Projected Health Care Costs	Total Expenses
1	2016	64	62	$62,000	N/A	N/A	N/A	$3,000	$65,000
2	2017	65	63	63,860	10,000	8,000	1,500	18,024	101,384
3	2018	66	64	65,776	10,000	8,240	1,545	17,652	103,213
4	2019	67	65	67,749	10,000	8,487	1,591	11,324	99,152
5	2020	68	66	69,782	10,000	8,742	1,639	11,196	101,359
6	2021	69	67	71,875	10,000	9,004	1,688	11,756	104,323
7	2022	70	68	74,031	-	9,274	1,739	12,344	97,388
8	2023	71	69	76,252	-	9,552	1,791	12,961	100,557
9	2024	72	70	78,540	-	9,839	1,845	13,609	103,833
10	2025	73	71	80,896	-	10,134	1,900	14,290	107,220
11	2026	74	72	83,323	-	10,438	1,957	15,004	110,722
12	2027	75	73	85,822	-	10,751	2,016	15,754	114,344
13	2028	76	74	88,397	-	11,074	2,076	16,542	118,089
14	2029	77	75	91,049	-	11,406	2,139	17,369	121,963
15	2030	78	76	93,781	-	11,748	2,203	18,238	125,969
16	2031	79	77	96,594	-	12,101	2,269	19,149	130,113
17	2032	80	78	99,492	-	12,464	2,337	20,107	134,399
18	2033	81	79	102,477	-	12,838	2,407	21,112	138,834
19	2034	82	80	105,551	-	13,223	2,479	22,168	143,421
20	2035	83	81	108,717	-	13,619	2,554	23,276	148,167
21	2036	84	82	111,979	-	14,028	2,630	24,440	153,077
22	2037	85	83	115,338	-	14,449	2,709	25,662	158,158
23	2038	86	84	118,798	-	14,882	2,790	13,473	149,944
24	2039	87	85	122,362	-	15,329	2,874	14,146	154,712
25	2040	88	86	126,033	-	15,789	2,960	14,854	159,636
26	2041	89	87	129,814	-	16,262	3,049	15,596	164,722
27	2042	90	88	133,709	-	16,750	3,141	16,376	169,976
28	2043	91	89	137,720	-	17,253	3,235	17,195	175,402
29	2044	92	90	141,852	-	17,770	3,332	18,055	181,008
		Totals:		$2,803,569	$50,000	$343,447	$64,396	$474,671	$3,736,084

Making It Better

Once you have a basic scenario in place, the next step is figuring out how to make it better. Improving your baseline scenario has two components: planning decisions and lifestyle decisions. I frequently tell people, "I can show you the numbers. You have to bring your values to the table and decide what's right for you."

It is my job to share with you the planning decisions that can improve your outcomes. Each decision affects another. For example, the age at which you take Social Security affects how much you need to withdraw from savings, which affects how much in taxes you will pay. It is your job to define what *better* looks like to you from a lifestyle perspective. I can show you how to crunch the numbers, but I can't tell you whether you'll be happier working longer and having more post-work income or having more free time sooner, which in turn may mean driving a less-expensive car and living in a smaller home.

Each family has its own values, and faced with the same set of financial circumstances different people make different decisions. This is part of what makes us human. It is also what makes planning fun. You have a choice, and your choice may be different than your neighbor's.

There is one decision that almost every U.S. worker looking at a transition out of the workforce will be faced with. That is the decision about when to begin your Social Security benefits. For the most part, it is an irrevocable decision.

Every day, people begin their benefits without prudently considering their choices. In many cases, one choice can yield far more lifetime income than another. About half of Social Security recipients rely on Social Security to provide more than half their total income. For many, it is the most important post-work financial decision they make. That is the decision we'll look at next, in Chapter 3.

Summary

By creating a few basic financial schedules, you can begin to play with alternative futures and choose a path that best suits you. This chapter provided examples of the following to get you started:

- Personal balance sheet

- Income timeline

- Expense timeline

- Deposit/withdrawal timeline

- Spending plan

These schedules will give you a 30,000-foot view on how well prepared you are to live off your acorns. You can then use these schedules to compare choices and see how to improve the view.

Chapter 3

Social Security

How to Make the Most of It

"It has long been recognized as an inescapable obligation of a democratic society to provide for every individual some measure of basic protection from hardship and want caused by factors beyond his control. In our own country, the obligation of the Federal Government in this respect has been recognized by the establishment of our Social Security system."

—*Harry S. Truman*

Since 2008, I have been writing an online advice column called *MoneyOver55*. One of my most popular topics is Social Security. Due to the large amount of content I have on this subject other financial planners will often reach out to me with Social Security questions of their own.

Most recently a good friend of mine who is a financial planner in Colorado called with a question about a client of hers who was widowed a few years back.

"Dana, my client went in to the Social Security office, but something about what they said doesn't sound right to me. Can I run this by you?"

Of course I said yes.

Let's take a look at the analysis I ran for my friend - and why it is so important to do an analysis.

The Impact of a Bad Decision

We'll call my friend's client Diane. Diane's husband, Paul, passed away at age 57. Diane is now 62 and is no longer working, but she had worked for much of her life and is eligible for her own Social Security retirement benefit amount or a widow benefit amount.

Diane heard that she could collect a widow benefit[9] as early as age 60, so at 60 she went to the Social Security office to pursue this. They told her she would get more if she waited until 62. Technically this was true.

Just before her 62nd birthday she went back to her local Social Security office. They told her at 62 she could collect her own benefit amount which would be $1,791 a month, or if she waited until 66 she could collect a widow benefit based on Paul's Social Security, which would be $2,706 per month (this is the amount Paul would have received if he filed at his age 66). Technically this was also true.

So what was the problem with this information given to Diane?

1.   There are additional claiming options that can provide substantially more money over her lifetime.

2.   With the info given, Diane has little way of comparing the impact of one benefit choice vs. another.

The claiming rules that Diane did not know about were:

•   Her ability to file what is called a *restricted application*.

•   The fact that she could claim a widow benefit now and later switch to receiving her own benefit amount.

To show how these rules work together, let's look at Diane's monthly retirement benefit and widow benefit amounts shown in Table 3-1 for ages 60, 62, 66 and 70. Inflation increases have been factored in to these numbers.

---

9   I am using the term "widow benefits" which may also be called *widower benefits* or *survivor benefits*.

Table 3-1 Diane's Retirement Benefit vs. Widow Benefit

Age	Retirement	Widow
60	N/A	$1,767
62	$1,791	$2,025
66	$2,571	$2,706
70	$3,674	$2,929

Based on Diane's numbers, when she visited her Social Security office at 60 and they told her she could get more if she waited and filed at 62, that was true. What Diane did not know is she could have started collecting her $1,767 monthly widow benefit at 60, and then at 70 switched over to receiving her $3,674 retirement benefit amount.

When Diane went back to the Social Security office at 62, it is true, she could have filed a restricted application for her own benefit amount of $1,791, or she could wait and at 66 collect a widow benefit of $2,706. What Diane did not know is she could start collecting her monthly widow benefit of $2,025 now at 62 and then at 70 switch over to receiving her retirement benefit amount of $3,674.

Note   There is no benefit to waiting past Full Retirement Age to collect a widow/widower benefit.

To compare the impact of one choice vs. another I put Diane's benefit amounts into a software package called Social Security Timing®. It calculates all the possible claiming combinations and delivers a suggested strategy – and allows you to compare this to other options.

The suggested strategy is for Diane to file a restricted application for a widow benefit at age 62 and begin collecting $2,025 a month. Then at age 70 she will file for her own benefit amount. This means her widow benefit will stop and she will switch over to her retirement benefit of $3,674 a month.

If Diane uses this plan and lives to her 90th birthday, and assuming benefits increase at 2% a year (there is an annual cost of living adjustment applied to Social Security benefits), she will receive a cumulative $1,279,500 from age 62 through 89. (This is shown in Figure 3-1 under the section labeled "Suggested" by adding her $208,500 of widow benefits and $1,071,000 of retirement benefits.)

Contrast that with $987,588, which is the cumulative amount she receives over her lifetime if she waits until 66 and files for her widow benefit with no restricted application, shown under the section labeled "Widow Only".

In Chapter 2 we covered the concept of *present value* – the amount needed today to provide a future cash flow stream. To provide a fair side-by-side comparison of Diane's claiming options, the numbers need to be translated into present value amounts using a discount rate that reflects a risk level[10] similar to the guaranteed nature of Social Security benefits.

In Figure 3-1 in the columns to the right of Diane's benefit amounts, you see the corresponding present value. These were calculated using a 3% discount rate.[11] If Diane had claimed based solely on the information from the Social Security office, as you see in the "Difference" column[12] she could easily have made a decision that could cost her $200,000 or more over her lifetime. Don't blame the Social Security staff for this[13] – they are not trained financial planners. Do be aware that the Social Security staff you speak with may not know all your options.

Note   For Divorcees - If Diane and Paul had been married for over ten years, but divorced before he passed away, and if Diane did not remarry prior to age 60, then even though they had divorced she would still be eligible to use the claiming options shown and could collect widow benefits.

---

10 Chapter 5 goes into greater depth on investment risk and expected returns.

11 In 2016 a safe guaranteed investment with risk characteristics similar to Social Security is not likely to deliver a 3% rate of return, however over 28 years, earning 3% on average in safe, guaranteed investments is more feasible, and so for this example I chose to use a 3% discount rate.

12 The Difference column is the difference in Present Value.

13 Social Security staff are not supposed to give you advice; they are trained only to tell you what amounts you can receive.

Figure 3-1
Widow Social Security Options

# of Years	Calendar Year	Diane (age)	Widow Only		Suggested			
			Widow Benefit @66	Present Value	Widow Benefit @ 62	Switch to her own @70	Present Value	Difference
1	2016	62	$0	$0	$24,300	$0	$24,300	$24,300
2	2017	63	0	0	24,780	0	24,058	24,058
3	2018	64	0	0	25,272	0	23,821	23,821
4	2019	65	0	0	25,776	0	23,589	23,589
5	2020	66	32,472	28,851	26,292	0	23,360	(5,491)
6	2021	67	33,120	28,570	26,820	0	23,135	(5,434)
7	2022	68	33,780	28,290	27,360	0	22,914	(5,377)
8	2023	69	34,452	28,013	27,900	0	22,685	(5,327)
9	2024	70	35,148	27,746	0	44,088	34,803	7,057
10	2025	71	35,844	27,471	0	44,964	34,461	6,990
11	2026	72	36,564	27,207	0	45,864	34,127	6,920
12	2027	73	37,296	26,943	0	46,776	33,792	6,849
13	2028	74	38,040	26,680	0	47,712	33,464	6,784
14	2029	75	38,796	26,418	0	48,672	33,143	6,725
15	2030	76	39,576	26,164	0	49,644	32,821	6,656
16	2031	77	40,368	25,911	0	50,628	32,496	6,586
17	2032	78	41,172	25,657	0	51,648	32,185	6,528
18	2033	79	41,988	25,403	0	52,680	31,872	6,469
19	2034	80	42,828	25,157	0	53,736	31,564	6,407
20	2035	81	43,692	24,917	0	54,804	31,254	6,337
21	2036	82	44,556	24,670	0	55,896	30,948	6,279
22	2037	83	45,456	24,435	0	57,024	30,653	6,218
23	2038	84	46,356	24,193	0	58,164	30,355	6,163
24	2039	85	47,292	23,962	0	59,316	30,055	6,092
25	2040	86	48,228	23,725	0	60,504	29,764	6,039
26	2041	87	49,200	23,498	0	61,716	29,476	5,978
27	2042	88	50,184	23,270	0	62,952	29,191	5,920
28	2043	89	51,180	23,041	0	64,212	28,908	5,867
	Totals:		$987,588	$620,193	$208,500	$1,071,000	$823,196	$203,003

The numbers calculated for Diane factor in all the following Social Security rules:

- The ability for widows/widowers to file a restricted application.

- The reduction factor that is applied when you claim before what is called your *Full Retirement Age* (FRA).

- Delayed retirement credits that increase your benefit if you wait and claim after your FRA.

- Inflation adjustments that are applied to benefits.

- The fact that FRA is defined differently for your own retirement benefit amount than for a widow/widower benefit.

- Widow/widower rules that apply if the deceased passed before filing but had worked long enough to be fully eligible for benefits (which are different than the rules that apply if the deceased passed after having filed for benefits).

- Any new rules that are in effect as a result of changes in Social Security law that were passed in November 2015.

Due to the complex nature of the rules, even if you are a widow or widower, you cannot take Diane's options and easily apply them to your own situation. I know the rules well, and I still won't make a recommendation without the use of software. Making an uninformed choice can mean less income for the rest of your life.

I cover the Social Security rules in greater depth in my book *Social Security Sense*. It's a perfect resource for those who want to do additional research, understand the "why" behind certain recommendations and see more practical examples. In this book, I want to focus on Wally and Sally's Social Security claiming choices, and explain how it will impact their retirement income plan.

WHAT IS FULL RETIREMENT AGE (FRA)?

Your FRA is based on your date of birth. If you were born in 1937 or earlier, your FRA is 65.

1938: 65 and 2 months

1939: 65 and 4 months

1940: 65 and 6 months

1941: 65 and 8 months

1942: 65 and 10 months

1943-1954: 66

1955: 66 and 2 months

1956: 66 and 4 months

1957: 66 and 6 months

1958: 66 and 8 months

1959: 66 and 10 months

If you were born in 1960 or later, Full Retirement Age is 67. If you were born on the 1st of the year, you are considered to have attained your age in the prior year, so someone born January 1, 1955 would have an FRA of 66, not an FRA of 66 and 2 months.

When I refer to claiming early, I mean claiming before you reach our FRA. When I refer to a delayed claiming strategy that means waiting until past your FRA.

Should You Claim at 62?

Age 62 is the earliest age you can begin drawing on Social Security retirement benefits, and like many people, you are probably inclined to start drawing benefits as soon as you can.

However, you will take a reduced benefit if you begin benefits at 62. That reduction will not only affect you, if you are married, it will also affect your spouse. An early claiming choice may permanently reduce your spouse's future survivor benefits.

Let's take a look at some of the factors that apply if you claim early by examining Wally and Sally's situation.

Table 3-2 shows the monthly amount of Wally and Sally's benefits depending on the age they begin claiming (including what they would have gotten if they had filed at 62). Inflation increases have been calculated in to these numbers.

Table 3-2. Wally and Sally's Social Security Benefits

Age	Wally	Sally
62	$1,471	$1,659
66	$2,065	$2,382
70	$2,950	$3,403

Wally and Sally didn't take Social Security at 62 because they read about something called the *earnings limit*.

The Earnings Limit

The earnings limit is a rule that reduces benefits if:

1. You are collecting benefits and you have not yet reached your FRA, and

2. Your earned income exceeds the current year's limit.

In 2016, the annual earnings limit is $15,720. If you are collecting benefits, have not reached your FRA, and have earned income in excess of this limit then Social Security will take back $1 of benefits for every $2 you earn in excess of the limit.

Here are a few additional rules:

*   During the year you reach FRA both a higher limit and different reduction factor are used.

*   Once you attain FRA the earnings limit *no longer applies*, and you can earn any amount with no concerns about your benefits being reduced.

*   If you have been impacted by the earnings limit and a reduction factor was applied – you may get it back over time. When you reach FRA a recalculation will be applied.

Whew! The rules are complicated, aren't they?

For those still working at 62, it rarely makes sense to collect Social Security early unless;

- Your earnings will be below the earnings limit.

- You have other extenuating circumstances, such as a shorter than average life expectancy, and no spouse dependent on your survivor benefits.

What if you're 62 and *not* working? Should you begin benefits right away? It then depends on factors such as:

- Eligibility for other benefits amounts such as spousal or widow benefits

- Health and longevity probabilities

- Other available resources such as savings and investments

- Your tax situation

For many folks, starting benefits early is not the best financial choice. When you factor in the impact of taxes it often makes sense to withdraw from savings and investments between the ages of 62 and 70 (if retired) and delay the start of Social Security benefits to 70.

As Wally and Sally were both still working at 62, they didn't want to begin benefits only to be required to give a large portion back due to the earnings limit. Instead, they decided to wait, and their plan was to claim on their first birthday after retirement. Much like Diane, Wally and Sally did not know about some of the alternative claiming options, such as the availability of spousal benefits.

Who Benefits From Delaying Social Security?

According to economists John B. Shoven and Sita Nataraj Slavov, "The gains from delaying are greater at lower interest rates, for married couples relative to singles, for single women relative to single men, and for two-earner couples relative to one-earner couples."[14]

---

14 John B. Shoven and Sita Nataraj Slavov, "The Decision to Delay Social Security Benefits: Theory and Evidence," NBER Working Paper No. 17866 (February 2012).

Who Can Get Spousal Benefits?

Spousal benefits were designed to provide income in retirement to a non-working spouse. They can also be utilized for spouses who did work and are eligible for their own Social Security retirement benefit. Many couples (or ex-spouses who were married over ten years) are not aware of this.

The bad news - you cannot receive your own retirement benefit and a spousal at the same time.

Here are a few basic rules about spousal benefits:

- Current spouses and ex-spouses (if you were married for over ten years and did not remarry prior to age 60) are eligible for a spousal benefit.

- You must be age 62 to qualify for either type of Social Security benefit (your own or a spousal).

- You are not eligible to receive a spousal benefit until your spouse files for his or her own benefit first. (Different rules apply for ex-spouses. You can receive a spousal benefit based on an ex-spouse's record even if your ex has not yet filed for his or her own benefits.)

Let's see how spousal benefits apply to Wally and Sally.

Figure 3-2 shows their suggested claiming strategy from Social Security Timing® software input to their income timeline.

This plan has Sally filing for her benefits at 64. Wally then files a restricted application for spousal benefits. Wally will collect the spousal benefit for four years, then at 70 he will switch to his own, then larger, benefit amount.

Due to changes in the Social Security rules that became law in November 2015, only those who turned 62 on or before January 1, 2016, can file a restricted application for spousal benefits.[15] And restricted applications cannot be filed before you reach FRA, which is age 66 for Wally. This means Wally has to wait until 66 to file the restricted application for spousal benefits – and Sally must have filed for her own benefits before Wally can collect a spousal benefit.

---

15 Restricted applications remain available for widows/widowers.

By filing a restricted application, Wally's own benefit amount will continue to accumulate delayed retirement credits, and at age 70 Wally will switch over to receiving this higher amount.

At Wally's death, his now larger amount becomes the survivor benefit for Sally. This larger survivor income provides what we call a longevity hedge. It is a way to hedge against one of the critical risks you face in retirement – the risk of living quite long.

RESTRICTED APPLICATIONS: SPOUSAL VS. WIDOW/WIDOWERS

Restricted Application for Spousal Benefits

- Not available for anyone born January 2, 1954 or later.

- Still available for anyone born January 1, 1954 or earlier.

- Must be FRA or older to file one.

Restricted Applications for Widows/Widowers

- Available regardless of date of birth.

- You do not have to be FRA to file one.

Notice the total amount expected from Social Security is now $1,649,872. Compare that to the total amount of Social Security they would get based on their original plan shown in Figure 2-2, which was $1,389,985.

Figure 3-3 shows how this alternate Social Security claiming plan affects their deposit/withdrawal timeline. In Figure 3-3 I used their original expense time-line numbers from Figure 2-3 – not the revised one in Figure 2-11. I did this intentionally, to illustrate the impact their Social Security decision has. In Chapter 4, you'll see revised scenarios that incorporate numerous changes including their revised expense timeline.

Figure 3-2
Income Timeline Taking Social Security According to a Plan

Fixed Sources Of Income

# of Years	Calendar Year	Wally (age)	Sally (age)	Wally Take Home Pay	Wally's Own SS	Spousal Benefit	Sally Take Home Pay	Sally's Own SS	Sally's Survivor Benefit	A Total Fixed Income
1	2016	64	62	$19,452	$0	$0	$67,485	$0	$0	$86,937
2	2017	65	63	0	0	0	0		0	0
3	2018	66	64	0	0	11,440	0	19,970	0	31,410
4	2019	67	65	0	0	14,004	0	24,444	0	38,448
5	2020	68	66	0	0	14,292	0	24,924	0	39,216
6	2021	69	67	0	0	14,568	0	25,428	0	39,996
7	2022	70	68	0	29,500	2,478	0	25,932	0	57,910
8	2023	71	69	0	36,108	0	0	26,448	0	62,556
9	2024	72	70	0	36,828	0	0	26,976	0	63,804
10	2025	73	71	0	37,560	0	0	27,516	0	65,076
11	2026	74	72	0	38,316	0	0	28,068	0	66,384
12	2027	75	73	0	39,084	0	0	28,632	0	67,716
13	2028	76	74	0	39,864	0	0	29,208	0	69,072
14	2029	77	75	0	40,656	0	0	29,784	0	70,440
15	2030	78	76	0	41,472	0	0	30,384	0	71,856
16	2031	79	77	0	42,300	0	0	30,984	0	73,284
17	2032	80	78	0	43,140	0	0	31,608	0	74,748
18	2033	81	79	0	44,004	0	0	32,244	0	76,248
19	2034	82	80	0	44,892	0	0	32,892	0	77,784
20	2035	83	81	0	45,780	0	0	33,540	0	79,320
21	2036	84	82	0	46,704	0	0	34,212	0	80,916
22	2037	85	83	0	47,628	0	0	34,896	0	82,524
23	2038	86	84	0	0	0	0	0	48,588	48,588
24	2039	87	85	0	0	0	0	0	49,548	49,548
25	2040	88	86	0	0	0	0	0	50,544	50,544
26	2041	89	87	0	0	0	0	0	51,552	51,552
27	2042	90	88	0	0	0	0	0	52,584	52,584
28	2043	91	89	0	0	0	0	0	53,640	53,640
29	2044	92	90	0	0	0	0	0	54,708	54,708
			Totals:		$653,836	$56,782		$578,090	$361,164	$1,736,809

Figure 3-3
Revised Deposit/Withdrawal Timeline Using Suggested Social Security Plan

				Income	− Spending	= Deposit or Withdrawal	
				A	B	C	D
# of Years	Calendar Year	Wally (age)	Sally (age)	Total Fixed Income	Total Expenses	$ To/ From Savings	Cumulative $ Needed
1	2016	64	62	$86,937	$65,000	$21,937	$21,937
2	2017	65	63	0	85,360	(85,360)	(63,423)
3	2018	66	64	31,410	88,161	(56,751)	(120,174)
4	2019	67	65	38,448	91,058	(52,610)	(172,783)
5	2020	68	66	39,216	94,054	(54,838)	(227,621)
6	2021	69	67	39,996	97,153	(57,157)	(284,779)
7	2022	70	68	57,910	100,360	(42,450)	(327,229)
8	2023	71	69	62,556	103,677	(41,121)	(368,349)
9	2024	72	70	63,804	107,109	(43,305)	(411,654)
10	2025	73	71	65,076	110,660	(45,584)	(457,238)
11	2026	74	72	66,384	114,334	(47,950)	(505,188)
12	2027	75	73	67,716	118,136	(50,420)	(555,608)
13	2028	76	74	69,072	122,071	(52,999)	(608,608)
14	2029	77	75	70,440	126,144	(55,704)	(664,312)
15	2030	78	76	71,856	130,359	(58,503)	(722,815)
16	2031	79	77	73,284	134,723	(61,439)	(784,254)
17	2032	80	78	74,748	139,240	(64,492)	(848,746)
18	2033	81	79	76,248	143,916	(67,668)	(916,413)
19	2034	82	80	77,784	148,757	(70,973)	(987,387)
20	2035	83	81	79,320	153,770	(74,450)	(1,061,837)
21	2036	84	82	80,916	158,961	(78,045)	(1,139,881)
22	2037	85	83	82,524	164,336	(81,812)	(1,221,693)
23	2038	86	84	48,588	169,903	(121,315)	(1,343,008)
24	2039	87	85	49,548	175,668	(126,120)	(1,469,128)
25	2040	88	86	50,544	181,641	(131,097)	(1,600,225)
26	2041	89	87	51,552	187,827	(136,275)	(1,736,500)
27	2042	90	88	52,584	194,236	(141,652)	(1,878,152)
28	2043	91	89	53,640	200,876	(147,236)	(2,025,387)
29	2044	92	90	54,708	207,755	(153,047)	(2,178,434)
	Totals:			$1,736,809	$3,915,243	($2,178,434)	

The cumulative number at the bottom of Figure 3-3, $2,178,434, represents the total amount Wally and Sally would need to withdraw from savings and investments over 29 years. You can compare this to the $2,438,322 shown in Figure 2-4 in Chapter 2 to see that the result of this Social Security claiming option is that Wally and Sally would need to use $259,888 less of their own savings and investments to spend the exact same amount over 29 years. That difference is a simple sum – to do a fair comparison of what the difference is in today's dollars we have to compare the options in terms of their present value.

Table 3-3 shows the present value of Column C based on various discount rates the same way it was done in Chapter 2, Table 2-1. In Table 3-3 you see the present value numbers from Table 2-1 under the heading "PV w/ Original SS Plan" compared to the present value numbers using this new suggested Social Security claiming plan.

Table 3-3. Present Value of 29 Years of Withdrawals

Discount Rate	PV w/ Original SS Plan (Table 2-1)	Present Value (PV) w/ New SS Plan	Difference
0%	$2,438,322	$2,178,434	(259,887)
1%	$2,021,409	$1,815,094	(206,315)
2%	$1,688,862	$1,525,548	(163,313)
3%	$1,421,992	$1,293,351	(128,641)
4%	$1,206,509	$1,105,944	(100,565)
5%	$1,031,440	$953,701	(77,739)
6%	$888,316	$829,205	(59,111)

Using Table 3-3 you can determine that if Wally and Sally think a 3% return on their savings and investments is a reasonable expectation, then by following their suggested Social Security claiming strategy they are ahead by $128,641.

The $128,641 represents the present value of the additional amount of money they have from following a smart plan. The lower the expected rate of return on savings and investments, the greater the value of their suggested claiming plan.

This makes this suggested claiming plan a great hedge against a time period where investment returns are below average. If you are using average historical returns in your planning, keep in mind average means half the time returns will be higher - and half the time they will be lower. It's smart to have a plan that protects you against outcomes that don't beat historical averages.

LENGTH OF MARRIAGE RULES

9 months: To be eligible for a survivor's benefit on your spouse's record.

1 year: To be eligible for a spousal benefit.

2 years: If your divorced spouse is 62, but has not yet filed, you must be divorced two years before you can claim a spousal benefit based on their record. If they have already filed for benefits, there is no two-year requirement for claiming on an ex-spouse's record.

10 years: To claim a spousal benefit on an ex-spouse's record.

Spousal Benefits for Those Born After January 1, 1954

What if Wally was two years younger, born on 3/15/1954 rather than 3/15/1952? In that case the ability to file a restricted application would not be available, and the claiming strategy likely to work out best for him and Sally would be one of the following:

1. Have Wally file at 66 for his own benefit and Sally file at 70 for her own benefit. As Sally is the higher earner of the two, this approach makes her higher age 70 benefit amount the survivor benefit for either one of them.

2. Have them each file on their own benefit amount at 70. This claiming option would provide the most cumulative benefits if they both live long.

For dual income households where both were born after January 1, 1954, the use of restricted applications and switching strategies for spousal benefits will not be available, but date of birth is not the only factor. Age differential and lifetime earnings differences are also factors. There will still be many scenarios where spousal benefits will apply and be of benefit to a married couple.

For married couples where one spouse had low earnings, or didn't work at all, spousal benefits will certainly be utilized. For example, if Sally had not worked at all, or had worked only a little and had a low benefit amount of her own, then the likely strategy would be for Wally to file at 70, at which time Sally would become eligible for a spousal benefit based on 50% of Wally's age 66 benefit amount.

More About Longevity

Naturally, many couples are concerned that if one of them were to delay the start of Social Security to age 70 and pass away before they began benefits, that this would have a detrimental effect. For example, what if Wally passes away right before he turns 70? As a survivor, Sally would continue to receive the larger of her own benefit amount or the amount Wally would have gotten had he filed at his date of death. In this case the larger amount would be what Wally would have gotten. This situation is shown in their income timeline in Figure 3-4.

Figure 3-4
Income Timeline if Sally Widowed Young

| | | | | Fixed Sources Of Income | | | | | | |
| | | | | Wally | | | Sally | | | A |
# of Years	Calendar Year	Wally (age)	Sally (age)	Take Home Pay	Wally's Own SS	Spousal Benefit	Take Home Pay	Sally's Own SS	Sally's Survivor Benefit	Total Fixed Income
1	2016	64	62	$19,452	$0	$0	$67,485	$0	$0	$86,937
2	2017	65	63	0	0	0	0		0	0
3	2018	66	64	0	0	11,440	0	19,970	0	31,410
4	2019	67	65	0	0	14,004	0	24,444	0	38,448
5	2020	68	66	0	0	14,292	0	24,924	0	39,216
6	2021	69	67	0	0	14,568	0	25,428	0	39,996
7	2022	70	68	0	0	2,478	0	4,322	29,500	36,300
8	2023	71	69	0	0	0	0	0	36,108	36,108
9	2024	72	70	0	0	0	0	0	36,828	36,828
10	2025	73	71	0	0	0	0	0	37,560	37,560
11	2026	74	72	0	0	0	0	0	38,316	38,316
12	2027	75	73	0	0	0	0	0	39,084	39,084
13	2028	76	74	0	0	0	0	0	39,864	39,864
14	2029	77	75	0	0	0	0	0	40,656	40,656
15	2030	78	76	0	0	0	0	0	41,472	41,472
16	2031	79	77	0	0	0	0	0	42,300	42,300
17	2032	80	78	0	0	0	0	0	43,140	43,140
18	2033	81	79	0	0	0	0	0	44,004	44,004
19	2034	82	80	0	0	0	0	0	44,892	44,892
20	2035	83	81	0	0	0	0	0	45,780	45,780
21	2036	84	82	0	0	0	0	0	46,704	46,704
22	2037	85	83	0	0	0	0	0	47,628	47,628
23	2038	86	84	0	0	0	0	0	48,588	48,588
24	2039	87	85	0	0	0	0	0	49,548	49,548
25	2040	88	86	0	0	0	0	0	50,544	50,544
26	2041	89	87	0	0	0	0	0	51,552	51,552
27	2042	90	88	0	0	0	0	0	52,584	52,584
28	2043	91	89	0	0	0	0	0	53,640	53,640
29	2044	92	90	0	0	0	0	0	54,708	54,708
			Totals:		$0	$56,782		$99,088	$1,015,000	$1,257,807

In this example the partial amounts shown in 2022 are reflective of the last two months of spousal benefits that Wally received before he passed, and the two months of her own benefits that Sally received before she began receiving widow benefits instead.

This is a simplified example. Each widow or widower situation will depend on whether the spouse passed away before or after filing for benefits, and before or after reaching their FRA. For a great summary of widow/widower rules see Social Security Timing's web page, *Social Security Widow Benefit explained* (https://www.socialsecuritytiming.com/index.cfm/knowledge-base/articles/social-security-widow-benefit-explained/).

One thing to keep in mind when considering the potential that one spouse passes at a young age; income will go down as the survivor no longer receives both Social Security amounts, but expenses also go down.

In Wally and Sally's case, let's assume expenses go down by 15% from what they outlined in their original expense timeline (Figure 2-3). Figure 3-5 shows Sally's new deposit/withdrawal timeline with the survivor Social Security benefit. In the row for year 2023, you see a box around the spending that year to highlight the year I assumed expenses went down.

Figure 3-5
Deposit/Withdrawal Timeline - If Sally Widowed Young

# of Years	Calendar Year	Wally (age)	Sally (age)	Income − Spending = Deposit or Withdrawal			
				A	B	C	D
				Total Fixed Income	Total Expenses	$ To/ From Savings	Cumulative $ Needed
1	2016	64	62	$86,937	$65,000	$21,937	$21,937
2	2017	65	63	0	85,360	(85,360)	(63,423)
3	2018	66	64	31,410	88,161	(56,751)	(120,174)
4	2019	67	65	38,448	91,058	(52,610)	(172,783)
5	2020	68	66	39,216	94,054	(54,838)	(227,621)
6	2021	69	67	39,996	97,153	(57,157)	(284,779)
7	2022	70	68	36,300	100,360	(64,060)	(348,839)
8	2023	71	69	36,108	88,125	(52,017)	(400,856)
9	2024	72	70	36,828	91,042	(54,214)	(455,070)
10	2025	73	71	37,560	94,061	(56,501)	(511,571)
11	2026	74	72	38,316	97,184	(58,868)	(570,439)
12	2027	75	73	39,084	100,416	(61,332)	(631,771)
13	2028	76	74	39,864	103,761	(63,897)	(695,668)
14	2029	77	75	40,656	107,222	(66,566)	(762,234)
15	2030	78	76	41,472	110,806	(69,334)	(831,568)
16	2031	79	77	42,300	114,514	(72,214)	(903,782)
17	2032	80	78	43,140	118,354	(75,214)	(978,996)
18	2033	81	79	44,004	122,328	(78,324)	(1,057,320)
19	2034	82	80	44,892	126,444	(81,552)	(1,138,872)
20	2035	83	81	45,780	130,704	(84,924)	(1,223,796)
21	2036	84	82	46,704	135,117	(88,413)	(1,312,209)
22	2037	85	83	47,628	139,686	(92,058)	(1,404,266)
23	2038	86	84	48,588	144,417	(95,829)	(1,500,095)
24	2039	87	85	49,548	149,318	(99,770)	(1,599,866)
25	2040	88	86	50,544	154,395	(103,851)	(1,703,716)
26	2041	89	87	51,552	159,653	(108,101)	(1,811,817)
27	2042	90	88	52,584	165,100	(112,516)	(1,924,334)
28	2043	91	89	53,640	170,744	(117,104)	(2,041,438)
29	2044	92	90	54,708	176,592	(121,884)	(2,163,322)
	Totals:			$1,257,807	$3,421,129	($2,163,322)	

Once again, we can calculate the present value required to meet these needed withdrawals. Table 3-4 shows these numbers.

Table 3-4. Present Value of 29 Years of Withdrawals, Sally as a widow.

Discount Rate	Present Value
0%	$2,163,322
1%	$1,821,680
2%	$1,546,668
3%	$1,323,853
4%	$1,142,151
5%	$993,004
6%	$869,777

By comparing the numbers in Table 3-4 to the numbers in Table 3-3 you can see that from a financial standpoint Sally is not worse off even if widowed at a younger age.

Your Social Security Statement

Social Security mails annual statements at five year increments 3 months before your birthday at ages 25, 30, 35, 40, 45, 55 and 60 - only if you do not have a my Social Security account and are not currently receiving benefits. You don't have to wait for a statement. You can create an online my Social Security account to access an estimate of your future Social Security benefits at www.socialsecurity.gov/mystatement/.

Some people mistakenly look at their statement and think that if they don't begin benefits at 62, they must wait until 66, and that if they don't begin at 66, they must wait until 70. This is not true. You can begin benefits anytime at 62 or later (age 60 if you are eligible for a widow or widower benefit). The formula that determines what you get is recalculated monthly, so your benefit increases for each month you wait.

Your statement also provides information on how your benefits are estimated and what assumptions are used – but inflation increases are not projected into your benefit estimates on your statement. Running calculations based on the numbers shown on your statement without factoring in the inflation increases that will be applied can cause you to underestimate what you will actually receive by claiming at a later age.

For Teachers, Law Enforcement, etc.

Many workers, such as fire fighters, law enforcement employees, postal workers or educators who work for government agencies or municipalities that have their own pension system, do not participate in Social Security. These workers can have years where they worked and did contribute to Social Security and years where they worked and did not participate in Social Security.

In you fall into this situation a modified formula may be used to calculate the amount of Social Security you are eligible for, and the benefit amount shown on your Social Security statement may not be what you will receive.

If you answer yes to any of the following questions, this situation may apply to you:

- Did you work for a government agency (federal, state or local)?
- Did you work for an employer in another country?
- If yes to either question, will you receive a pension from this government agency or employer in another country?

Note   If you were a federal employee after 1956 and were covered under the Civil Service Retirement System (CSRS) this provision affects you. If you were a federal employee covered under the Federal Employees' Retirement System (FERS) where Social Security taxes are withheld, this provision does not affect you.

There are two different rules:

- *Windfall Elimination Provision (WEP):* If you receive a pension from work that was not subject to Social Security taxes, WEP may reduce your own Social Security benefit and may affect your dependents' benefits that are based on your earning's record.[16]

- *Government Pension Offset (GPO):* If you receive a pension from work that was not subject to Social Security taxes, then GPO may reduce the Social Security spousal benefit you receive (or benefit you receive as an ex-spouse) and may reduce the widow/ widower benefit you receive.

If you think WEP or GPO will affect you, you cannot rely on standard estimates of your Social Security retirement, spousal or widow benefits. Personalized calculations will need to be done.

SOCIAL SECURITY SOFTWARE AND CALCULATORS

As you've learned, Social Security is complex. I'd advise you use an online tool or calculator to help you evaluate your options. It is beyond the scope of this book to provide a comprehensive analysis of the different methods that online Social Security calculators use. Some tools use different methodologies than others, which can change the advice. In addition, online tools are continuously being improved, so at different times in the software development cycle, one tool may have more advanced capabilities than another, but that can change rapidly. This section contains a brief list of online resources that includes the tools I am most familiar with at the time of writing.

From the Social Security Administration: You can download a free, detailed Social Security calculator from the Social Security website (www.ssa.gov/OACT/ anypia/anypia.html). However, it does not evaluate claiming options for you and a spouse. If are the engineer type you may find it useful for understanding the factors that affect your own benefits.

---

16 The WEP calculation affects your PIA. Dependent benefits are calculated based on your PIA. However, in the case of a widow/widower, when the worker dies, the WEP reduction is removed.

From the AARP: AARP offers a free calculator (www.aarp.org/work/social-security/social-security-benefits-calculator/) that can help you see some of your claiming options. It does not allow you to see the numbers that lead to the final recommendation, nor at the time of writing does it deliver some of the more advanced claiming strategies that some of the fee-for-service software products provide.

As for software that charges a fee, there are a few options:

Maximize My Social Security: Maximize My Social Security (www.maximizemy socialsecurity.com) was developed by Boston University economics professor Laurence Kotlikoff, software engineer Richard Munroe, and other professionals at Economic Security Planning, Inc., which markets personal financial-planning programs. This calculator covers all the Social Security claiming scenarios one might encounter: retiree, spousal, survivor, divorcee, parent and child benefits, as well as calculations for the windfall elimination provision and government pension offset. (These will affect you if you receive a pension from an employer who did not withhold Social Security tax from your earnings, such as state employers.)

Financial advisors have options as well. My favorite Social Security tool is the one I used to run examples throughout this book, Social Security Timing®.

Social Security Timing: Social Security Timing (www.socialsecuritytiming.com) was developed by Joe Elsasser, an Omaha-based financial planner. Joe is also the Director of Advisory Services for Senior Market Sales, Inc. In his work as a financial advisor, Joe began testing a variety of Social Security calculator tools in search of a solution that would help his clients make the best decision about when to elect to take Social Security benefits. What he found was that every tool he tested, including the government's, was woefully incapable of providing a thorough analysis that took all of the election strategies for married couples into account. This calculator provides a free look into what is at stake between a poor claiming choice and a planned claiming choice and generates three strategies you may want to consider. To see the full strategy and the full report, you have to agree to be contacted by an advisor who subscribes to the full version of the software.[17]

---

17 Author disclosure: at the time of writing, I subscribe to Social Security Timing.

Taxes on Your Social Security Benefits

If Social Security is your sole source of income, you do not pay taxes on it. If you have sources of income in addition to Social Security, up to 85% of your Social Security benefits may become subject to federal income taxes. The formula used to determine the amount of taxes you might pay is complex, and I cover it in Chapter 4.

When you learn how to factor in taxes, you see that many people have their plan completely backwards. They take Social Security early and leave their retirement money alone, waiting until age 70½, when required minimum distribution rules require them to begin taking withdrawals. From a tax perspective, for some people this can be one of the worst ways to get their retirement income. It is beyond the scope of this chapter to get into the details of why, but I cover it in Chapter 4.

What If Social Security Goes Away?

When I read online articles about Social Security claiming strategies, I always find it fascinating to read the comments from readers. A number of them attempt to negate the information in the article by suggesting that Social Security won't be around, and therefore you should take your money and run.

Often, the same people who say this have their money in the bank (backed by FDIC insurance, which is backed by the U.S. Government), collect unemployment or other forms of benefits, or own U.S. bonds of some kind. Why would you be willing to count on the government for one form of sustenance but not another?

Yes, there will likely be changes to the Social Security system to make it viable for younger generations. Small changes like adjusting the full retirement age up by one month can have a big impact on the overall system but a negligible impact on any one person. Those are the types of changes I foresee.

No one is required to stay in the United States. If you find another country which you believe provides more security, and you can juggle the visa requirements and immigration laws to make it happen, then go. That is your right. It is also your right to say whatever you want as publicly as you wish. If you are near retirement age today, it is my right to think you are a fool if you are making your decision about Social Security based on a belief that it is going to go away.

Summary

The Center for Retirement Research offers a short brochure titled "The Social Security Claiming Guide." On the front page it says, "A guide to the most important financial decision you'll likely make."[18]

It is important to do analysis before you make this important and often irrevocable decision.

A smart Social Security decision that is integrated with the rest of your retirement plan can help provide a solid floor of guaranteed income.

The evidence is clear that everyone has something to gain from developing a Social Security plan.

I think it is important to use software to advise you on your options. The rules are complex, and important nuances can be missed by trying to work through this decision on your own.

Be smart and design a claiming plan. Build it into your Income Timeline. Then you can begin to align your investment decisions around your plan. I examine potential investment choices in Chapter 5.

Before you start to look at investing, there is one more thing to incorporate into your timeline – taxes. Let's move on to Chapter 4 to see how a tax timeline helps you plan for this expense in retirement.

---

18 http://crr.bc.edu/special-projects/books/the-social-security-claiming-guide/

Chapter 4

Taxes

Plan and Pay Less

"The conventional view serves to protect us from the painful job of thinking."

—John Kenneth Galbraith

Browsing through an online article on retirement income one day, I came across a paragraph similar to this:

> The other consideration is which accounts to withdraw from first. In general, if you have a taxable investment account, you should withdraw from this account before you touch your retirement accounts. Why? Because the longer the investments in your retirement accounts continue to grow tax deferred, the better.

That paragraph reflects what is called *conventional wisdom*, and many people who follow this particular conventional wisdom are paying far more in taxes than they would be if they took a different approach.

In the case of this article, I knew the journalist, so I sent an e-mail suggesting that the paragraph be replaced with something like this,

> Which accounts should you withdraw from first? It depends on your individual tax situation. Choosing which accounts to withdraw from in a way that matches your tax situation can result in significant savings.

I am happy to say that my e-mail was well received!

I took the time to send the e-mail because incorporating meaningful tax planning with your retirement plan can mean big bucks for you.

Note   My intent with this chapter is not to provide a laundry list of the tax rules. Those are readily available online. Instead, I'd like to focus your attention on the type of tax planning that can save you money.

What matters is not how much income you have; it's how much you have available to spend. If, after paying taxes, you are expecting to have $60,000 a year available to spend in retirement, and proper tax planning can increase it to $63,000 a year, that's a meaningful increase.

Research papers have begun to quantify the results that can be delivered by incorporating tax planning with investment management.

In a paper titled "Tax Alpha: The Importance of Active Tax Management,"[19] put out by a Canadian wealth management firm, author Tim Cestnick says, "It's possible to reliably and consistently add 200 to 300 basis points annually through attention to taxes."

In layman's terms that means it's possible to add the equivalent of an additional return of 2–3% a year by using a strategy to minimize taxes. One of the challenges with this; these types of returns don't show up in investment performance results. This type of return is received by paying less in taxes, which means less withdrawals needed in retirement, which means your money does more for you. Too many eager investors focus on performance results which are stated in terms of gross returns of an investment – in many cases investments that appear to be high performers can deliver less in after-tax returns than other more conservative approaches.

An Ernst & Young study[20] commissioned by LifeYield (a company that builds software to help advisors deliver advice that is more tax conscious) looked at the results over 40 years of managing assets using LifeYield's methodology (which pays attention to taxes) versus using a Pro Rata approach (where taxes are not considered in the investment management process) and concluded that the LifeYield methodology would have generated up to:

- 44% more retirement income; and

---

19 Available online at www.waterstreet.ca/data/WSG_Tax_Overlay_Management.pdf.
20 Available online at www.lifeyield.com/research-paper/. Study conducted using 10,000 scenarios on four different hypothetical households of asset levels of $200,000, $400,000, $1 million, and $10 million, covering 40 years, including 15 years prior to retirement and 25 years in retirement.

- 39% fewer taxes.

LifeYield's methodology looks at a few key things such as asset location, capital gains management, and tax-managed income distributions. In this chapter, I explain what these things are.

Without knowing your situation, it is impossible to tell you how much increased income tax planning can deliver, but it can likely make a difference.

Unfortunately, incorporating smart tax planning isn't easy. Putting together a retirement income plan that considers all these pieces is like putting together a complex jigsaw puzzle where each time you decide where to place one piece it instantly changes the shape of some of the other pieces.

I break it down into the types of tax planning that apply to three situations:

- While you are still contributing to savings

- When you are taking withdrawals

- How you allocate your investments

While You Are Contributing

Many people get serious about saving as they reach their 50s. This is good! They often begin putting as much away in tax-deferred accounts as possible. This is better than not saving at all, but it might not always be the best strategy based on taxes. To understand why, you have to take a look at the tax brackets.

Table 4-1 shows the U.S. 2016 federal tax brackets. The ranges you see refer to the amount of taxable income you have. *You can find taxable income on the second page of your 1040 tax form on line 43.* Taxable income is calculated after taking all applicable personal exemptions and standard or itemized deductions.

Table 4-1. U.S. Tax Code Brackets

Taxable income that falls in this range:		Applicable Marginal Tax Rate (%)	Long Term Capital Gains Rate[4] (%)
Single	Married		
$0 - $9,275	$0 - $18,550	10	0
$9,276 – $37,650	$18,551 – $75,300	15	0
$37,651 – $91,150	$75,301 – $151,900	25	15
$91,151 – $190,150	$151,901 – $231,450	28	15
$190,151 – $413,350	$231,451 – $413,350	33	15
$413,351 – $415,050	$413,351 – $466,950	35	15
$415,051 +	$466,951+	39.6	20

Note   The long-term capital gains rate also applies to qualified dividends.[21] These rates are not tiered in exactly the same way the marginal rates are. For a detailed explanation, see the September 30, 2014 article "Qualified Dividends and Capital Gains Flowchart" by Kevin H. Koehler, CPA, MBT at http://www.thetaxadviser.com/issues/2014/oct/tax-clinic-04.html.

Here is what you must know about how tax brackets work: only the next dollar that falls into a range is taxed at that marginal rate. For example, if you are single and have $37,651 of taxable income, the first $9,275 is taxed at 10%, the next $28,375 is taxed at 15%, and the next $1 is taxed at 25%.

In 2016, each person gets a personal exemption of $4,050 and a standard deduction of $6,300.

- This means in 2016 a single filer can have at least $10,350 of income (their personal exemption plus their standard deduction) that will not be taxed.

21 A dividend is *qualified* if it was paid by a U.S. or qualified foreign corporation, and you held the investment for "more than 60 days during the 121-day period that begins 60 days before the ex-dividend date," per IRS website: www.irs.gov/publications/p17/ch08.html#en_US_2011_publink1000171584. The 1099-DIV form you receive each year should show you what amount of dividends are qualified versus non-qualified.

- A married couple can have at least $20,700 of income that will not be taxed. [22]

If you itemize deductions[23] (you can see the amount of itemized deductions on page 2 of the 1040 on line 40), you may have additional income that is not subject to taxation. For example, if you are married and have $30,000 of itemized deductions, this amount will replace your $12,600 of standard deductions. Add $30,000 to your combined $8,100 of personal exemptions and you can have up to $38,100 of income that will not be taxed.

Tip   If you want to get the most out of this chapter, grab your last tax return and look up the line items as I reference them.

You can use your tax rates and an estimate of your taxable income to determine the most advantageous types of retirement accounts to contribute to.

To simplify things, let's break your choices into two categories:

1. Traditional tax-deferred retirement account contributions (Traditional IRA, 401(k), or 403(b) contributions for example).

2. After-tax retirement account contributions (such as Roth IRA or designated Roth account contributions).

I will refer to these choices as traditional or Roth.

With traditional contributions, money goes in on a tax-deductible basis,[24] grows tax-deferred, and you pay taxes at your ordinary income tax rate when you withdraw it.

---

22 Those 65 and older get an additional standard deduction of $1,550 if single and $1,250 if married. This means a couple whom are both age 65 or older can have $23,200 of income that will not be taxed, even if they do not itemize deductions (based on 2016 deduction/exemption amounts).

23 Itemized deductions take the place of standard deductions. Normally you only use itemized deductions if they are greater than your standard deduction, but there are cases where for someone covered by the AMT (Alternative Minimum Tax), it makes sense to intentionally use itemized deductions, even when they are lower than the standard deduction.

24 If you contribute $1,000 on a tax-deductible basis, you will report $1,000 less of taxable income. If that $1,000 falls in the 25% marginal rate, that $1,000 contribution will reduce your current year taxes owed by $250.

With Roth contributions, money goes in after-tax, grows tax-free (if you follow the rules[25]), and withdrawals are tax-free when you take them.[26]

Using these rules, let's look at an example. Suppose you are a single tax filer and you do not itemize deductions. You make $55,000 a year. You have downsized your lifestyle so you can save as much as possible, and you plan on contributing $15,000 a year to your 401(k) plan.

Note   2016 401(k) Salary Deferral Limits: The 2016 401(k) contribution limits are $18,000 plus an additional $6,000 of allowable contributions for those age 50 or older.

The first $10,350 of your income is not taxed (due to your personal exemption and standard deduction), so you have $44,650 of taxable income. By looking up your taxable income and tax brackets in Table 4-1, you see that of the $15,000 that goes into your 401(k) plan, the first $7,000 of it saves you taxes at the 25% tax rate. The next $8,000 saves you taxes at the 15% rate.

Maybe it would make more sense to put the money that is only saving you taxes at the 15% rate into a Roth (or designated Roth account if your 401(k) plan offers this). You'll learn why this might make sense throughout this chapter as you see how Roth distributions are treated when you take withdrawals.

If you are expecting to be in a higher tax bracket in retirement, it is likely the Roth will be a better long-term solution for you. But to know for sure, you need a multiple-year tax projection that incorporates your future sources of income (such as Social Security and pension income) as well as retirement account values.

Retirement account values are necessary because traditional IRA accounts and other types of retirement accounts, in which the money went in tax-deferred, require you to start taking withdrawals at age 70½. These withdrawals are taxed as ordinary income in the year they occur. In many cases, these re-

---

25 See IRS Publication 590-B for rules on Roth distributions. This can be found at: https://www.irs.gov/publications/p590b/ch02.html.

26 With both traditional retirement account withdrawals and Roth retirement account withdrawals, a 10% early withdrawal penalty may apply on withdrawals taken before you reach age 59 1/2.

quired withdrawals also end up making more of your Social Security benefits subject to taxation.

Roth accounts do not require withdrawals at any age, and when you do take withdrawals, they are tax-free. In addition, Roth IRA withdrawals are not included in the formula that determines how much of your Social Security benefits will be subject to taxation.

When you put all this together in a comprehensive plan, it means that a smart strategy during your savings years may result in substantial tax savings throughout your retirement years.

Tax Planning Triggers

If your income and deductions stay fairly consistent from year to year, you can figure out your best strategy and stick with it until something major changes.

When you have a year in which your income or deductions change, you want to pay special attention to your tax planning that year. Here are some triggering events that should cause you to do additional tax planning in the year these events occur:

- Change in amount of mortgage interest you pay (maybe you paid off a mortgage, refinanced, or took on a mortgage)

- Variations in income because you work on commissions, have varied bonuses, or your income varies from year to year. (For one real estate agent I work with, in low income years we have her fund Roth accounts, and in high-income years we have her make deductible 401(k) contributions.)

- Loss or change of job

- Year of retirement

- A year with a lot of health expenses and/or charitable contributions that may increase your itemized deductions

- Change in number of dependents you claim

- Move to a different state with a different tax structure

Excellent tax-planning opportunities exist during low-income/high-deduction years. I am going to talk about two of them that are relevant to those nearing retirement: Roth conversions and IRA withdrawals.

Tip   Excellent retirement tax-planning opportunities exist during low-in-come/high-deduction years.

Roth Conversions

As mentioned, with traditional retirement accounts you put the money in pre-tax. It grows tax-deferred (meaning you don't get a 1099 tax form each year showing you the amount of interest, dividends and capital gains to re-port—because you don't report them). When you withdraw from these ac-counts, you pay tax at your ordinary income tax rate, only on the amounts you withdraw, in the year you withdraw it. Your tax rate is determined by all your combined sources of income.

With a Roth IRA, you put the money in after-tax. It grows tax-free (meaning if you follow the rules you never pay tax on the interest, dividends, and capital gains that are earned in the Roth). When you withdraw the money, you pay no tax on withdrawals.

You can convert money in traditional retirement accounts to a Roth. You pay tax on the amount that you convert (but no penalty taxes for early withdraw-als) in the year you do the conversion. After that, the money is in the Roth, and Roth tax rules apply.

During the 2008–2009 Great Recession, I had several high-income clients who found themselves out of work. They had deductions because they still had a mortgage and all their other expenses. They had savings to use to pay their expenses, so they didn't need to worry about day-to-day living money.

We put together a tax projection (an estimate of what we think someone's tax return will look like) and realized they would have about $40,000–$50,000 of negative taxable income. What does that mean? It means they had more deductions[27] than income. With $40,000 of deductions, they could have up to

---

27 The word *deductions* here really means a combination of deductions and exemptions.

$40,000 of income and pay no tax. We used up their deductions by converting about $40,000 of IRA money to a Roth IRA.

In addition to converting an amount sufficient to offset deductions, it may make sense to "fill up" the 10% or 15% tax brackets if projections show you are likely to pay taxes at a higher rate later on. Also, Roth-conversion strategies make the most sense if you have money outside of retirement accounts that you can use to pay the additional taxes owed.

The Roth IRA is such a powerful planning tool; it deserves a few more words.

Roth IRAs: The Superhero of Retirement Accounts

I consider a Roth IRA the superhero of the retirement account world. It has some amazing features, and I think it is currently underutilized as a planning tool.

First of all, who can contribute to a Roth IRA?

- Single filers who have less than $117,000[28] of adjusted gross income

- Married filers who have less than $184,000 of adjusted gross income

- Employees whose employer offers a designated Roth account as part of the company retirement plan offering, regardless of income level

- Self-employed persons who establish a 401(k) that offers a designated Roth account, regardless of their income level

What makes Roth IRAs so great? Roth IRAs have several features that give them superhero status:

---

28 Roth contribution limits begin to phase out for single filers with adjusted gross income in the $117,000–$132,000 range and for married filers in the $184,000–$194,000 range. This means if your AGI falls in that range, you may be able to contribute some money to a Roth —just not the maximum allowable amount (2016 limits quoted).

- First of all, you can always withdraw your original contributions[29] from your own Roth IRA without tax or penalties. This gives you liquidity that other retirement accounts don't have.

- Interest and dividends earned are tax-free.

- Roth IRA withdrawals do not count in the formula that determines the amount of your Social Security benefits subject to taxation.

- Roth IRA withdrawals do not count in the formula that determines how much your Medicare Part B premiums will be.

- With a Roth, there are no required minimum distributions at age 70½.

For 2016, the maximum amount you can contribute to a Roth IRA is $5,500, plus an additional $1,000 for those age 50 and older.[30] If your 401(k) plan offers a designated Roth account, the maximum 401(k) contribution limits apply.

Note   Spousal IRA contributions: To make either a traditional or Roth IRA contribution, you must have earned income in an amount equal to or exceeding the amount of your IRA contribution. If you have a sufficient amount of earned income, you may also make a spousal IRA contribution for a nonworking spouse (either traditional[31] or Roth, depending on which is most advantageous for you). These earned income rules do not apply to Roth conversions. You do not have to have earned income to convert IRA assets to a Roth.

IRA Withdrawals Before Official "Retirement"

Between the ages of 55 and 70, you may find yourself temporarily unemployed or forced into retirement earlier than you had planned. Conventional wisdom

---

29 Contributions are not the same as conversions. There are limitations on withdrawing amounts converted to a Roth, and on withdrawals from designated Roth accounts offered through a 401(k) plan.
30 Limits are indexed to inflation in $500 increments.
31 If you are an active participant in a company retirement plan, and your income exceeds $184,000 (this the 2016 limit which is indexed to inflation), you may not be able to fully deduct a traditional IRA contribution made for a non-working spouse.

would suggest you should not take IRA or 401(k) withdrawals for income in such a situation. This isn't always true.

If you find yourself in this predicament, it may pay to look at your tax situation before making any decisions. You may be able to take money out of your tax deferred retirement accounts and pay no tax. [32]

It makes sense to create enough taxable income (in the form of retirement account withdrawals if you have no other sources of taxable income) to at least offset the amount of your deductions.

Let's look at an example. Suppose you are married, age 60, and find yourself unemployed. You have mortgage interest, charitable contributions, state taxes, and other items that add up to about $34,000 of itemized deductions. In addition, you have your personal exemption of $4,050 for each of you. Now let's say you were laid off at the beginning of the year. You have almost no income and $42,100 of deductions.

You decide to run a tax projection and realize that if you withdraw $50,000 from your IRA, the first $42,100 will be tax-free because of your deductions, and the next $7,900 of your withdrawal will only be taxed at the 10% rate. As a matter of fact, you realize the 10% bracket goes up to $18,550 for a married couple. If you wanted to fill up the 10% tax bracket, you could take a total IRA withdrawal of $60,650. You take the withdrawal, and pay $1,855 of income taxes on a $60,650 IRA withdrawal (a 3.1% effective rate).

Because you had a long-term plan in place, you know if you had followed conventional wisdom and taken that IRA withdrawal later when you were required to—when you had other sources of income, like Social Security—you would have paid taxes at the 15% rate at a minimum. That would be $9,097 in taxes.

This strategy thus permanently saved you over $7,000 in taxes.

This is not a manufactured example for the sake of writing a book. I have encountered these planning opportunities several times within a small sample of

---

32 For additional information on the most efficient way to withdraw IRA money, see Alan R. Sumutka, CPA; Andrew M. Sumutka, Ph.D.; and Lewis W. Coopersmith, Ph.D., "Tax-Efficient Retirement Withdrawal Planning Using a Comprehensive Tax Model," Journal of Financial Planning.

about 100 people. The key to recognizing the opportunity is that you must do a tax projection before the end of the year.

A similar situation may exist for someone who is laid off after age 55 but before 59½. It has to do with the age-related rules on 401(k) withdrawals.[33] One of those rules may allow you to take withdrawals from your 401(k) between ages 55 and 59½, and not have to pay the 10% early-withdrawal penalty. This rule only applies if you left the company after you reached the age of 55.

Rather than remembering all the rules, what you want to remember is that if you have a change of job or a year where your income and deductions change, that is also the year you want to put together an accurate tax projection before the end of the year so you can see if any tax savings opportunities exist.

Tip   To take advantage of tax opportunities when you have a life-changing event (like losing your job or buying a new house), you have to do some projections before year's end. It is well worth your time.

When You Are Taking Withdrawals

Prior to retirement, you should create what I call a *withdrawal strategy*. A withdrawal strategy helps you strategically decide which accounts to withdraw from and how to coordinate that with your other sources of income (such as part-time work, Social Security, or pensions) in a way that improves your outcome.

The simplest way to look at it is to realize that all sources of retirement income are not equal when viewed on an after-tax basis.

For example, for each dollar you withdraw from a Roth IRA, you get to spend the entire dollar. No taxes are owed on Roth IRA withdrawals. For each dollar you withdraw from a traditional IRA or 401(k), a portion will be owed to Uncle Sam. Maybe you only get to keep 60 to 90 cents, depending on your tax bracket (maybe even less after factoring in state taxes).

Then you have Social Security. Depending on how much other income you have, you may get to keep all your Social Security benefits or you may owe taxes on them. Taking extra money out of a traditional IRA can have a double

---

33 I cover these in Chapter 7.

whammy effect by suddenly making more of your Social Security subject to taxation. As a matter of fact, if your income and Social Security fall into certain ranges, you can find yourself paying about 46 cents of every extra dollar of IRA withdrawals in taxes. [34]

Figuring Taxes on Social Security Benefits

To understand how Social Security taxation works, you have to look at the formula that is used to calculate the portion of your benefits that will be taxed. The formula starts by determining something called *combined income*. [35]

For tax purposes, combined income is calculated as the total of your adjusted gross income[36] (page 1 of the 1040 tax form line 37), plus non-taxable interest, plus one half of your total Social Security benefits.

If your combined income is less than the threshold amounts in Table 4-2, you will not pay income tax on any of your Social Security benefits. If your combined income is over the lower threshold amount, then a formula is used to determine how much of your Social Security is subject to taxation.

The formula applied is a three-part test that determines the amount of your Social Security benefits subject to taxation. You pay taxes on the lower of:

- 85% of your Social Security benefits

- 50% of the benefits plus 85% of the amount of combined income over the second threshold amount

- 50% of the amount of combined income over the first threshold amount, plus 35% of the amount of combined income over the second threshold amount

These threshold amounts in the formula are shown in Table 4-2.

---

34 For an example of when this 46% rate may apply, see The Bogleheads article "Taxation of Social Security benefits," available online at www.bogleheads.org/wiki/Taxation_of_ Social_Security_benefits.

35 You will also see this called *provisional income*.

36 For this calculation it is adjusted gross income calculated *without* including the taxable portion of your Social Security.

Table 4-2. Combined Income Thresholds for Social Security Taxation Formula

	First Threshold ($)	Second Threshold ($)
Single filers	25,000	34,000
Married filers	32,000	44,000

How would this work for a single woman, age 66, who has $25,000 of Social Security income and $25,000 of IRA withdrawals? Her combined income would be her IRA withdrawals plus half her Social Security, which comes to $37,500. Using these numbers in the three-part test provides these results:

- 85% of her benefits would be $21,250.

- $12,500 (which is 50% of her Social Security benefits) + $2,975 (85% of the amount over the second threshold of $34,000) equals $15,475.

- $6,250 (which is 50% of the amount of combined income she has in excess of the $25,000 first threshold) + $1,225 (35% of the amount of combined income in excess of the second $34,000 threshold amount) equals $7,475.

The lower of the three amounts is subject to taxation, so $7,475 of her Social Security benefits (or about 30% of the benefits) are taxed. This $7,475 then goes into line 20b on the 1040 tax form under the taxable amount of Social Security benefits. When you then calculate your taxable income and tax liability, the results are:

- *Taxable income:* $20,575 (after applicable deductions and exemptions)

- *Tax liability:* $2,623[37]

Now, what happens if she takes an extra $25,000 out of her IRA? You would think at most her tax liability would double, right? Not in this case. Her combined income now comes to $62,500 because of her additional IRA with-

---

37 These numbers were calculated using 2016 tax rates. You can verify these numbers by using the "How much of my Social Security benefit may be taxed?" calculator at http://www.calcxml.com/calculators/how-much-of-my-social-security-benefit-may-be-taxed. Take the result and plug it into DinkyTown's 1040 Tax Calculator at www.dinkytown.net/java/Tax1040.html.

drawals. Using this combined income amount, the three-part test is applied to determine how much of her Social Security is subject to taxation. With the new, higher combined income amount, the results look like this:

- 85% of her benefits would still be: $21,250.

- The final two tests result in a number larger than 85% of her benefits, and the maximum amount of Social Security benefits subject to taxation is 85%, so 85% of her benefits become taxable.

This $21,250 then goes into line 20b on the 1040 tax form and is used to calculate taxable income and tax liability. With the additional IRA withdrawal, the results are:

- *Taxable income:* $59,350

- *Tax liability:* $10,609

Now if you go back to Table 4-1, with taxable income of $59,350, she should be in the 25% marginal rate. Yet she paid an additional $7,986 of taxes on her additional $25,000 IRA withdrawal—an effective rate of 31.9%. Her additional IRA withdrawal meant that an additional $13,775 of her Social Security became included as taxable income.

When you look at how all this works, it shows that you can design a withdrawal strategy that can save money. The most comprehensive analysis of this interaction between Social Security, taxes, and retirement account withdrawals that I have found is a chapter titled "Rethinking Social Security Claiming in a 401(k) World" from the book *Recalibrating Retirement Spending and Saving* by James I. Mahaney and Peter C. Carlson (Pension Research Council, 2008).[38] In this chapter, the authors provide detailed examples and conclude:

> When considering the after-tax dollars actually available for the retirement lifestyle, the break-even age for comparing early Social Security versus delayed Social Security is often lowered to somewhere between 75 and 76 years old. The actual age varies depending on the tax situation of the individual. It is important to note that the tax advantages created by delaying Social Security may be even more advantageous for a married couple after the death of the primary worker.

---

38 Chapter available online at http://www.pensionresearchcouncil.org/publications/document. php?file=904.

When you use this research to take a close look at your claiming options on an after-tax basis, and you account for the fact that after the death of the first spouse, filing status will change from married to single (and thus the lower combined income threshold amounts will apply to determine how much of a surviving spouse's Social Security is subject to taxation), for many singles and couples it meaningfully affects when you should begin taking your Social Security benefits.

The type of tax planning which takes a detailed look at the interaction of your Social Security benefits with your other sources of income is beneficial for those with expected after-tax retirement income of around $90,000 or less.

Here are the key takeaways when looking into a withdrawal plan that minimizes taxes:

- Marrieds have a higher combined income amount than singles. While married you may pay little tax on your Social Security benefits, but a surviving spouse who becomes a single tax filer may suddenly see his or her income reduced by taxes because the lower threshold amounts now apply.

- Roth IRA withdrawals do not count in the Social Security taxation formula, but traditional IRA withdrawals do. With traditional IRAs, you must take required minimum distributions starting at age 70½. Each year thereafter, you are required to take a slightly larger withdrawal.

- You have the ability to convert traditional IRA assets to a Roth IRA. By doing so, you reduce your required minimum distributions later, and you can now take Roth IRA withdrawals at any time without affecting the amount of Social Security benefits subject to taxation.

- When doing your planning, if you expect your after-tax retirement income to be $100,000 a year or less, evaluate the potential benefits of a strategy that involves starting your Social Security benefits later and converting traditional IRA assets to a Roth over multiple tax years before you start Social Security.

For many (like Wally and Sally, whose situation we will look at in a few pages) a tax-conscious strategy will result in lowering the cumulative amount of taxes paid over their retirement years by a meaningful amount.

Another factor that plays into withdrawals in retirement is the required minimum distribution rules.

Required Minimum Distributions

Once you reach age 59½, you may take distributions from an IRA or other qualified retirement plan without being subject to the 10% early-withdrawal penalty tax. Once you reach age 70½, you have to begin taking withdrawals from IRAs and other qualified retirement accounts. These withdrawals are called *required minimum distributions* (RMDs).

The amount of your required distribution is based on two things:

- Your prior year's December 31st account balance

- An IRS table that provides a divisor based on your age

There are three separate IRS tables; a description of each follows. The appropriate one to use depends on your situation:

- *Uniform Lifetime Table:* This table is used for singles and marrieds whose spouse is within ten years of their own age.

- *Joint and Last Survivor Table:* This table is used if you have a spouse who is younger than you by ten years or more.

- *Single Life Expectancy Table:* This table is used if you are taking distributions from an IRA you inherited as a non spouse beneficiary.

At age 70, using the Uniform Lifetime Table, the divisor is 27.4. Assuming a prior year end account balance of $200,000, you take $200,000 divided by 27.4, and the RMD at age 70 is $7,299.27. RMDs cannot be rolled over into another retirement account, although you can reinvest them in an after-tax savings or investment account.

Note   You can find the full tables detailing required distributions in IRS Publication 590-B at https://www.irs.gov/uac/about-publication-590b.

Each year, you are required to take a larger portion of your remaining retirement accounts as a required minimum distribution. At age 85 the divisor is 14.8 and someone with a $200,000 balance would be required to take $13,514. For those with large retirement account balances who don't need the larger withdrawals for income purposes, this can have the effect of steadily increasing their taxable income in retirement. This is one of the reasons strategic planning—and potentially taking IRA withdrawals earlier than you might think—might lower your cumulative tax bill in retirement.

If you miss an RMD, a 50% penalty tax applies to the amount that should have been—but wasn't—withdrawn. This is one of several reasons I think it makes sense to consolidate retirement accounts near retirement. If you have numerous accounts, it can be easy to miss a required withdrawal or overlook important notices or paperwork that may have been mailed to you.

Exactly when must the RMD begin?

Your first required minimum distribution must occur by April 1st of the year after you reach age 70½.

Example: Tom's birthday is in March, and he will turn 70½ in September. His first distribution must occur by April 1st of the following year, although he could take his first distribution in the current year. If Tom waits until April 1st of the year following the year he turns 70½, he will have to take an RMD for both years.

His decision whether to wait and take two distributions in the second year or take his first distribution in the year he turns 70½ would be made based primarily on his tax situation. Depending on the amount of his required distributions, two distributions in a single year may cause Tom to pay taxes on a portion of the distribution at a higher rate than if he took the first distribution in the year he turned 70½.

What types of retirement plans require minimum distributions?[39]

The RMD rules apply to all employer-sponsored retirement plans, including profit-sharing plans, 401(k) plans, 403(b) plans, and 457(b) plans. The RMD rules also apply to traditional IRAs and IRA-based plans such as SEPs, SARSEPs, and SIMPLE IRAs.

The RMD rules also apply to Roth 401(k) accounts (which are called Designated Roth Accounts). However, the RMD rules do not apply to Roth IRAs while the owner is alive. And remember, you can roll your Roth 401(k) into a Roth IRA after retirement.

Wally and Sally

Let's put some of these tax rules together and see how they impact Wally and Sally's plan.

If you recall, Wally and Sally worked with their tax professional to estimate taxes in retirement based on $40,000 of Social Security income, $5,000 of investment income and $30,000 of annual IRA withdrawals. This resulted in an estimate of $8,000 of federal tax and $1,500 of state taxes. In Chapter 2, Figure 2-3 they used this estimate as a starting place and then assumed taxes went up by 3% each year.

This calculation is sufficient for getting a general idea of whether your current savings and investments are likely to meet your retirement income needs. However, to accurately create a withdrawal strategy, you must get far more detailed when it comes to taxes.

Some sources of taxable income, like RMDs, can begin later and cause you to have additional taxable income at age 70½ and beyond. Some deductions, like mortgage interest, go away if you pay your mortgage off partway into retirement.

---

39 From the IRS website: https://www.irs.gov/retirement-plans/retirement-plans-faqs-regarding-required-minimum-distributions#2

Tax rates are tied to inflation, but some components of the tax code—such as the combined income thresholds used in the formula that determines how much of your Social Security is taxable—are not tied to inflation.

To accurately tie all this together, you must create a projection that inflates the things that inflate, that has an estimate of your RMDs based on the projected future balances of your IRA accounts, and that accurately taxes things depending on the tax characteristics of the income they generate.

For Wally and Sally, I have shown you three possible scenarios. All scenarios use the living expenses shown in the timeline in Figure 4-1, which incorporates their revised spending numbers which include:

- Extra travel money in years 2017 - 2021

- Customized health care expenses as they transition out of work and on to Medicare

- Lower projected expenses for Sally as a surviving spouse as Wally's health care costs drop off and living expenses go down by 15% (In Figure 4-1 you see these changes marked by a box around the corresponding expense in the row for 2038.)

This expense timeline does NOT include taxes. This is intentional, as taxes will vary depending on the Social Security plan and withdrawal strategy that Wally and Sally use.

Figure 4-1
Revised Expense Timeline w/ Extra Travel & Reduction for Survivor

| | | | | Living Expenses | | |
# of Years	Calendar Year	Wally / Sally Ages		Desired Annual Spending	Extra Travel	Projected Health Care Costs	Expenses NOT Including Taxes
1	2016	64	62	$62,000	N/A	$3,000	$65,000
2	2017	65	63	63,860	10,000	18,024	91,884
3	2018	66	64	65,776	10,000	17,652	93,427
4	2019	67	65	67,749	10,000	11,323	89,072
5	2020	68	66	69,782	10,000	11,195	90,977
6	2021	69	67	71,875	10,000	11,755	93,630
7	2022	70	68	74,031	-	12,343	86,374
8	2023	71	69	76,252	-	12,960	89,212
9	2024	72	70	78,540	-	13,608	92,148
10	2025	73	71	80,896	-	14,288	95,184
11	2026	74	72	83,323	-	15,003	98,326
12	2027	75	73	85,822	-	15,753	101,576
13	2028	76	74	88,397	-	16,541	104,938
14	2029	77	75	91,049	-	17,368	108,417
15	2030	78	76	93,781	-	18,236	112,017
16	2031	79	77	96,594	-	19,148	115,742
17	2032	80	78	99,492	-	20,105	119,597
18	2033	81	79	102,477	-	21,111	123,587
19	2034	82	80	105,551	-	22,166	127,717
20	2035	83	81	108,717	-	23,274	131,992
21	2036	84	82	111,979	-	24,438	136,417
22	2037	85	83	115,338	-	25,660	140,998
23	2038	86	84	100,979	-	13,473	114,452
24	2039	87	85	104,008	-	14,147	118,155
25	2040	88	86	107,128	-	14,854	121,982
26	2041	89	87	110,342	-	15,597	125,939
27	2042	90	88	113,652	-	16,376	130,029
28	2043	91	89	117,062	-	17,195	134,257
29	2044	92	90	120,574	-	18,055	138,629
	Totals:			$2,667,025	$50,000	$474,647	$3,191,673

The amount of taxes Wally and Sally will pay depends on when they collect Social Security and the order in which they withdraw from their savings and investments. The tax results of three different withdrawal strategies are shown in Figure 4-2, where you see total estimated federal and state taxes each year for each option.[40]

- Option A – Shows estimated taxes over 29 years if Wally and Sally take their Social Security early, while withdrawing from their non-retirement accounts first, and only withdrawing from retirement accounts when their RMDs begin.

- Option B – Shows estimated taxes if they use their suggested Social Security claiming plan and use the same withdrawal order as Option A.

- Option C – Shows estimated taxes if they use their suggested Social Security claiming plan while converting retirement account assets to a Roth IRA during low tax years, and withdrawing from IRAs before RMDs begin.

In the cumulative columns you see that over 29 years they pay the least amount of taxes using Option C, and the most using Option B. Of course with Option C they pay more taxes early in retirement, with 2032 being their "breakeven" year – the year that the cumulative taxes using Option C are less than using the other two options.

Option C has Wally converting $95,000 of his 401(k) to a Roth IRA in 2017, and then each year from 2018 to 2021 converting another $25,000.[41] Each Roth conversion is reported as taxable income. This is causing the substantial increase in taxes in 2017 in Option C relative to Options A and B.

By using the Roth conversions Wally and Sally fill up the 15% tax bracket in 2017, and have some income that falls into the 25% bracket. In 2018 – 2021, their conversion amounts fill up the 10% bracket.

---

40 Finance Logix financial planning software was used to calculate these estimates.
41 Technically Wally would likely first roll his 401(k) to an IRA, then convert the IRA assets to a Roth as described.

Figure 4-2

Taxes calculated based on three different withdrawal plans.

	Total Annual Fed & State Taxes			Cumulative Taxes		
	A	B	C	A	B	C
Calendar Year	Early SS	Suggested SS	Suggested SS + Roth			
2016	N/A	N/A	N/A	N/A	N/A	N/A
2017	182	168	14,593	182	168	14,593
2018	181	127	2,686	363	294	17,279
2019	135	91	2,580	498	385	19,859
2020	109	57	2,151	607	442	22,010
2021	81	0	1,601	687	442	23,611
2022	1,364	3,412	7,425	2,051	3,854	31,036
2023	1,437	3,791	7,846	3,488	7,645	38,881
2024	11,251	11,268	8,012	14,739	18,913	46,893
2025	12,067	12,061	8,300	26,806	30,974	55,194
2026	12,914	12,891	8,954	39,720	43,865	64,148
2027	14,023	13,756	9,636	53,743	57,621	73,784
2028	14,737	14,658	10,347	68,479	72,279	84,131
2029	15,297	15,558	11,064	83,776	87,837	95,195
2030	15,903	16,537	11,835	99,679	104,373	107,030
2031	16,466	17,442	12,550	116,145	121,816	119,580
2032	17,083	18,549	13,352	133,228	140,364	132,932
2033	17,675	19,650	14,113	150,903	160,014	147,045
2034	18,279	20,447	14,895	169,183	180,461	161,940
2035	18,895	21,258	15,695	188,078	201,719	177,635
2036	19,522	22,094	16,518	207,599	223,814	194,153
2037	15,937	17,448	16,131	223,537	241,262	210,284
2038	32,658	35,005	27,871	256,194	276,266	238,156
2039	32,913	35,284	28,806	289,108	311,550	266,961
2040	33,092	35,479	29,732	322,200	347,029	296,693
2041	32,939	35,320	30,598	355,139	382,349	327,292
2042	32,711	35,172	31,431	387,850	417,521	358,722
2043	32,382	34,956	32,201	420,232	452,478	390,924
2044	31,722	34,497	32,843	451,953	486,974	423,767
	$451,953	$486,974	$423,767			

Why Roth Conversions Can Be So Effective

Suppose you can take $1,000 out of your IRA today and pay 10 cents on the dollar in tax, or you can wait until you reach age 70½, where you have to take the funds out. At that point your balance is larger because you didn't withdraw anything yet, and so the amount you have to take out is larger. These larger required distributions often put you in the 25 percent tax rate once you and your spouse are both over age 70. For some of you, by taking some money out earlier than required, you pay 15 cents on the dollar less in taxes than you'll pay by waiting and taking it out later.

Let's take a look at some of the numbers behind these tax calculations. Tax brackets, deductions and exemptions are indexed to inflation, so in the tax calculations I assume a 2% inflation adjustment each year for these items.[42] (Social Security and Medicare Part B & D thresholds are not indexed to inflation.)

Figure 4-3 shows how the indexing is applied to personal exemptions and the standard deduction for Wally and Sally over the next 29 years.[43] In 2017 the number in the standard deduction column jumps up as Wally turns 65, and it jumps up again in 2019 as Sally is 65 that year. In 2038 you see the exemption and deduction numbers decrease as we assume Sally is a surviving spouse at that point.

All the numbers end in round numbers as the IRS indexing methodology that adjusts the tax code to inflation uses the Consumer Price Index to measure inflation and rounds to the nearest $10, $25, or $100 (depending on which item is being indexed).

---

42 See the Tax Foundation for details on what is indexed and how the indexing methodology works: http://taxfoundation.org/article/2016-tax-brackets

43 For years through 2041 these numbers were calculated using the software program BNA Income Tax™ Planner, Years 2042 – 2044 are estimated by author.

Figure 4-3
Inflation Indexing of
Exemptions/Deductions

Calendar Year	Personal Exemptions	Standard Deduction
2016	$8,100	$12,600
2017	8,200	14,150
2018	8,400	14,400
2019	8,600	16,000
2020	8,700	16,400
2021	8,900	16,800
2022	9,100	17,000
2023	9,300	17,400
2024	9,500	17,700
2025	9,700	18,100
2026	9,800	18,400
2027	10,000	18,800
2028	10,200	19,200
2029	10,500	19,600
2030	10,700	20,000
2031	10,900	20,400
2032	11,100	20,800
2033	11,300	21,200
2034	11,500	21,700
2035	11,800	22,000
2036	12,000	22,500
2037	12,300	23,000
2038	6,250	12,250
2039	6,400	12,500
2040	6,500	12,750
2041	6,600	13,000
2042	6,750	13,250
2043	6,850	13,500
2044	7,000	13,800

Quick recap: your taxes start by calculating your Adjusted Gross Income (AGI) then subtracting out your personal exemptions and deduction (standard or itemized) to determine your taxable income. Your taxable income is plugged into the tax brackets to determine your final tax rate. If a portion of your taxable income is composed of long-term capital gains and qualified dividends, an alternate tax calculation is run, and thus you pay tax at a lower rate on that type of income.

Figure 4-4 shows how all of this impacts Wally and Sally in their Option A scenario over 29 years.[44] You see their:

- Adjusted gross income (AGI)

- Taxable income

- Total Social Security (SS) received

- Taxable portion of their SS

- % of SS that is taxable[45]

- Federal and state marginal rates

From 2017 to 2021 you see a box around their taxable income, which shows a negative number. During those years Wally and Sally have more deductions than income. These years present an opportunity. Wally and Sally can withdraw money from tax-deferred retirement accounts (and/or convert tax-deferred retirement account assets to Roth account) up to the amount of negative taxable income and pay no additional tax.

Starting in 2024 Wally and Sally have over $60,000 a year in taxable income and will remain in the 15% marginal tax bracket until such time as one of them becomes a surviving spouse filing at single rates.

Over these 29 years, $888,550 of the Social Security benefits they are projected to receive are taxable, leaving $474,694 received tax-free.

---

44 For years through 2041 these numbers were calculated using the software program BNA Income Tax™ Planner. For years 2042 – 2044 they were manually calculated.
45 Simply take the taxable portion of SS divided by total SS to calculate the % taxable.

Figure 4-4
Option A - Tax Characteristics

| Calendar Year | AGI | Taxable Income | Social Security Taxation | | | Marginal | |
			Total SS	Taxable Portion	% SS Taxable	Fed Rate	State Rate
2016	$137,300	$114,860	$0	$0	0%	25%	4%
2017	12,140	(10,210)	38,646	0	0	0	3
2018	11,402	(11,398)	45,108	652	1	0	3
2019	8,992	(15,608)	46,008	0	0	0	0
2020	7,258	(17,842)	46,932	0	0	0	0
2021	5,370	(20,330)	47,868	0	0	0	0
2022	31,896	5,796	48,828	8,899	18	10	3
2023	32,441	5,741	49,800	9,373	19	10	3
2024	91,827	64,627	50,796	36,887	73	15	3
2025	96,997	69,197	51,816	39,497	76	15	3
2026	102,334	74,134	52,848	42,186	80	15	3
2027	107,861	79,061	53,904	44,968	83	15	3
2028	112,453	83,053	54,972	46,726	85	15	3
2029	116,214	86,114	56,076	47,665	85	15	3
2030	120,240	89,540	57,204	48,623	85	15	3
2031	124,051	92,751	58,344	49,592	85	15	3
2032	128,177	96,277	59,508	50,582	85	15	3
2033	132,186	99,686	60,696	51,592	85	15	3
2034	136,280	103,080	61,908	52,622	85	15	3
2035	140,453	106,653	63,144	53,672	85	15	3
2036	144,711	110,211	64,416	54,754	85	15	3
2037	125,541	90,241	39,020	33,167	85	15	3
2038	151,056	132,556	34,356	29,203	85	25	4
2039	152,459	133,559	35,040	29,784	85	25	4
2040	153,597	134,347	35,736	30,376	85	25	4
2041	153,559	133,909	36,456	30,988	85	25	4
2042	153,266	133,266	37,189	31,611	85	25	4
2043	152,596	132,246	37,933	32,243	85	25	4
2044	150,658	129,858	38,692	32,888	85	25	4
			1,363,244	888,550			

Figures 4-5 and 4-6 lay out the tax characteristics of Option B and Option C.

Figure 4-5
Option B - Tax Characteristics

| Calendar Year | AGI | Taxable Income | Social Security Taxation | | | Marginal | |
			Total SS	Taxable Portion	% SS Taxable	Fed Rate	State Rate
2016	$137,300	$114,860	$0	$0	0%	25%	4%
2017	11,186	(11,164)	0	0	0	0	3
2018	8,436	(14,364)	31,540	0	0	0	0
2019	6,038	(18,562)	38,604	0	0	0	0
2020	3,784	(21,316)	39,384	0	0	0	0
2021	1,346	(24,354)	40,164	0	0	0	0
2022	49,815	23,715	58,028	19,246	33	15	3
2023	52,699	25,999	62,664	21,636	35	15	3
2024	90,525	63,325	63,924	39,305	61	15	3
2025	95,509	67,709	65,196	41,887	64	15	3
2026	100,708	72,508	66,504	44,576	67	15	3
2027	106,122	77,322	67,836	47,370	70	15	3
2028	111,756	82,356	69,192	50,270	73	15	3
2029	117,399	87,299	70,560	53,177	75	15	3
2030	123,497	92,797	71,976	56,304	78	15	3
2031	129,204	97,904	73,416	59,257	81	15	3
2032	135,491	103,591	74,880	62,482	83	25	3
2033	140,867	108,367	76,380	64,923	85	25	3
2034	145,193	111,993	77,916	66,229	85	25	3
2035	149,611	115,811	79,464	67,544	85	25	3
2036	154,149	119,649	81,060	68,901	85	25	3
2037	133,723	98,423	53,468	45,448	85	15	3
2038	158,392	139,892	48,576	41,290	85	25	4
2039	159,986	141,086	49,548	42,116	85	25	4
2040	161,325	142,075	50,532	42,952	85	25	4
2041	161,536	141,886	51,540	43,809	85	25	4
2042	161,516	141,266	52,584	44,696	85	25	4
2043	161,247	140,597	53,640	45,594	85	25	4
2044	160,120	153,120	54,708	46,502	85	25	4
			1,623,284	1,115,514			

Figure 4-6
Option C - Tax Characteristics

Calendar Year	AGI	Taxable Income	Social Security Taxation Total SS	Taxable Portion	% SS Taxable	Marginal Fed Rate	State Rate
2016	$137,300	$114,860	$0	$0	0%	25%	4%
2017	105,872	83,522	0	0	0	25	3
2018	42,429	19,629	31,540	9,767	31	10	3
2019	40,681	16,081	38,604	10,587	27	10	3
2020	36,524	11,424	39,384	8,856	22	10	3
2021	34,647	8,947	40,164	8,173	20	10	3
2022	68,074	41,974	58,028	27,635	48	15	3
2023	70,951	44,251	62,664	30,022	48	15	3
2024	72,435	45,235	63,924	30,993	48	15	3
2025	74,615	46,815	65,196	32,287	50	15	3
2026	78,838	50,638	66,504	34,528	52	15	3
2027	83,231	54,431	67,836	36,852	54	15	3
2028	87,806	58,406	69,192	39,266	57	15	3
2029	92,431	62,331	70,560	41,705	59	15	3
2030	97,377	66,677	71,976	44,303	62	15	3
2031	102,022	70,722	73,416	46,768	64	15	3
2032	107,182	75,282	74,880	49,475	66	15	3
2033	112,121	79,621	76,380	52,089	68	15	3
2034	117,201	84,001	77,916	54,776	70	15	3
2035	122,409	88,609	79,464	57,524	72	15	3
2036	127,755	93,255	81,060	60,347	74	15	3
2037	128,405	93,105	53,468	45,448	85	15	3
2038	135,396	116,896	48,576	41,290	85	25	3
2039	140,054	121,154	49,548	42,116	85	25	3
2040	144,900	125,650	50,532	42,952	85	25	3
2041	149,869	130,219	51,540	43,809	85	25	3
2042	155,026	135,426	52,584	44,696	85	25	3
2043	160,339	140,339	53,640	45,594	85	25	3
2044	165,769	145,419	54,708	46,502	85	25	3
			1,623,284	1,028,360			

Using Option B or C, where Wally and Sally follow a suggested Social Security claiming strategy, they not only receive more income from Social Security over twenty-nine years, they receive more tax-free income.

In both scenarios B & C, they receive $1,623,284 of Social Security from 2018 – 2044, but using Option C, $594,924 of it is tax-free whereas with Option B, only $507,770 is received tax-free.

In Option C, Wally and Sally have no years with negative taxable income as they convert tax-deferred retirement assets to Roth IRAs, withdrawing from retirement account during years where they would otherwise have negative taxable income.

For this illustration I used a $95,000 Roth conversion in 2017 in order to get more money growing tax-free early on in their plan, even though that meant some of the converted amount was taxed at a 25% marginal rate, which is higher than their marginal rate is projected to be for many of their later re-tirement years. Some couples may wish to front-load their Roth conversions in this way, particularly if they are concerned about higher future tax rates and/or want to do everything possible to put a surviving spouse in a better financial situation. Others may wish to use Roth conversions to fill up a tax rate that is lower than their tax rate is expected to be later in retirement. These nuances are where each person's values impact which planning strategy they implement.

The Impact on Financial Accounts

Each of these different withdrawal strategies will lead to a differing result in the amount of financial assets that are consumed. The deposits or withdraw-als and subsequent balances are projected for each option in Figures 4-7, 4-8 and 4-9.

- Figure 4-7 – shows their beginning of year (BOY) financial ac-count values and deposit/withdrawal timeline based on Option A.

- Figure 4-8 – shows their BOY financial account values deposit/ withdrawal timeline based on Option B.

- Figure 4-9 – shows their BOY financial account values deposit/ withdrawal timeline based on Option C.

Scenario Assumptions

Here are the assumptions used in the withdrawal planning to estimate the financial account balances each year.

- Their non-retirement account earns a 5% return (net of all investment fees). Of this 5%, 50% is taxed as interest income, with the remaining 50% taxed as long-term capital gains and qualified dividends – which means all gains are assumed to be taxed each year. (Additional planning involving investment allocations and gain/loss harvesting may further lower the amount of taxable income this account generates each year.)

- IRA accounts earn a 5% return (net of all investment fees).

- Living expenses increase by 3% a year, while health care expenses go up at 5% a year.

- Tax brackets are indexed to inflation using a 2% inflation rate.

- In these scenarios, Wally passes away at age 85.

- These scenarios assume Wally and Sally do not itemize deductions.

- In the Deposits or W/D column for Sally's retirement account there is a deposit of $35,800 in 2016. This is composed of the $24,000 of contributions Sally made through payroll deduction and $11,800 of employer contributions that went into her plan.

- In all three scenarios you will see years where there are deposits going back into the non-retirement account. This occurs when IRA withdrawals exceed what Wally and Sally need to spend that year. All deposits to the non-retirement account, including the 2016 savings, are directed within the software to a non-interest bearing savings account.

- Upon the death of the first spouse, the software assumes that RMDs increase due to being calculated on the single life expectancy of the survivor. You see this in the deposits or W/Ds column for Wally's retirement assets in the year 2038 in all the scenarios. In reality a surviving spouse has the option to continue distributions based on their deceased spouse's previous RMD schedule so those large increases would not have to occur.

- In Figure 4-9 you see a box around a selection of years for Wally's retirement and Roth accounts. This is a reminder that behind the scenes Roth conversions are happening. In 2017 at the beginning of the year Wally has a zero account balance in his Roth but on January 1, 2017 he converts $95,000 to his Roth so $95,000 is removed from his retirement account, deposited in his Roth, earns 5%, and so by January 2018 he has $99,750 if his Roth. In years 2018 – 2020 the same thing is happening, with $25,000 being converted each of those years.

Figure 4-7
Financial Account Deposit/Withdrawal Timeline for Option A

Calendar Year	Non Retirement Account		Wally Retirement		Sally Retirement	
	BOY Balance	Deposits or W/Ds	BOY Balance	Deposits or W/Ds	BOY Balance	Deposits or W/Ds
2016	$246,000	$21,841	$365,000	$24,000	$546,000	$35,800
2017	280,141	(53,420)	407,843	0	609,984	0
2018	238,861	(48,500)	428,235	0	640,483	0
2019	201,111	(43,199)	449,647	0	672,507	0
2020	166,904	(44,154)	472,129	0	706,133	0
2021	130,008	(45,843)	495,735	0	741,439	0
2022	89,535	(19,913)	520,522	(18,997)	778,511	0
2023	73,623	(20,959)	527,082	(19,890)	817,437	0
2024	55,841	(455)	533,055	(20,822)	858,309	(31,325)
2025	58,178	(842)	538,371	(21,796)	869,126	(32,797)
2026	60,241	(1,244)	542,955	(22,813)	878,975	(34,335)
2027	61,997	(1,879)	546,726	(23,874)	887,741	(35,941)
2028	63,196	(2,103)	549,598	(24,982)	895,299	(37,618)
2029	64,220	(2,257)	551,480	(26,013)	901,518	(39,368)
2030	65,132	(2,311)	552,398	(27,212)	906,254	(41,193)
2031	66,034	(2,655)	552,134	(28,315)	909,356	(42,894)
2032	66,628	(2,851)	550,727	(29,451)	910,870	(44,870)
2033	67,051	(3,258)	548,085	(30,619)	910,435	(46,689)
2034	67,079	(3,706)	544,114	(31,820)	908,115	(48,562)
2035	66,648	(4,203)	538,715	(33,050)	903,759	(50,489)
2036	65,687	(4,745)	531,784	(34,309)	897,211	(52,468)
2037	64,121	(28,066)	523,217	(35,353)	888,307	(54,497)
2038	38,579	7,172	513,153	(63,352)	876,879	(56,573)
2039	47,679	4,621	473,894	(62,354)	862,753	(58,294)
2040	54,325	1,757	433,694	(61,084)	846,157	(60,011)
2041	58,209	(2,083)	392,787	(58,625)	826,972	(61,714)
2042	58,359	(6,242)	352,353	(55,929)	805,082	(63,392)
2043	54,462	(10,694)	312,661	(52,993)	780,379	(65,032)
2044	46,107	(15,814)	273,992	(49,817)	752,760	(66,032)
Totals:		($336,005)		($809,470)		($988,296)

Figure 4-8					
Financial Account Deposit/Withdrawal Timeline for Option B					
	Non Retirement Account		Wally Retirement		Sally Retirement	
Calendar Year	BOY Balance	Deposits or W/Ds	BOY Balance	Deposits or W/Ds	BOY Balance	Deposits or W/Ds
2016	$246,000	$21,841	$365,000	$24,000	$546,000	$35,800
2017	280,141	(92,052)	407,843	0	609,984	0
2018	199,275	(62,014)	428,235	0	640,483	0
2019	145,697	(50,559)	449,647	0	672,507	0
2020	101,176	(51,650)	472,129	0	706,133	0
2021	53,311	(53,466)	495,735	0	741,439	0
2022	1,191	(1,220)	520,522	(30,539)	778,511	0
2023	0	0	515,311	(31,063)	817,437	0
2024	0	10,959	509,304	(19,895)	858,309	(31,325)
2025	10,959	11,573	514,383	(20,825)	869,126	(32,797)
2026	22,532	11,419	518,762	(21,797)	878,975	(34,335)
2027	33,951	11,256	522,366	(22,811)	887,741	(35,941)
2028	45,207	11,083	525,110	(23,869)	895,299	(37,618)
2029	56,290	10,807	526,907	(24,854)	901,518	(39,368)
2030	67,097	10,615	527,785	(25,999)	906,254	(41,193)
2031	77,712	10,179	527,533	(27,053)	909,356	(42,894)
2032	87,891	9,743	526,188	(28,138)	910,870	(44,870)
2033	97,634	9,087	523,664	(29,255)	910,435	(46,689)
2034	106,721	8,716	519,870	(30,402)	908,115	(48,562)
2035	115,437	8,281	514,711	(31,577)	903,759	(50,489)
2036	123,718	7,797	508,089	(32,780)	897,211	(52,468)
2037	131,515	(16,703)	499,904	(33,777)	888,307	(54,497)
2038	114,812	16,222	490,288	(60,529)	876,879	(56,573)
2039	131,034	13,980	452,778	(59,576)	862,753	(58,294)
2040	145,014	11,444	414,370	(58,362)	846,157	(60,011)
2041	156,458	8,008	375,285	(56,013)	826,972	(61,714)
2042	164,466	4,200	336,654	(53,437)	805,082	(63,392)
2043	168,667	78	298,730	(50,632)	780,379	(65,032)
2044	168,745	(4,801)	261,784	(47,597)	752,760	(66,032)
		($125,175)		($796,780)		($988,296)

Figure 4-9							
Financial Account Deposit/Withdrawal Timeline for Option C							
	Non Retirement Account		Wally Retirement		Sally Retirement		Roth
Calendar Year	BOY Balance	Deposits or W/Ds	BOY Balance	Deposits or W/Ds	BOY Balance	Deposits or W/Ds	BOY Balance
2016	$246,000	$21,841	$365,000	$24,000	$546,000	$35,800	$0
2017	280,141	(106,477)	407,843		609,984	0	0
2018	184,535	(64,573)	328,485		640,483	0	99,750
2019	127,624	(53,048)	318,659		672,507	0	130,988
2020	79,669	(53,744)	308,342		706,133	0	163,787
2021	28,593	(29,299)	297,509	(25,768)	741,439	0	198,226
2022	0	4,282	286,020	(10,439)	778,511	(30,000)	208,138
2023	4,282	6,535	289,625	(10,929)	786,696	(30,000)	218,544
2024	10,818	5,206	292,907	(11,442)	795,290	(30,000)	229,472
2025	16,024	4,039	295,828	(11,977)	804,314	(30,351)	240,945
2026	20,063	3,534	298,347	(12,536)	813,428	(31,775)	252,992
2027	23,598	3,004	300,419	(13,119)	821,541	(33,261)	265,642
2028	26,602	2,447	301,997	(13,727)	828,536	(34,812)	278,924
2029	29,048	1,805	303,031	(14,294)	834,290	(36,432)	292,870
2030	30,853	1,198	303,535	(14,952)	838,673	(38,122)	307,514
2031	32,051	378	303,390	(15,558)	841,544	(39,695)	322,890
2032	32,430	(362)	302,617	(16,183)	842,945	(41,524)	339,034
2033	32,067	(1,288)	301,166	(16,825)	842,543	(43,207)	355,986
2034	30,780	(2,271)	298,984	(17,484)	840,396	(44,941)	373,785
2035	28,509	(3,338)	296,017	(18,161)	836,365	(46,724)	392,474
2036	25,171	(4,467)	292,208	(18,852)	830,305	(48,556)	412,098
2037	20,704	(20,704)	287,501	(32,524)	822,065	(50,433)	432,703
2038	0	0	268,599	(41,752)	811,489	(52,354)	454,338
2039	0	0	239,292	(43,991)	798,417	(53,947)	477,055
2040	0	0	206,246	(46,412)	783,058	(55,536)	500,908
2041	0	0	169,094	(48,948)	765,304	(57,112)	525,953
2042	0	0	127,520	(51,675)	745,046	(58,665)	552,251
2043	0	0	81,115	(54,574)	722,185	(60,182)	579,863
2044	0	0	29,470	(30,198)	696,626	(89,079)	608,857
		($285,300)		($568,319)		($1,000,910)	

Comparing Scenarios

Remember in each scenario Wally and Sally consume the same amount – the expenses shown in Figure 4-1. But each scenario requires a differing amount of their savings and investments to accomplish that goal. The total net withdrawals for each scenario are as follows:

- Option A: $2,133,771

- Option B: $1,910,250

- Option C: $1,854,529

In order to do a fair comparison, we need to take each deposit/withdrawal pattern and compare the outcome based on present value. Table 4-3 shows the present value of the three options based on various discount rates.

Table 4-3. Present Value of All Deposits/Withdrawals

Discount Rate	Option A	Option B	Option C
0%	2,133,771	1,910,250	1,854,529
1%	1,768,029	1,591,153	1,548,378
2%	1,475,202	1,335,857	1,303,528
3%	1,239,352	1,130,337	1,106,455
4%	1,048,249	963,848	946,810
5%	892,468	828,120	816,637
6%	764,714	716,760	709,794

By taking the difference in present value of financial assets needed when using one option versus another, you can calculate that at a 3% discount rate with Option C they would need to use $132,897 less of their own money, or need $132,897 less at the start of retirement than if they used Option A.[46]

For those who aren't quite grasping present value, what this means is that if Wally and Sally had an additional $132,897 in financial assets earning 3% a year, and used Option A, it would provide the same result as Option C. But

---

46 In the 3% row the difference between the $1,106,455 under Option C and the $1,239,352 under Option A is $132,897.

they don't have an additional $132,897 – Option C provides an outcome as if they did.

For each potential withdrawal strategy you can total all the account values each year to see the impact on financial wealth. Figure 4-10 graphs their gross beginning of year (BOY) account values for each withdrawal strategy.

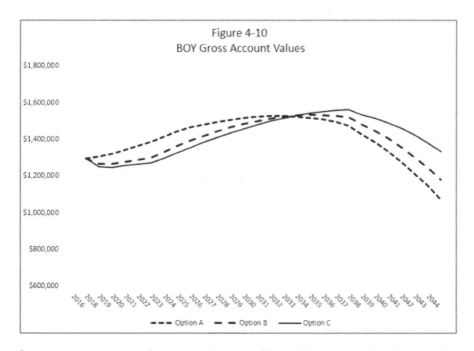

Gross account values, however, do not offer a fair comparison. Each dollar in the Roth IRA can be withdrawn (or inherited) tax-free. I have assumed all gains in the non-retirement account were taxed each year, so every dollar remaining in the non-retirement account can be withdrawn (or inherited) tax-free. The retirement accounts are different. Each withdrawal from a tax-deferred retirement account will be taxed - and if inherited by heirs, the heirs will pay tax on withdrawals from these accounts. To factor this in, I calculate the liquidation value which is a rough approximation of the remaining after-tax financial assets. To calculate liquidation value, I assume that 25% of any tax-deferred retirement accounts are not available (as that amount is going right to Uncle Sam for taxes), and that the full amount of Roth and non-retirement accounts are available.

Figure 4-11 graphs the resulting liquidation value using each of the three strategies. The year that the liquidation value using Option C is projected to be higher than using Option A or B is 2028.

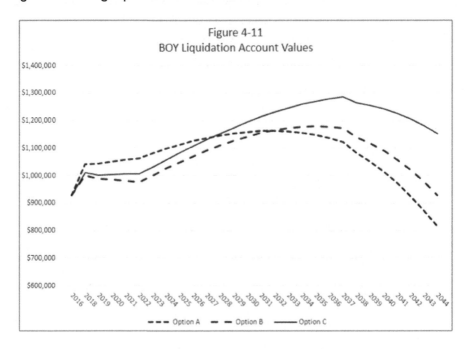

You may think, who cares if I have more assets later? I want to spend more now. Using this planning methodology, you can calculate how much more Option C allows you to spend from day one of retirement while resulting in the same liquidation value as Option A.

In Wally and Sally's situation, if they use Option C, it would allow them to continue their $10,000 a year travel expense all the way through 2030 (instead of through 2021), and end up with about the same liquidation value as if they used Option A.[47]

Option C has other benefits that don't show up in the graphs. Here are a few of them:

---

47 This was calculated in Finance Logix by using the Option C withdrawal strategy and increasing their vacation spending to the point that the liquidation value of assets at end of plan matched the Option A liquidation value. These kind of calculations can also be done using E$Planner®. See http://www.esplanner.com/.

- If tax rates go up, having more assets in the Roth will provide Wally and Sally even greater results. They will have tax-free money to use.

- The Roth is a far more beneficial account for a surviving spouse to have, as they will be filing at single tax rates and will only have their own personal exemption and deduction.

- In these scenarios I assume all accounts earn the same rate of return.[48] If the Roth is intended to be an account that won't be tapped anytime soon then it can be invested more aggressively giving it the potential to earn higher returns, which would result in even more tax-free funds available.

Smart Planning Delivers Positive Results

The bottom line is that smart planning can deliver measurable results. You can measure the results in terms of the values that are most important to you: higher liquidation values if you want to leave more to heirs or increased spending along the way if you want to leave less to heirs. Either way, smart planning provides longevity protection (a better outcome if you are long-lived).

Once Wally and Sally decide on a withdrawal strategy, they can begin to allocate their investments in a way that matches up with their plan. This is covered in Chapter 5.

The scenarios shown for Wally and Sally reflect results independent of any investment or allocation changes.[49] Additional attention to building a portfolio that reduces taxable investment income from their non-retirement accounts may be able to deliver further improvement.

---

48 With the exception noted before: all deposits into the non-retirement account are allocated to a non-interest bearing savings account. The starting principal value is assumed to earn 5%.

49 Some advisors and/or online planning tools imply that by changing your asset allocation, you can increase your return, and your situation looks more secure. I have often seen this approach used in what I consider to be a completely inappropriate way. You need to isolate all the planning decisions that can improve your outcome and then make investment decisions based on cash flow needs and comfort level with risk.

Asset Allocation and Location Decisions

Regardless of whether you are accumulating or withdrawing, if you have savings and investments in both after-tax and tax-deferred accounts, you want to look at how to position those assets to reduce the annual tax impact. The technical term for this process is *asset location*.

Note   Asset location is different than asset allocation. Asset allocation is the process of determining how much of your money should be in asset classes like stocks, bonds, or cash. Asset allocation can be applied at a household level or on an account-by-account basis. Asset location is the process of strategically deciding which asset belongs in which type of account to make the overall outcome more tax-efficient. To apply asset location, you must look at your asset allocation from a household view rather than on an account-by-account basis.

Asset location makes a difference, because not all investment income is taxed at the same rate. Interest income and non-qualified dividends are taxed at your applicable marginal tax rate, whereas long-term capital gains and qualified dividends are taxed at a lower rate. This differential in tax rates provides some opportunities for you.

To understand this, keep three things in mind:

- Your IRA withdrawals are taxed at your marginal tax rate, regardless of the characteristics of the investment income inside the IRA.

- Your Roth IRA withdrawals are tax-free, regardless of the characteristics of the investment income inside the Roth IRA.

- Mutual funds, stocks, bonds, and other investments owned in a regular account (not a designated retirement account of any kind) generate interest, dividends, and capital gains that will be reported to you each year on a form 1099.

Suppose you have two accounts, a traditional IRA and a non-IRA mutual fund. In your IRA, you own a stock index fund that pays a dividend yield of about 2% and accumulates a long-term gain of about 4% a year. Your non-IRA mutual fund is a corporate bond fund that yields about 4% (or it could just as easily be a brokerage account that owns individual corporate bonds).

For the sake of simplicity, let's say you own $100,000 of each fund.

In your IRA, all interest is tax-deferred. But someday, when you take withdrawals, it will be taxable to you. You have $2,000 a year of dividend income in your IRA, and $4,000 a year of gain accumulating. Let's assume it will be taxed at the 25% marginal rate when it is withdrawn, which means when you take $6,000 of withdrawals you will receive $4,500 net of tax.

In your non-IRA account, you have $4,000 of interest income that is being taxed at the 25% marginal rate each year, so you keep $3,000 after taxes. On an after-tax basis, you accumulated $7,500 over both accounts for the year.

If you flip-flopped the two investments (meaning you own the bond fund in your IRA and the stock index fund in your non-IRA), what would happen?

Now you would have $4,000 of interest income in your IRA that someday would be taxed as ordinary income. On an after-tax basis you would receive $3,000; same as the first scenario.

In your non-IRA account, you would have $2,000 of income that is taxed at the qualified dividend rate of 15% and $4,000 of long-term gain realized when you sell shares, which is also taxed at 15% (assuming you are in the 25% tax bracket). On an after-tax basis, you keep $5,100.

Combined, and on an after-tax basis, you have accumulated $8,100; $600 more than the initial allocation choice delivered.

Now maybe an extra $600 doesn't seem like much to you, but when you add up the tax savings that can be achieved by compounding this result over many years, it can quickly turn into thousands.

In addition, in the second scenario, where you own the bonds funds in your IRA and the stock funds in your non IRA account, say you have a year with less taxable income (perhaps a job transition or larger itemized deductions because of medical expenses). If you end up in the 10% or 15% tax brackets, your long-term capital gains could end up being taxed at zero (see the long-term capital gains rates in Table 4-1).

While you are in accumulation mode, once you set your emergency fund aside, I think it makes sense to design an allocation that is as tax-efficient as possible. And for those in higher tax rates, asset location can have a larger impact than in the example here.

As you near retirement, you may need to forsake some tax-efficiency in your allocation in order to most appropriately align the investments in each account (according to risk) with the withdrawals you will need to take from that account.

Tip   You have numerous opportunities to save on taxes by allocating assets in specific ways. But you need to run some projections to identify the allocation that will save you the most in the long run.

Capital Gains Management

Capital gains management is another area where paying attention to taxes can make a difference.

To illustrate how it works, let's make a few assumptions. Let's assume you use an index-fund investing philosophy. You have allocated your growth-oriented stock index funds to your non-retirement accounts based on the asset location guidelines we just discussed.

Now, you are a savvy investor, and so you clearly recognize that the market will not go up in a straight line. You expect that in some years you will have a negative return. Suppose you look at your statement near year end and realize that you have invested $50,000 in one of your stock index funds, but it is currently worth $45,000. You exchange it for a similar stock index fund on the same day, so your overall allocation does not change at all. Yet by exchanging it you realize a $5,000 capital loss. This loss flows through to your tax return. First, it is used to offset capital gains. Then $3,000 of it can be used to offset ordinary income, and you are able to carry forward any remaining loss to offset capital gains and ordinary income in the future.[50]

---

50 Capital losses and capital-loss carryforward amounts offset long-term capital gains first, and then short-term capital gains. Any remaining losses up to $3,000 can be used against ordinary income.

Your ordinary income rate is higher than your capital gains rate—anywhere from 10% to 19.6% higher, depending on your tax rate. That means that tax loss, if used against ordinary income, is worth anywhere from $300 to $588 in reduced taxes. Once again, that may not sound like much to you, but when such strategies are used consistently, the savings can add up.

When it comes to your allocation plan, tax savings can be realized by:

- Looking at your investment allocation on a household basis rather than by allocating each account on its own.

- Intentionally harvesting capital losses when appropriate.

The smart way to do this, as always, depends on your individual situation. It also depends on when you will need to use your money. Your allocation needs to match your risk tolerance, be designed to be tax-efficient, and match your future withdrawal needs. Particularly for couples with age differences, this can lead to some interesting allocation designs.

Let's take Mark and Holly as an example. They were about seven years away from retirement. When we ran their projections, in their case it made sense to follow conventional wisdom (yes, sometimes that does make sense) and defer traditional retirement account withdrawals until they were each required to take them at 70½. Mark is ten years older than Holly. They also had substantial assets outside of retirement accounts. In their allocation plan, we decided to allocate all of Holly's retirement accounts to growth investments, because there would be no withdrawals for 17 years. We placed their taxable bond funds in Mark's retirement accounts, as well as some stock index funds. Then, in their non-retirement account, we used tax-exempt municipal bonds as well as additional stock index funds. When viewed as a household, their allocation was about 45% stock index funds and 55% bonds, CDs, and bond funds. This allocation was appropriate for their risk tolerance, it was tax-efficient, and it matched up with their future withdrawal needs.

Special Considerations for High-Income Tax Filers

There are a few tax rules that high-income tax filers should be aware of. Some of them are new; some have been around for a while. This section discusses a few I want to draw your attention to.

3.8% Net Investment Income Tax (NIIT)

If your adjusted gross income (AGI) is in excess of $200,000 for singles and $250,000 for marrieds, the 3.8% NIIT may apply to some of your investment income.[51] Proper asset location can help reduce the effects of this tax.

Phaseout of Exemptions and Deductions

If you are single with AGI of $259,400 a year or more, or a married couple filing jointly with AGI of $311,300 or more, you may not be able to use all your deductions and exemptions. A phaseout of the deductions and exemptions begins to apply at these income levels.

The Alternative Minimum Tax

The alternative minimum tax (AMT) is a calculation that runs parallel to the regular tax calculation. If the result of the AMT tax calculation says you owe more tax than the regular tax calculation, then you must pay the difference. AMT is most likely to affect singles with incomes of about $200,000–$350,000 and married couples with incomes in the $250,000 to $475,000 range. (You may be more likely to have to pay AMT tax if you have a large family with many dependents, pay high state taxes or high property taxes, or have large miscellaneous itemized deductions.)

When you take a look at the highest tax bracket, add on the NIIT as well as any state and local taxes, and factor in the potential loss of deductions, a high-income tax filer may be paying taxes at a marginal rate of 50% or more.

If you are a high-income tax filer, you'll therefore want to spend more time finding appropriate ways to use tax-deferred products. You'll also want to look at your savings and investments in terms of their after-tax yield.

After-Tax Yield

Assume you own a CD (certificate of deposit) or bond fund, which pays annual interest of 3%.

If you are at the 39.6% tax rate, pay the 3.8% NIIT, and pay state taxes of 5%, for every dollar of taxable interest you earn, 48.4 cents go to taxes.

Your after-tax yield is 1.55% (Calculated by: 3% × (1–.484).

---

51 NIIT went into effect January 1, 2013. You can learn more on the IRS website at: https://www.irs.gov/uac/Newsroom/Net-Investment-Income-Tax-FAQs

You might consider investing in tax-exempt municipal bonds issued by your state as an alternative. Interest paid is not subject to federal or state taxes—but it may be subject to AMT. Although yields are low in today's interest-rate environment, on an after-tax basis a municipal bond yielding 3% is paying you nearly double what you may be getting in something that pays taxable interest income.

Another possibility would be to use a flat-fee variable annuity and tuck your taxable bond investments inside of it. I discuss this in Chapter 8.

There is one additional item that affects high-income tax filers in retirement, and many of them are not aware of it. It is the means-testing that applies to Medicare Part B and Part D premiums.

Medicare Part B and D Premiums

Many people who fall in the high-income category are caught off-guard when they reach age 65 by something that is not technically categorized as a tax, although I would certainly call it a tax.

It has to do with how Medicare Part B premiums are calculated. In Chapter 10, I provide an overview of how Medicare works and what Medicare Part B premiums are. For now, accept that when you turn 65 you will enroll in Medicare and pay a premium for what is called Medicare Part B.

The amount you pay is means-tested, meaning the more income you have, the higher your premiums. Table 4-4 shows you the monthly premium you pay depending on your modified adjusted gross income.[52]

---

52 For those who were already receiving Social Security and enrolled in Medicare as of 2015, the 2016 Part B premiums are lower than the 2016 chart shown in Table 4-4.

Table 4-4. Medicare Part B & D Premiums Based on Modified Adjusted Gross Income

Single ($)	Married ($)	Monthly Medicare Part B Premium ($)	Monthly Medicare Part D Premium ($)
Based on Modified Adjusted Gross Income (MAGI) as follows:			
Up to $85,000	Up to 170,000	121.80	Your plan premium
85,001–107,000	170,001–214,000	170.50	12.70 + your plan premium
107,000–160,000	214,001–320,000	243.60	32.80 + your plan premium
160,000–214,000	320,001–428,000	316.70	52.80 + your plan premium
214,001+	428,001+	389.80	72.90 + your plan premium

Your Medicare Part B premium are assessed based on your modified adjusted gross income (MAGI) from your tax return two years prior. So if your MAGI exceeds one of the threshold amounts in 2016, then in 2018 you would begin paying the next higher premium amount. Note that those in the highest range are paying $4,090 more per year ($340.90 more a month) for their combined Medicare Part B and D premiums[53] than those in the lowest range.

Qualified Roth IRA and Health Savings Account withdrawals are not included in MAGI. By planning ahead, you may be able to avoid paying the higher Medicare Part B & D premiums in retirement.

So far, I have covered what I call tax-planning strategies. I have discussed various concepts and looked at specific examples to see how tax planning can make a difference. Before I wrap up this chapter, I'd like to discuss a few other miscellaneous tax-related items that didn't quite fit in anywhere else.

---

53 Your plan premium for Part D will depend on the type of coverage you select in retirement. Additional details are provided in Chapter 10.

Taxation of Annuities

Many years ago in Colorado, I was out with a small group of friends, and one of my girlfriends brought along a date, someone we hadn't met before. I'll call him Evan. As she introduced us, she told us we were in the same line of work, financial planning.

As he and I started chatting, he said he worked with seniors on their estate planning. I asked if he was an attorney. He said, no, but they had an attorney in their office, and once the attorney had a list of the senior's account and asset information, he would suggest they set an appointment with Evan.

Evan would then show them how they could save money on taxes by repositioning their taxable investments into annuities. I asked Evan how long he'd been doing this. He said about a year. I asked Evan to estimate the average age of his clients. He said about 70.

I said to Evan, "Well I suppose you inform them that with annuities, heirs will not get a step-up in cost basis upon their death, and as a matter of fact will have to pay taxes at their ordinary income tax rate on any accumulated gains in the annuity?"

I got a blank stare.

I went on. "And I suppose you inform them that if they invest after-tax money in a variable or fixed annuity (not the immediate annuity) and take withdrawals, all gain will be taxed as ordinary income at their current tax rate? Whereas it might be taxed at a lower capital gains or qualified dividend tax rate, or possibly even be tax-free[54] if they built a portfolio of investments that were not in the annuity?" Another blank stare.

I went on. "And I suppose you provide a thorough estimate of the tax consequences of selling any of their existing investments in order to move them into the annuity so they aren't surprised come April 15th?" At this point Evan decided not to talk to me anymore.

Unfortunately, there are far too many people like Evan selling investment and insurance products—well-intentioned yet perhaps uninformed.

---

54 If they invested in municipal bonds.

I have no problem with annuities when they are used properly and placed thoughtfully. For example, Chapter 5 discusses the use of an immediate annuity for Wally and Sally. The purpose of this would be to hedge against longevity risk. Based on their tax situation, and using a scenario analysis similar to the examples in this chapter, if they buy the immediate annuity it will be to their benefit to buy it with Wally's IRA money. If they buy it with their joint account assets, it will be a less tax-efficient solution.

What I do have a problem with is people selling these products without doing an objective analysis to show someone how it affects their situation in terms of taxes, liquidation value, or various types of risk. If you buy a product, it should offer an improvement to your situation, and that improvement needs to be shown in quantifiable terms.

Remember   Some investment "professionals" mistake a retirement tool for a plan. After reading this book, you're likely to be better informed about retirement finances than many, if not most, financial advisors.

Mortgages

Many people have an inflated view of the value of their mortgage interest deduction. You either claim your standard deductions or itemized deductions. If you and your spouse are both age 65 or older, in 2016 your combined standard deduction amount would be $15,100.

A mortgage of $375,000 at a 4% interest rate would generate $15,000 a year of deductible mortgage interest—less than your standard deduction. But say you have other itemized deductions, like charitable contributions, state taxes or sales taxes, real estate and personal property taxes, health care expenses (only to the extent that they exceed 10%[55] of your adjusted gross income), and miscellaneous deductions (like tax preparation and investment management fees) that add up to $10,000. In that case, you would add the $15,000 of mortgage interest paid to come up with total itemized deductions of $25,000 (assuming your income is not high enough to be subject to the phaseout of

---

55 Up from 7.5% in 2012.

deductions rule). If you're beginning to think our tax code is overly complex, I agree.

If you want to compare the "return" of paying off your mortgage to that of other investments, you can calculate your mortgage cost on an after-tax basis, but because the full extent of your mortgage interest may not be deductible (as it depends on other itemized deductions you might have), it may not be as simple as taking your mortgage rate multiplied by one minus your tax bracket.

Once retired, when you factor in additional tax intricacies, like the necessity of taking additional IRA withdrawals to continue making mortgage payments, it gets even more complicated.

For example, conventional wisdom would tell you it doesn't make sense to take a large, lump sum IRA withdrawal to pay off a remaining mortgage. In some cases conventional wisdom is wrong.

One case I ran for a retired client—who was already taking Social Security— showed that taking about $100,000 out of his IRA to pay off a $75,000 remaining mortgage, allowed him to lower his future IRA withdrawals. That also lowered the amount of his Social Security benefits subject to taxation. The end result was an estimated cumulative federal tax savings of about $45,000 over a 20-year period.

Cumulative tax savings aren't the only thing to look at. In this tax-planning scenario, as well as with Roth conversions, you are paying a chunk of taxes up front, so the other consideration is the break-even point. In the situation where the mortgage was paid off with a large IRA withdrawal, the break-even point was about nine years out. This was acceptable based on the person's age and health status.

Note   State taxes: As of 2016, thirty-seven states don't tax Social Security benefits. For the thirteen states that do tax Social Security, many have exemption limits, so if your income falls under the limits the benefits won't be taxed. Retirement Living's Taxes by State webpage provides details on each state at: https://www.retirementliving.com/taxes-by-state.

Some states don't tax pension income either, and some have no state income taxes. Property taxes also vary widely from state to state. If you're considering relocating, maybe taxes should play a part in your decision. Use Kiplinger's Retiree Tax Map to find out the tax-friendliest states for retirees: www.kiplinger. com/tools/retiree_map/.

Health Savings Accounts

If Roth IRAs are the superheroes of retirement accounts, health savings accounts (HSAs) are their sidekicks. Together, they make up a dynamic duo.

The basic premise behind the HSA is that you lower your insurance premiums by choosing a health insurance plan that has a higher deductible. Then you contribute the premium savings on a tax-deductible basis to a health savings account. An HSA is not to be confused with an FSA (flexible savings account):

- With an FSA (usually offered through an employer) it's a "use it or lose it" proposition. Money not used during the year is forfeited.

- With an HSA, even if you don't use it, the money stays in the account and continues to grow tax-deferred.

To establish a health savings account, you must have an HSA-qualified high deductible plan. Any health insurance provider can provide you with details on such a plan, and I provide additional information in Chapter 10.

As with an IRA, there is a maximum allowable contribution to an HSA. In 2016, the maximum contribution per single plan is $3,350 (plus an additional $1,000 catch-up for those age 55 and older). The maximum contribution for a family plan is $6,750.

As with an IRA, HSA money goes in on a tax-deductible basis and grows tax deferred (no need to report the annual investment income earned). Unlike an IRA, you can use the funds any time for eligible medical expenses on a tax-free basis.

Even if you spend the full amount of your HSA contribution each year, you still save a fair amount of money in taxes. For example, if you contributed the $3,350 and used it all the next year, doing so saved you $837 at the 25% tax bracket.

One key difference between HSAs and IRAs is the early-withdrawal penalty. With an HSA, a 20% penalty tax applies for early withdrawals not used for medical reasons. For HSAs, an early withdrawal is one that occurs before age 65. For IRAs it is a 10% penalty tax for early withdrawals, and an early with-drawal is one that occurs before 59½.

I have an HSA myself and think they are a great choice for those eligible for them. Ideally you use the HSA as an additional retirement savings account. You would fund it each year, let it accumulate for retirement, and during your working years pay for your health care from other sources – not out of the HSA.

The Value of Advice

Ellen heard me speak at a women's event and called the next day to set up an appointment. She was 82, and her husband had passed away about nine months earlier. She was trying to sort out the finances. Her husband was an engineer and had left his 401(k) plan with his employer throughout his retire-ment. He had about $300,000 of company stock in his plan.

I knew there was a way to distribute this stock that would potentially result in $20,000 or more of tax savings for Ellen and her heirs, but some analysis needed to be done to make sure it was the right strategy for her. The strategy is the use of something called *net unrealized appreciation*.

The net unrealized appreciation (NUA) rule allows you to distribute stock from a company retirement plan and pay ordinary income taxes on its cost basis. (You have to get the cost basis from the company, which, if you have worked for the company for a long time, is often significantly lower than the market value of the stock.)

NUA is the difference between the cost basis and the market value of the stock when distributed from the plan. Once the stock is outside the plan, as you sell the stock, you pay taxes on the NUA gain at capital gains tax rates.[56] Or, if you are age 82, after you distribute the stock, perhaps you hang on to

---

56 Any additional appreciation beyond the market value price at time of distribution will not eligible for long-term capital gains treatment unless held for one year.

it and then upon your death your heirs get a step-up in cost basis[57], so taxes on gain are avoided altogether. If you leave the stock in the retirement plan, this type of tax treatment does not apply. When heirs inherit retirement plan assets, no step-up in basis applies.[58]

Ellen did not want to pay for advice, because her husband had never paid for advice. She wanted to keep things simple: call up a mutual fund company and roll over the 401(k) plan to her IRA. We called her mutual fund company together, and this particular tax strategy came up in the conversation. The mutual fund company representative told her that they could not offer tax advice and recommended she consult with someone about the tax implications before making a decision.

Despite this, Ellen decided she did not want to pay me—nor anyone else—to do the analysis.

Paying for advice is a personal choice. Perhaps in the long run, you'll pay just as much to professionals who can show you how to save in taxes as you would pay in taxes if you simply did no planning. I don't think so, but I do understand that is how some people look at it.

Personally, I'd rather pay for professional advice and be sure that I was taking advantage of all the legal tax strategies available to me. Even if I knew it was a break-even proposition, it would then be a matter of where I'd rather see my money go.

Summary

You can't control tax rates. You can manage taxes. Managing taxes can result in a measurable improvement to your bottom line.

When you are saving, managing taxes means strategically deciding which accounts to fund based on your tax rates now and your projected tax rates

---

57 A step-up in cost basis means the value of the asset upon your date of death becomes the heir's value—or basis—for tax purposes. For example if you bought a stock for $10,000 and it is worth $20,000 upon your death, for tax purposes the $20,000 value becomes the cost basis for your heirs. If they sell it for $20,000 no capital gains taxes are owed on the gain.

58 In this scenario, I am referring to federal income tax, not estate taxes. With the 2013 tax changes, as of 2016 a single person can pass along $5.45 million that is exempt from estate taxes ($10.9 million for marrieds). However, an heir—spouse or non-spouse—must still pay income taxes on withdrawals from inherited traditional retirement plan accounts. (Roth IRAs are tax-free, so heirs do not pay tax on withdrawals from inherited Roth accounts.)

in retirement. It also means paying attention to how you locate investments between after-tax and tax-deferred accounts as well as managing your capital gains and losses.

As you near retirement, managing taxes means creating a withdrawal strategy that lowers your cumulative tax bill. By projecting your tax rates and account withdrawals over your future life expectancy, and designing a plan that is tax efficient, your savings and investments can deliver more cumulative income.

Tax planning results in savings that you actually can take to the bank.

Chapter 5

Investing

How Much Risk to Take

"The safe way to double your money is to fold it over once and put it in your pocket."

—*Frank Hubbard*

Many years ago, I was sitting on a flight headed to see my family in Des Moines, Iowa. As we were waiting to take off, I noticed the guy sitting in the seat next to me reading a publication called *Computerized Investing*, published by the American Association of Individual Investors. I asked him if I might take a look at it when he was done. He said sure. Then he asked me a question that, at the time, I hated. It's a common enough question, but all the same, it is one I hated.

"So, what do you do for a living?"

I could feel a cringe creep over me as I replied, "I'm a financial advisor."

Why is it that I cringed at this oh-so-normal question? I am certainly not ashamed of what I do. I am, however, ashamed at the way a lot of so-called financial advisers do what they do. A lot of misconceptions arise in people's minds when they hear the term *financial advisor*.

Most people assume that if I'm a financial advisor, I sell investments. Somehow this also leads them to believe I might have a stock tip for them. Upon hearing my profession, they almost always ask some version of the same question: "What do you recommend people invest in right now?"

He didn't let me down. He asked, "So, what are you buying these days?" The absurdity of the question hit me all at once, and I was silent for an uncomfortable length of time. I could not think of a rational reply.

After the unusually long pause, I looked at my airplane buddy with a puzzled expression and said, "I'm really not sure how to answer that. It all depends on your goals."

When someone asks me this question, it makes me wonder if they think they would get a different answer if they asked me tomorrow, or the day after. A good investment strategy should not change daily—or even monthly.

I can think of a hundred questions you can ask that will have a bigger impact on your financial success than asking a financial advisor what investment they are recommending. As you reach age 50 and beyond, asking the right questions becomes particularly important.

The first thing you need to learn is how to measure risk. As you transition toward using your savings, your primary goal becomes the development of a strategy that delivers reliable monthly paychecks. This requires a new mindset and a new way of looking at investing. You need to have a way to compare the potential results of one strategy or investment choice to another. You need to make sure you are doing an apples-to-apples comparison, and this means you must have something objective to measure against.

Measuring Risk

Before putting your money somewhere, the first question to ask is "Can I lose all my money?" The second question is "Can I lose any money?"

Every investment can be logged somewhere on such a scale (Figure 5-1).

Figure 5-1. A Simple Investment Risk Scale

The investment risk scale in Figure 5-1 can help you compare the relative risk in one investment choice versus another.

However, you need to be careful with questions like "Can I lose any money?" You would think the definition of losing money would be simple, but it isn't always so.

Suppose you were to put all your money in a five-year, bank-issued certificate of deposit (CD) paying 2% a year. You invest $10,000. Five years later, it is worth $11,041. Inflation over those five years averaged 3% a year. If I were to ask you if you lost money, what would you say?

After adjusting for inflation, your $11,041 would buy only $9,524 of goods and services. Although you didn't lose any actual dollars, you did lose purchasing power. This is inflation risk in action.

In today's investing world, the word risk is often used only to refer to one type of risk: volatility. *Volatility* is the variation of returns from their average. For example, from 1926–2015, U.S. stocks, as measured by the S&P 500 Index, averaged a return of 10% a year. But that average encompassed years where it was down 43.3% (1931) and up 54% (1933), as well as more recent years like 2008 when it was down 37%, and 2009 when it went up 26.5%.[59] This variation of returns from the average shows up as sequence risk. You may project one outcome based on your expected average return but experience an entirely different outcome because of the volatility of the actual returns incurred.

Nassim Taleb, in his book *The Black Swan* (Penguin, 2008), has a section titled "Don't cross a river if it is (on average) four feet deep." It is a statement worth pondering. Many financial projections use averages. There is no guarantee that your investments will achieve the average return. When it comes to aligning your investments toward the objective of producing reliable income, you need to decide whether you want to rely on averages and whether you think they provide an accurate representation of risk.

James Montier, a member of GMO's asset allocation team, has a definition of risk that I like. He says, "Let us forsake the false deity of volatility as a measure of risk. Risk isn't a number. It is a far more complex and multifaceted concept. Risk is the permanent impairment of capital."[60]

---

59 Returns sourced from Dimensional Fund Advisors, *Matrix Book 2016*
60 James Montier, "The Flaws of Finance," GMO White Paper (May 2012). GMO is a global investment management firm. Additional info at www.gmo.com.

The real measure of risk is not losing or gaining money; it is the risk of not achieving your goals. If your money no longer buys the necessary amount of food, clothing, and shelter, conceptual views of risk—whether it is inflation risk, sequence risk, or some other form of risk—become irrelevant.

A one-to-five (1-5) risk scale is useful for comparing the relative amount of risk in one investment to another, but how do you compare an investment choice against the risk of not achieving your goals?

• First you must clearly identify and quantify the goals.

• Next you must determine a risk-free way to achieve those goals.

• Then you can compare your alternatives relative to the risk-free choice. Once you have done this, you can decide whether the riskier alternatives have the potential to improve your outcome enough to warrant taking on the risk.

Identifying goals can be challenging in and of itself. We are all different. I do not want to work and then reach a particular age and "retire." Planning toward that end is not inspiring to me. However, I do want choices, and I do realize there may come a day when I cannot work. I want to make sure I have my finances in order when that time comes.

You may be planning a traditional retirement, or you may choose to simply identify a point in time where you don't have to go to work to earn a living each day—a point where you may still choose to work, but on your terms.

Regardless of how you define your goals, you will reach a point where your financial capital needs to provide reliable income to take the place of your former paycheck. Success at this point is no longer defined as achieving a higher rate of return. You need a different measure of success and a different measure of risk.

Measuring requires a benchmark, something to compare against. When your goal is reliable income, start by looking at what can be achieved by using safe, guaranteed choices. Then compare alternatives relative to your risk-free choices.

Benchmarking Against a Risk-Free Choice

There's only one response when someone asks you, "Hey, is that a safe investment?" And that is: "Safe compared to what?"

A benchmark gives you something to compare to.

If you are interested in having life-long inflation-adjusted income, then compare investment alternatives to risk-free choices that provide guaranteed life-long inflation-adjusted income.

This means measuring against such choices as:

- I Bonds

- TIPS (Treasury Inflation-Protected Securities)

- Inflation-adjusted immediate annuities

Let's take a look at each one of these options.

I Bonds

My interest in I Bonds started after I met Zvi Bodie, professor of economics at Boston University. We were both guest lecturing at a class for upcoming Retirement Management Analysts®. I flew in a few days before my presentation because I wanted to meet Zvi and a few other presenters.

In his presentation, Zvi said he believes that any financial advisor who does not advise their clients about the benefits of I Bonds is committing malpractice. That certainly caught my attention. As I began looking into I Bonds, I could see why he said this. They offer features that in many cases are more attractive than some of the financial products advisors sell. How can an advisor in good faith sell their client a financial product like a fixed annuity without first educating them about a free option that may have similar qualities? Let's take a look at what makes I Bonds attractive:

- I Bonds are issued directly by the U.S. Treasury and have been around since 1998.

- Their primary advantage is tax-deferred, inflation-adjusted interest and complete liquidity after 12 months.[61] In addition, interest earned is exempt from state and local taxes, making them even more attractive for those who live in states with high income taxes.

- You can buy I Bonds by opening a TreasuryDirect account online at www.treasurydirect.gov. Note that you can only buy them in non-retirement accounts (not in IRAs[62]). You do have the option to title your account as a trust.

- I Bonds are issued with a fixed interest rate that stays with the bond for its full term and a variable interest rate which is adjusted every six months based on inflation.

Table 5-1 shows historical I Bond rates[63] for the ten years from November 2006 to May 2016. Using the bonds issued November 1, 2006 as an example, the fixed rate of 1.4% stays with the bond for its entirety, and in the right-hand column you see the inflation rate for the six-month period beginning on that date. The inflation rate is updated every six months and is applied in addition to the fixed rate.

---

61 You cannot redeem I bonds within first 12 months of purchase. For redemptions that occur before five years of ownership, you forfeit the interest from the three most recent months.

62 IRAs require a custodian to provide annual reporting for tax purposes. This requires additional administrative time, paperwork, and costs. It is likely not practical or cost effective for the Treasury to go down this path and offer TreasuryDirect IRA accounts.

63 Treasury Direct I Savings Bonds Rates and Terms at: http://www.treasurydirect.gov/indiv/research/indepth/ibonds/res_ibonds_iratesandterms.htm.

Table 5-1. Historical I Bond Rates

Issue Date	Fixed Rate (%)	Inflation Rate (%)
1-Nov-06	1.40	1.55
1-May-07	1.30	1.21
1-Nov-07	1.20	1.53
1-May-08	0.00	2.42
1-Nov-08	0.70	2.46
1-May-09	0.10	-2.78
1-Nov-09	0.30	1.53
1-May-10	0.20	0.77
1-Nov-10	0.00	0.37
1-May-11	0.00	2.30
1-Nov-11	0.00	1.53
1-May-12	0.00	1.10
1-Nov-12	0.00	0.16
1-May-13	0.00	0.16
1-Nov-13	0.20	0.36
1-May-14	0.10	0.26
1-Nov-14	0.00	0.16
1-May-15	0.00	0.16
1-Nov-15	0.10	0.26
1-May-16	0.10	0.26

If you bought an I Bond in September 1998 when they were first issued and held on to it, by my calculations as of May 2016 you would have earned about a 5.36% annualized rate of return.[64] If bought November 2007 and held until May 2012, about 3.36%.

Unfortunately, the returns have continued to go down as both the fixed interest rates at issue and the inflation rate component are lower now than they have been in the past. A bond bought in May 2016 is yielding about .62%. Of course if the inflation component increases in the future, the yield will participate in that increase.

There is some flexibility offered; if you buy an I Bond that is issued with a fixed rate of zero, after holding it 12 months, you can cash it in and repurchase new I Bonds if the newer issues have a higher fixed rate.

The maximum purchase amount is $10,000 per year per person. You can purchase an additional $5,000 a year by directing your tax refund directly toward the purchase of I Bonds.

Because of the annual maximum purchase limitations and the cumbersome nature of the way TreasuryDirect accounts work,[65] it can be impractical to build a retirement income portfolio with I Bonds, but as they earn inflation-adjusted interest, and their redemption value can never be less than their value the preceding month, this makes them an attractive baseline, or ruler, against which you can measure alternative strategies.

When comparing alternatives to I Bonds, or to anything, you should ask two questions:

- What return in excess of this safe, inflation-adjusted return do you think you will achieve?

- How certain is it?

---

64 An I Bond's composite rate changes every six months and is determined by the following formula: [fixed rate + (2 × semiannual inflation rate) + (fixed rate × semiannual inflation rate)]. Sept. 1998 bonds were issued with a fixed rate of 3.40%.

65 I opened my own TreasuryDirect account. When you log in, they email a one-time password (OTP). You have 24 hours to use it. This would be fine except the email often takes many hours before it shows up in your inbox, and if you're like me, you are on to something else, and often it is more than 24 hours before you come back to find it. Then you have to start over again.

When comparing safe investments like I Bonds to riskier alternatives, keep in mind that there is no guarantee that a traditional portfolio of stocks and corporate bonds will earn a higher rate of return than safer options. The majority of people in the financial services industry will tell you that you must own stocks to have some growth in your portfolio—as if it is a certainty that stocks will outperform safer choices over the long term. It is not a certainty. Japan's large cap stock market index provides a good example. From the beginning of 1992 through the end of 2011, the 20-year annualized return was −.50%.[66] (This means for every $1 invested in 1992, you lost one half of one percent a year each year for 20 years.) Any sane person must acknowledge that any stock market could follow a similar path.

Personally, I believe that over the long term, stocks will provide a higher return than safer alternatives. Yet I acknowledge that my belief will not make it so. If it were a certain thing, there would be no need for safe investments.

Once you embrace an objective view of risk, you can make smarter and more personal decisions about how to allocate your money across both safe and risky choices.

TIPS: Treasury Inflation-Protected Securities

TIPS are another type of bond issued by the U.S. Treasury. The Treasury began issuing TIPS in 1997.

TIPS are issued with a fixed interest rate, and the principal value is adjusted upward (or downward) based on inflation. In a deflationary environment, your TIPS principal value may decline. (This is not the case for I Bonds.)

Both the interest paid and any principal increases are reported as taxable income in the year in which they occur. This makes them tax inefficient. They are best owned inside tax-deferred accounts, like IRAs, which means you need a brokerage account to purchase them for that purpose.[67] There are also mutual funds that specialize in TIPS.

---

66 Dimensional Fund Advisors, *DFA Matrix Book* (2012) p 45.

67 You can purchase TIPS directly with a TreasuryDirect account, but only non-retirement account options are offered. To purchase them in an IRA you must have a brokerage account, which can either be a self-directed brokerage account such as one you might open with Schwab, Vanguard, Scottrade, or E*TRADE, or one you open through a traditional brokerage firm such as Merrill Lynch.

Owning Individual Bonds vs. a Bond Fund

If you buy a bond when it is issued, you get the same amount back when it matures (in nominal, not real terms[68]). Your return is then composed of the interest rate, or coupon rate, that the bond pays.

Note, however, that between the issue date and maturity date, bond prices fluctuate.

For example, assume you buy a $1,000 bond that matures in ten years and pays an interest rate of 5%. The bond's *yield to maturity* is 5%.[69] Three years later, interest rates have gone down, and new bonds being issued (of similar quality and with about seven years left to maturity) are paying 3%. At that point an investor would be willing to pay you more than $1,000 for your bond because of its higher yield. This higher price would have the effect of making this bond's yield to maturity about 3%. In other words, the price increase made it equivalent to other bonds with similar characteristics being sold the day of the transaction. If you hold the bond to maturity you will receive $1,000, regardless of its market value any time before it matures.

On the other hand, if interest rates had gone up to 6%, and you wanted to sell your bond before maturity, an investor would offer you less than $1,000 for it because your coupon rate is lower than current rates. Again, if you hold it to maturity you receive your $1,000.

To summarize, if you sell your bond before it matures, you may get more or less than you paid for it, which will change the total return you earn. But if you hold it to maturity, you will get its face value when the issuer redeems it.[70]

When you buy a mutual fund that owns bonds, your return will depend on the collective pricing and coupon rates of all the bonds the mutual fund owns, and on the timing of when those bonds are bought and sold, which is up to the management team that runs the mutual fund.

---

68 *Nominal* means in today's dollars. Real means in inflation-adjusted dollars. If you buy a $1,000 bond today, and it matures in ten years, you get $1,000. But it may not buy $1,000 of goods and services because of price increases due to inflation.

69 *Yield to maturity* is a calculation that shows your expected rate of return on a bond if you hold the bond to maturity. It takes into account the current price of the bond, the interest rate, and the time left to maturity and assumes all interest is reinvested at the same rate, which in reality is not always possible.

70 Assuming the issuer does not default on its bonds.

I am explaining this because it affects how you measure the return on an investment. To measure the return on a category of investments, financial companies create an index. An index is like a ruler; it is a measuring stick. The S&P 500 Index, for example, measures the collective performance of 500 large-company U.S. stocks. It is not reflective of the performance of any one stock. Think of it as a family with 500 children – some will behave better than others.

There is an index for TIPS. It measures the performance of owning lots of TIPS with varying maturity dates. You can look at this index return to see how TIPS have performed, but keep in mind it is not the same as tracking the performance of buying individual bonds.

The annualized total return[71] for the Barclays Capital U.S. TIPS Index for the ten years from the beginning of 2006 through the end of 2015 was 4.5%.[72] A 4.5% return in a safe investment is not bad. Before you run out and buy TIPS keep in mind this is measured over a time period where interest rates have gone down, and so the corresponding increase in bond prices is included in that total return number.

TIPS have not been around long enough to measure their performance over a prolonged period of rising interest rates. If real interest rates rise (real meaning a rate increase beyond the rate of inflation), prices on existing TIPS bonds may go down.

To use TIPS to create future income, you could buy bonds today that mature in the year you want to spend the money. This is called building a *bond ladder*. When the bond matures you spend the principal and the interest it has accumulated. Building a bond ladder with TIPS can be challenging because you cannot always find TIPS with maturity dates that match your spending needs.

Owning TIPS by purchasing individual bonds offers an attractive and safe option for tax-deferred accounts. However, I find that unless you have multiple millions, it can be impractical to build an effective bond ladder entirely with TIPS.

---

71 Annualized total return means you earned a return equivalent to earning 7.6% a year, but in reality that return was composed of some years where the TIPS Index was down (2008, for example, was down –2.4%) and other years where it was up significantly (2002, up 16.6%).
72 Dimensional Fund Advisors, Matrix Book *2016*, p.48.

As an alternative to TIPS or I Bonds you can accomplish a laddering strategy by using a combination of CDs, agency bonds, municipal bonds and packages of bonds called BulletShares®.[73] I will collectively call such investments "fixed income". Using such a strategy is a smart way to guarantee the cash flows that need to come out of each account in the first five to ten years of retirement. With current cash flows guaranteed, you will never be in a position where you are forced to liquidate riskier investments at an inopportune time.

As an alternative to buying individual bonds, you can buy bond funds. In that case, your return is dependent on the collective pricing and yields of lots of bonds.

Both I Bonds and TIPS provide a safe investment option and protect your future purchasing power, but may be impractical to use. They do give you something to measure other choices against. You can use fixed income choices for all of your investments, a small portion, or none of them. It's your choice regarding how much risk you want to take and how much work you want to put into building and managing your portfolio. Later in this chapter, you'll learn more about deciding how much to put in these types of investments.

Immediate Annuities

An immediate annuity is another safe option, but it is not an investment. An *annuity* is a contract with an insurance company. I've included it in the investment chapter because so many people think of it as an investment – but an annuity is insurance. You are insuring an outcome.

With an immediate annuity you give the insurance company a lump sum of money, and they pay you guaranteed life-long income. An inflation-adjusted immediate annuity pays you a lower amount initially, but then your income increases over time according to a predetermined inflation rate.

---

73 Learn more about Guggenheim BulletShares® at: http://gi.guggenheiminvestments.com/products/etf/bulletshares.

Note   The term *annuity* is used to describe many types of contractual guarantees. There are fixed annuities, immediate annuities, variable annuities, index annuities, and the type of annuity provided by a pension plan. In this section I am speaking specifically about immediate annuities. The characteristics I am describing do not apply to all types of annuities. Other annuity types will be covered in Chapter 8.

Think of an immediate annuity as a jar of cookies. You give the insurance company the whole jar, and they hand you back a cookie each year. If the jar becomes empty, they promise to keep handing you cookies anyway, for as many years as you need them. In return, you agree that once you hand them the jar, you can't reach in it anymore. If one year you want three cookies, you'll have to get them from somewhere else.

This unending supply of cookies means a life payout annuity is a good hedge against longevity risk. No matter how long you live, and no matter how much of your other money you spend early in retirement, you'll still get a cookie each year.

With an inflation-adjusted immediate annuity, you start off getting a smaller cookie and it gets a little bigger each year thereafter. With a non-inflation-adjusted annuity, your cookie is the same size each year.

The amount of monthly income you receive from an annuity will also depend on your age, whether you purchase the annuity for a single life or joint life, and the inflation option you choose.[74]

TERM-CERTAIN ANNUITIES FOR OLDER HUSBAND/YOUNGER WIFE SCENARIOS

You can purchase an annuity for a specific term, such as a five-year payout. This is called a *term-certain* annuity. Contrast this with a life-long annuity, which pays out for as long as you live. You can also buy an annuity that combines both options. An example of combining the two would be a single life annuity with

---

74 Additional features such as a return of principal or cash refund rider will also affect pricing.

a five-year term certain, which means the annuity will pay monthly income for as long as you live. If you die within the first five years after purchase, it is guaranteed to pay out for at least that full five years (you would name a beneficiary to receive the remaining payments). If you die after the term-certain period, the annuity stops when you stop.

This can be an appropriate option for couples where the wife is much younger than the husband, because women tend to live longer. In a few such cases with the annuities offered by a pension plan, I have advised that the couple choose a life-long annuity on the wife, with a term-certain payout for 10 or 15 years. This option provides more income than a joint life annuity, and it provides a hedge, so that if the wife should die unexpectedly at a young age, the husband still has income for a specific amount of time. The risk in this option is that the wife dies first, and the husband lives many years past the term-certain period.

Here are a few immediate annuity basics to know:

- The older you are when you purchase the annuity, the more monthly income you will receive.

- Single-life annuities will have a higher payout than annuities that must cover two lives.

- Joint life annuities can be purchased for same-sex couples.

- With an immediate annuity, you are trading in your principal in return for a guaranteed income stream.

Let's look at an example. For a 65-year-old, in a low-interest-rate environment, it costs about $200,000 to buy $1,000 a month of lifelong income in the form of an immediate annuity. In a higher-interest-rate environment it would cost less to purchase this income.

Table 5-2 shows quotes[75] that cover two different ages, as well as male, female, and joint annuity options.

---

75 Table 5-2 quotes run on Annuities.direct (https://annuities.direct/) on May, 11, 2016 for nonqualified annuity purchases. Numbers rounded down to the nearest dollar.

Table 5-2. How Much Monthly Income Does a $200,000 Immediate Annuity Purchase Buy?

	No refund ($)	With refund ($)
Born 1/1/1951 (age 65 in 2016)		
Single Female	1,033	961
Single Male	1,091	990
Married couple	912	895
Born 1/1/1944 (age 72 in 2016)		
Single Female	1,253	1099
Single Male	1,374	1,126
Married couple	1,067	1,024

Using Table 5-2 you can see that for a married couple, each age 65 in 2016, it takes $200,000 to purchase $912 a month of guaranteed income with no guarantee as to return of principal, and $895 a month if they want a balance refund option.[76]

What about inflation-adjusted annuities? As discussed in Chapter 1, when studying actual retiree behavior, total spending in retirement may not keep pace with inflation as people age, particularly as they reach age 85 and beyond. Decreases in spending on travel, clothing, and entertainment seem to offset increases in spending on health care.

If you want to create a plan that allows you to spend more real dollars today, the non-inflation-adjusted annuity is a better choice. You're making a choice that spending now is more important than spending later.

If you are concerned that inflation will eat away at your standard of living, the inflation-adjusted annuity can provide protection against this, but your payout amount will be less than with a non-inflation-adjusted annuity, and it will take about twelve years until your payout amount is equivalent to what you would have received had you bought the plain vanilla non-inflation-adjusted product.

76 With a balance refund option if you should pass before the entire lump sum you originally put into the annuity has been paid out then the insurance company will pay a lump-sum payment of whatever is left in the account upon your death.

For example, for someone age 65, if you want your annuity income guaranteed to go up at 3% a year, your starting payout would be about 25 – 30% less than what you see in Table 5-2. Instead of getting $1,000 a month, you would get about $700 a month and each year it would go up by 3% until about 12 years later you would be getting the $1,000 a month. In my first edition of this book I quoted inflation-adjusted annuities. I didn't quote them in this edition as they are rarer and rarer, and most experts agree that you're better off buying the non-inflation-adjusted product and accounting for inflation in other ways in your planning.[77]

For someone who wants guaranteed income, my personal preference is for them to build a Social Security plan first, because that allows them to take advantage of the inflation-adjusted income that Social Security provides.[78] Then fill in additional needs for guaranteed income by using laddered bonds and non-inflation-adjusted annuities.

Now that you've examined three safe options for generating retirement income, you can compare riskier alternatives to these safe choices to see whether the potential additional returns are worth the risk.

The traditional, riskier alternative is the stock market. When used as part of your plan, stocks (particularly stock index funds, which I discuss in a bit) have their place in your retirement income portfolio. For stocks to be used as an effective tool, you must know where they fit into your plan and invest in them in a way such that the normal monthly and yearly ups and downs of the market have little to no effect on your long-term plan. I rarely see people use stocks as part of their plan in this way.

Instead, I see them used as speculative instruments. Attempting to achieve higher returns, many people fall for the big investment lie—the idea that someone out there can pick winning stocks and time the market. This approach can cause serious damage to your retirement plan.

---

77 See Stan the Annuity Man's article on combating inflation with annuities at: http://www.stantheannuityman.com/annuity-resources/annuityman-articles-columns/ combating-inflation-with-annuities/.

78 There are discussions to amend the way the inflation adjustments are applied to Social Security benefits. If changes are made to this formula, the effectiveness of Social Security as an inflation hedge would need to reconsidered based on the new rules.

Let's take a look at what the big investment lie is, how to avoid it, and what you can realistically expect to see if you use stocks as part of your retirement portfolio.

Don't Fall for the Big Investment Lie

In 2011, I ran an analysis for a client I'll call Bruce. As part of the analysis, I made recommendations for his investment portfolio. A year later he came back. His portfolio was entirely in cash.

"What happened?" I asked.

"I listened to one of those radio gurus who said the market was going to crash."

It is times like these when I am glad my inside voice cannot be heard. My internal commentator said:

> What? And you believed him? I gave you clear recommendations. You are a fool. You deserve to miss out on the gains that your investments would have experienced if only you had stuck with the plan. And of course the market is going to crash. The market crashes about once every four years. But no one knows exactly when it is going to happen. That's why you design your portfolio so those market movements have no effect on your cash flow.

Although I said nothing aloud, my expression must have said it all.

"I know, I know," he said.

The question I always like to ask is, why are so many people prone to believe the radio guru?

The book *Future Babble: Why Expert Predictions Are Next to Worthless—and You Can Do Better* by Dan Gardner (Dutton, 2011) may have the answer.

In a review of the book, Michael Edesess, an accomplished mathematician and economist, had this to say about predictions:

> Watching experts predict the future is like watching professional wrestling. You assume everybody knows it's a put-up job but can't

resist it anyway. Then you discover that most people don't even know it's a put-up job in the first place.

. . . Lacking other information—as with a coin-toss—the chances of a stock outperforming its benchmark are 50-50. Whether it does so or not isn't merely a matter of the interaction of forces obeying rigid physical laws; it's the result of an even more complex interaction of economic and human forces that do not even approximately obey laws. Yet while we would be hard pressed to find a theoretical physicist claiming to be able to predict the result of a coin toss, we can readily find thousands of people who claim to know whether a stock or stock portfolio will outperform its benchmark.[79]

Every week I talk to people who believe in this put-up job. They believe someone can consistently predict the outcome of the coin toss. They seek expert opinions by subscribing to investment newsletters and searching for actively managed funds, "hot" investment managers, or the next "beat the market" strategy. They think by finding such solutions they can achieve superior returns. Think about it—if anyone could deliver these superior returns, why would they be doing it for you and not acting solely on the information for themselves?

Anyone who has read the academic work on this return-seeking behavior finds it ludicrous that so many people continue to engage in it. Edesess goes on to describe this societal need to seek expert predictions:

Why are there so many "expert" predictions? And why do so many people believe them?

One reason, Gardner points out, is that predictions get attention. If they happen to succeed, they win attention and plaudits—even celebritization if the prediction is wildly successful. And there's not much downside. If a recognized expert succeeds, he or she can make page one. If the expert fails, the story may make the back page.

. . . The media needs forecasters to help make the news, the public needs predictors to give them hope or an anchor for the future and experts need to believe they can predict to validate that they are

79   Michael Edesess, "No More Stupid Forecasts!" Advisor Perspectives (July 2011). Used with permission. Available online at: www.advisorperspectives.com/newsletters11/pdfs/No_More_Stupid_Forecasts.pdf.

experts. The fact that the whole thing is mostly a sham is almost irrelevant.

After reading Michael's comments, I went on to read his book, *The Big Investment Lie*.[80] His introduction in the book is fabulous. He talks about his Ph.D. in mathematics and shares his thoughts on his first job with an investment firm. He didn't know anything about the stock market when he began his job, but at the time he thought . . .

> *I may as well learn about it. Besides, I should easily be able to get rich using my knowledge of mathematics, and why not? I'm smart; surely I can figure out how to beat the stock market. Little was I to know how many people I would meet over the years with the same idea, all of whom would be wrong.*

I cannot tell you how many engineers I have had walk into my office thinking the same thing. They're super smart. They understand math. They think they can chart stock patterns, moving averages or some other such thing, and instantly make a fortune. Or if they can't do it, their definition of a financial advisor is someone who can. If only it were so easy.

Michael's introduction goes on to say,

> *But within a few short months I realized something was askew. The academic findings were clear and undeniable, but the firm—and the whole industry—paid no real attention to them.*

The academic findings he refers to show that professional money managers do not add additional returns over what can be achieved by investing in a well-designed portfolio of index funds.

When I say *professional money managers*, what I mean are actively managed mutual funds and actively managed stock accounts. Actively managed means the money manager is trying to hand-pick the investments that will deliver the highest returns.

For example, you could own an S&P 500 Index fund, which owns all 500 stocks on Standard & Poor's large cap stock list, or you could own a mutual fund that tries to pick and choose among the 500 stocks to select only those that their research shows might deliver the highest returns. The active approach has

---

80 Michael Edesess, *The Big Investment Lie* (Berret-Koehler Publishers, 2007).

higher investment fees because research and analysis - including the salaries of the researchers and analysts - costs money.

Paying more for actively managed mutual funds would be fine, if it resulted in higher returns. However, it does not. Statistics show that funds with higher fees deliver lower returns.

Note   Data shows that mutual funds with higher fees have lower returns. There is rarely a need to pay for "active management" of a stock fund.

Fund fees are measured by an expense ratio. Each fund reports its expense ratio on an annual basis. An expense ratio of .50 means the fund costs one half of one percent a year. That means, for every $100,000 invested, you are paying $500 a year.

A 2010 Morningstar study showed that expense ratios are the best predictor of fund performance. One Morningstar article concluded, "Expense ratios are strong predictors of performance. In every asset class over every time period, the cheapest quintile produced higher total returns than the most expensive quintile."[81] In other words, it is the reverse from what it should be – more expensive funds do worse.

Actively managed funds have high expense ratios and have been proven to collectively deliver lower performance than their lower cost peers. If you have a proven way of selecting funds that are most likely to have higher performance, why would you choose anything else?

With your market-based portfolio you can avoid the big investment lie by following two rules:

1.   Buy investments based on risk, not return. If you encounter someone selling you on their ability to predict what the market is going to do, and when it will do it, run. No one can do this, and anyone who thinks they can is not the person you want giving you advice on your retirement money.

2.   Buy low-fee funds (index funds make a good choice).

---

81 Russell Kinnel, "How Expense Ratios and Star Ratings Predict Success," Morningstar Advisor (August 2010).

Let's take a look at both of these rules in more detail, starting with a look at how to classify investments according to risks rather than returns.

Risk Choices on the 1–5 Scale

The smart way to build a portfolio is by making choices based on risk. The 1–5 risk scale (Figure 5-1) is helpful in classifying the common investments you encounter. It starts with the question; can I lose any money? If the answer is no, the risk level is 1. The risk scale ends with the question; can I lose all my money? If the answer is yes, the risk level is 5.

This risk scale is not an industry standard; rather, it is something I use to help people develop realistic expectations. I am sure other professionals may disagree with some of my classifications, which is fine. The list is meant to be used only as a guideline to help you understand how one investment compares to another in terms of risk.

Risk Level 1: Investing for Safety

- I Bonds

- Series E/EE Bonds

- Certificates of deposit/bank savings accounts

- Money market accounts[82]

- Fixed annuities

- Fixed immediate annuities

- TIPS (Treasury Inflation-Protected Securities) and other government-issued bonds held to maturity

Risk Level 2: Investing for Safety and Some Income

- Short- or intermediate-term corporate and municipal individual bonds and bond funds using high-quality bonds.[83]

- Some funds that are classified as income funds—if the income comes from interest from short- or intermediate-term bonds, and not from stock dividends.

---

82 Technically a money market account is not risk-free, but I do consider it to fall in the "investing for safety" category.

83 Rated AA or better by Moody's or S&P rating services.

- TIPS mutual funds. When owned in a mutual fund format, I have chosen to classify TIPS as a 2 rather than a 1.

Risk Level 3: Investing for Income

- Individual long-term corporate bonds, bond funds, and high-yield bonds and bond funds

- Long-term bond funds that are classified as income funds—if the income comes from interest from bonds and not from stock dividends

- Asset allocation funds

- Balanced funds

- Retirement income funds

- International bond funds

Risk Level 4: Investing for Growth

- Stock funds (sometimes called "equity funds")

- Most growth-and-income funds

- International equity funds

- Unleveraged real estate (with no mortgage)

Risk Level 5: Investing for Growth

- Individual stocks

- Leveraged real estate

- Business ownership

- Alternative investments, limited partnerships, private placements, etc.

You can use this list to make appropriate risk-based choices.

For example, when you buy an individual stock, can you lose all your money? Yes, you can. You've heard the stories of what once were great companies who went under: Bethlehem Steel, Trans World Airlines, Montgomery Ward, Enron,

WorldCom, Lehman Brothers, Wachovia, Washington Mutual . . . the list goes on.

What about when you own an S&P 500 stock index fund? Can you lose all your money? An S&P 500 Index fund owns stock in 500 of the largest companies in the U.S. In order for you to lose all your money, all of those companies would have to go bankrupt at once. If that happened, I think we would have bigger problems on our hands than what a portfolio might be worth.

Because you can lose all your money, I rule out individual stocks as an option for the average person. If you want to build a portfolio with a number of dividend paying stocks, I am not saying that won't work. It might work quite well. But it takes a good deal of time and research to do it right. If you enjoy that, take classes and learn all you can before you do it. For the average person, I don't think this is the way to go. A lower-maintenance approach using index funds will fare just as well.

Index Funds

You can build a portfolio in numerous ways. If one way were certain to deliver better results, everyone would do it. I think most people are best served by a simple and effective strategy. Index funds fit the bill. Index funds allow you to invest in an entire stock or bond market, or segment of a market, with the purchase of a single fund.

Index funds are an effective way to manage risk, and they have low fees. As I mentioned, low fees have been proven to be the best indicator of fund performance. You can find great index funds at the following places:

- Vanguard (www.vanguard.com)

- iShares Exchange Traded Index Funds (www.ishares.com)

- Charles Schwab Index Funds (search "Schwab index funds" to get to the index fund section of the Schwab website)

There is one additional mutual fund company worth mentioning in this section: DFA (Dimensional Fund Advisors). DFA funds do not actually track an index, because they have their own way of defining certain sectors of the market. The funds are not actively managed and focus on low costs. DFA believes you can't "beat" the market, so its funds are equivalent to traditional index funds in that regard.

DFA offers its funds through fee-only advisors[84] or through institutions (such as a pension plan or as a choice in your 401(k) plan). I include DFA on this list because it has great educational material on its website (www.dfaus.com). Many reputable fee-only investment advisors use DFA funds, and you may encounter them within a 401(k) plan offered by your employer. They are a great choice.

Now that you understand what the big investment lie is, and how to avoid it, let's take a look at what you might experience when using stock and bond index funds to reach your goals.

Past Performance of Index Fund Portfolios

When I started my career as a financial advisor in 1995, the other advisers and I frequently used a version of a chart like Figure 5-2 to persuade clients to invest in stock mutual funds, particularly the ones we sold.

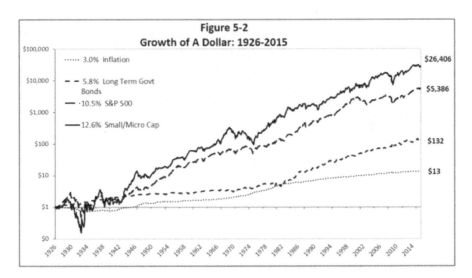

Figure 5-2
Growth of A Dollar: 1926-2015

The bottom dotted line on Figure 5-2, inflation, shows you that it would take $13 at the end of 2015 to buy the same goods and services that $1 would

---

84 Fee-only advisors are not compensated by commissions on the sale of investment or insurance products. They provide advice for a fee, which may be structured as an hourly rate, project fee, or as a percentage of assets managed.

purchase in 1926. The three lines above it show you what your dollar would be worth if you had invested it in either long-term government bonds, large cap[85] U.S. stocks (as measured by the S&P 500 Index), or U.S. small-cap stocks (as measured by CRSP 9-10 index). The results do not reflect any deductions for transaction costs, investment management fees, or taxes.

The chart makes owning a collection of stocks look great. Why wouldn't you put all your money in the line where it grows the most?

It took me years to come to the belief I hold today: that this chart, when used on a stand-alone basis as you see it here, has caused more harm to investors than just about anything else I can think of. There is nothing on it that is not true; yet when viewing it you begin to form a set of expectations about what you might experience as an investor that is far from true.

When you zoom in and look at shorter time periods, investment results can vary significantly from the averages you see in Figure 5-2. Look at returns during the 1990s, when the Cold War ended and the Internet took off (Figure 5-3).

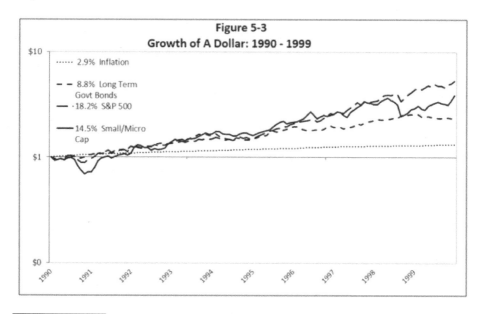

Figure 5-3
Growth of A Dollar: 1990 - 1999

---

85 *Cap* refers to capitalization or the total value of a company calculated by taking the share price multiplied by the total number of outstanding shares. Companies worth $5 billion or more are generally categorized as large cap. Small caps might be companies worth $2 billion or less. Dollar limits used for categorization can be defined differently by different organizations and may change over time.

In Figure 5-3 the line on the chart that finishes at the top shows the results of the S&P 500 Index. It averaged an annualized return of 18.2% a year from 1990–1999. Even long-term government bonds did well, averaging 8.8% a year.

Using that decade to set rate-of-return expectations on a portfolio that was 50% invested in stock funds and 50% in bond funds, you get the following:

- Stocks: .50 × 18.2% = 9.1%

- Bonds: .50 × 8.8% = 4.4%

- Expected return on this portfolio: 13.5%.[86] Net of investment fees it would be perhaps 12–13%, depending on the amount of fees you pay.

Instead of the 12–13% returns people had come to expect, the next decade delivered a mess. One of my clients shared with me her view that as a nation we are all suffering from PTSD (Post Traumatic Stress Disorder). Based on the 1990s, we all expected to be wealthy and retire at a young age. The events of the 2000–2009 decade shattered this expectation, and we are still recovering. Resetting expectations can take time.

The media occasionally refers to the ten years ending in 2009 or 2010 as "the lost decade" due to the poor performance of stocks during that time. Certainly, it was nothing like the stellar returns we became accustomed to in the 1990s, but was it truly lost? Figure 5-4 shows the returns for 2000–2009.

---

86 This calculation assumes half the portfolio is in stocks and half in bonds and that it is rebalanced annually. I am not saying this should be the expected return; I am saying behaviorally this is how people use past returns to begin to develop expectations about future returns.

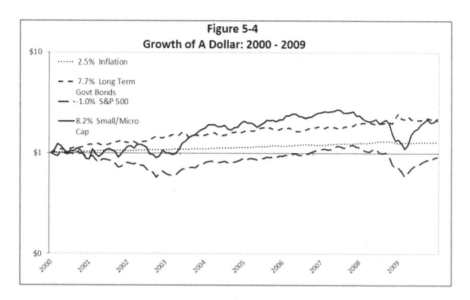

Figure 5-4
Growth of A Dollar: 2000 - 2009

Notice that small-cap stocks and long-term government bonds did just fine over this lost decade. Additional asset classes such as real estate and emerging markets also did quite well.[87]

Carl Richards, author of *Behavior Gap: Simple Ways to Stop Doing Dumb Things with Money* (Portfolio/Penguin, 2012), wrote about the lost decade in his New York Times Bucks Blog on August 31, 2011. He assumed from 2001 to 2010 an investor invested 1/5th of their portfolio in each of the following asset classes:

- U.S. large stocks (the S&P 500)

- U.S. small stocks (the Russell 2000 Index)

- U.S. real estate stocks (the Dow Jones US REIT index)

- International stocks (MSCI EAFE Index)

- Emerging markets stocks (MSCI Emerging Markets Index)

He concluded, "The return for this diversified stock portfolio … was an annualized 8.35 percent. That is a far cry from a lost decade."

Today I often meet people who tell me that, because of recent events, they don't believe investing works. A little fact-finding often shows they've been

---

87 Real estate as measured by the Dow Jones US Select REIT Index averaged 10.7% a year from 2000–2009, and emerging markets stocks as measured by the MSCI Emerging Markets Index averaged 10.1% a year.

investing in a completely illogical manner. They might own five mutual funds that all own the same asset class. If that asset class isn't having a good decade, their performance looks poor.

I've been known to say, "If you're doing it wrong, of course it doesn't work. It's like trying to use a hammer to drive a screw into the wall. You get a mess. So what are you going to do, blame the hammer?"

Whether investing for accumulation or to take regular withdrawals, you must diversify. Diversifying means owning different types of asset class. It does not mean having accounts in many different places.

Proper diversification involves building a portfolio model that matches your investment choices up with the point in time where you need to use the money. When done right, the allocations among different asset classes will be aligned to your goals. A good financial plan will clarify those goals and will tell you, among other things, approximately how much money you should have in the various types of investments available on the market, such as large-cap U.S., small-cap U.S., international, emerging markets, long-term bonds, short-term bonds, and so on.

I can't tell you exactly how much should be where, because I don't know you. But I can provide an example of what a diversified index fund portfolio looks like, and you can see how it held up while taking withdrawals during the "lost decade".

Index Fund Portfolios with Withdrawals

Let's take a look at what happened to a retiree who was taking withdrawals from a diversified index fund portfolio over the last decade. Suppose she invested $500,000 on January 1, 2000 and withdrew $25,000 a year, each year through 2011 for a total of 12 years of withdrawals. It was the "lost decade"; I bet she ran out of money, right?

First, this investor built a portfolio that was 50/50 bonds and stocks, rebalanced annually,[88] and reinvested all dividends and capital gains. The bond por-

---

88 As the market moves, if stocks go up and bonds stay flat, stocks may now represent more than 50% of your portfolio value. In this situation, rebalancing would involve selling stocks and buying bonds to bring the allocation back to 50/50. This would also work in reverse if stocks went down.

tion of her allocation included short-, intermediate-, and long-term bonds. The stock portion included U.S. large and small cap, real estate, international large cap, and emerging markets.

Table 5-3 shows the specific index funds used, how much was allocated to each, and how much was withdrawn each year.

Table 5-3. Fund Choices, Allocation, and Amounts Withdrawn From Each

Fund	Investment Amount ($)	Annual Withdrawal ($)	Rebalanced Annually to this %
Vanguard Short Term Bond Index (VBISX)	100,000	−5,000	20
Vanguard Intermediate Term Bond Index (VBIMX)	100,000	−5,000	20
Vanguard Long Term Bond Index (VBLLX)	50,000	−2,500	10
Vanguard 500 Index (VFINX)	90,000	−4,500	18
Vanguard International Growth (VWIGX)	75,000	−3,750	15
Vanguard REIT Index (VGSNX)	30,000	−1,500	6
Vanguard Explorer (VEXPX)	30,000	−1,500	6
Vanguard Emerging Markets (VEIEX)	25,000	−1,250	5

Table 5-4 shows their remaining balances[89] each year after taking a $25,000 withdrawal. This approach is often referred to as building a *total return portfolio* with *systematic withdrawals*.

This retiree has taken $300,000 of cumulative income (12 years x $25,000 a year) and has almost the same amount of principal she started with.

Today, a non-inflation-adjusted annuity that provides $25,000 a year of guaranteed income would cost about $460,000.[90] The difference is: with the market-based portfolio, you still have access to the cookie jar; at the end of the 12 years, you still have full access to the $488,000.

---

89 Calculated using the hypothetical illustration option in Morningstar Workstation.
90 Estimated by running quotes on Annuities.direct, using non-qualified funds, joint life couple both age 65 in May 2016.

Table 5-4. Portfolio Balance After Withdrawing $25,000 a Year

Calendar Year	End of Year Balance After Withdrawals ($)
2000	488,943
2001	459,451
2002	414,183
2003	468,494
2004	489,790
2005	494,517
2006	527,048
2007	540,078
2008	414,984
2009	472,964
2010	504,450
2011	488,128

Now, in this example the retiree's withdrawals have not kept pace with inflation. There is a reason for this. I advise people to use a flexible approach to withdrawals from market-based portfolios. If investment returns are below expectations, be prepared to forgo inflation raises or spend more principal. If you spend principal too fast, you could run out of money later. During the recent time periods of lower-than-expected market returns, I have advised people to forgo inflation raises.

On average, I suggest if you are willing to forgo inflation raises as needed, and if you are willing to spend some principal over your life expectancy, then as a rough rule of thumb, a diversified market portfolio should deliver about $5,000 a year of income per $100,000 invested over your expected lifetime.

If you get a period of above-average returns, your $5,000 may increase with inflation, and you may retain all principal. If you get a period of below-average returns, you may need to forgo all inflation raises, take a reduction in the level of withdrawals, and/or be willing to spend principal. There is no free lunch.

Market-based portfolios that are diversified and rebalanced are an effective strategy for retirement income, but they do come with uncertainty.

This decision to take inflation raises or adjust withdrawals should be evaluated each year in light of the portfolio return and future expected cash flow needs as measured over remaining life expectancy. This flexible approach makes a market-based portfolio a viable option for retirement income.

If you don't want uncertainty, plan on saving more and using choices like annuities, CDs, and bonds.

Let's compare safer choices side by side with riskier options. Then I look at how you might combine some of these strategies to accomplish your retirement income goals.

Cost of $1,000 a Month

Income isn't free. You pay a price to receive it. While working, the price of your income is your time and knowledge—what's called your *human capital*.

You may also receive benefits from the society you participate in and contribute to, such as Social Security or pensions. This is your *social capital*.

Then you have your *financial capital*: the savings and investments you have accumulated.

When considering your financial capital, you can compare alternatives by looking at how much capital you must use to generate a reliable $1,000 a month of income. The key word is reliable.

You may find a high-yield investment that generates a 10% dividend and decide it will only cost you $120,000 to buy $12,000 a year of income. When compared to the $200,000 price tag of an immediate annuity delivering a similar amount, this may sound great. However, the 10% is not guaranteed. The company could reduce its dividend, which would also result in a lower share price, leaving you with less income and less principal.

When comparing investment strategies, make sure you understand the reliability factor of the various choices you are considering and the assumptions you are making. The estimated price of an income stream will vary, depending on the assumptions you make. The two key assumptions are the rate of return you think is achievable and your estimated life span.

- When determining realistic rates of return, think in terms of what return you will earn in excess of inflation (called your *real rate of return*). If inflation is 3%, and your portfolio earns 7%, your real rate of return is 4%.

- When determining a realistic length of life, think in terms of the longevity table in Chapter 1 and in terms of probabilities.

For example, if you think stocks will average a 7% rate of return, and bonds will average a 4% rate of return, if half of your investments are in stocks and half are in bonds, the math works like this:

- .50 × 7% = 3.5%

- .50 × 4% = 2.0%

- Total estimated annual portfolio return: 5.5%[91]

You will likely have some investment fees. If you own index funds, your investment fees will run about one quarter of one percent up to one half of one percent, so your net return would be about 5.0%. If you pay an investment advisor who uses actively managed funds, you may be paying fees of 2% or more a year, which reduces your net return to 3.5%.

Next subtract out inflation expectations. If you think inflation will be about 3% that leaves you with a real rate of return of .5%–2% depending on how much in fees you pay.

To put all of this together, see Table 5-5, which was compiled by Moshe Milevsky[92] and originally published in *Research Magazine*.[93] It outlines the costs of $1,000 a month of real income by both assumed real rate of return and estimated life span.

---

91 When using conservative return estimates I think this calculation provides an appropriate way to set long-term rate-of-return expectations based on your portfolio allocation.

92 Moshe Milevsky, Ph.D., is the executive director of the Individual Finance and Insurance Decision (IFID) Centre, associate professor of finance at York University in Toronto, and author of the book Are You a Stock or a Bond? Create Your Own Pension Plan for a Secure Financial Future (FT Press, 2008).

93 Data from Moshe Milevsky, "What Does Retirement Really Cost?" Research Magazine (September 2011). Reprinted with permission of Summit Business Media. Article available online at www.advisorone.com/2011/09/01/what-does-retirement-really-cost.

Table 5-5. What Size Nest Egg Do You Need?

Retiring at age 65 Needing $1,000 of Monthly Income for Life					
		REAL inflation-adjusted returns (interest rates)			
	Age	0.0%	1.5%	4.0%	6.5%
Plan to Life Expectancy	84.2	$230,490	$200,300	$160,900	$131,600
Plan to 75th Percentile	90.1	$301,700	$251,300	$190,300	$148,600
Plan to 95th Percentile	97.1	$385,100	$305,600	$216,900	$161,700
Cost of REAL Annuity*	N.A.	N.A.	$230,000	N.A.	N.A.

*Quote run in 2011 for single life, male age 65, inflation-adjusted payout.

Using Table 5-5, if you assume your real[94] rate of return is zero, meaning your savings are going to earn the rate of inflation but no more, you can see that if you live to a life expectancy of 84.2, the cost of $1,000 a month of real income is $230,490. If you live to 97.1, that cost goes up to $385,100. A real rate of return of zero would be comparable to what you might receive from I Bonds or TIPS.

The bottom row labeled Cost of REAL Annuity is an inflation-adjusted immediate annuity quote run on a single life male. It shows that (in 2011) an immediate annuity that provides $1,000 a month of inflation-adjusted life-long income would cost a 65-year-old male $230,000.

In the far right column of Table 5-5, you see that if you could be assured of earning a 6.5% real rate of return (which means if inflation was 3%, your total return would be 9.5%—not something I think you should at all be assured of), the cost of achieving that same $1,000 of income goes down substantially. I think you should throw the 6.5% column out the window and focus on the remaining three columns. It is included here as I suspect some people have been told such returns exist over the long run – they rarely do.

The difference in cost in these choices reflects a difference in how much risk you retain. If you want to retain market risk and inflation risk, you may be able to accomplish your retirement income goals with less principal.

---

94 Remember, real return means the return you earn in excess of the inflation rate. Real income means income that has kept pace with inflation.

If you want to guarantee the outcome, you will need to save more to accomplish your goals. Saving more means spending less now.

When viewing such comparisons, keep in mind a bumper sticker I saw years ago. It said, "Fast, Cheap, or Reliable. Pick two out of three."

With a potentially lower price comes uncertainty and the possibility that you may not achieve your goals. You do not get "$1,000 a month," "life-long guarantee," and "low price." You must pick two out of those three.

A combination of the choices discussed in this section is often the best solution because it helps you hedge against a variety of risks.

Such a combination would involve taking on investment risk with a portion of your portfolio. The reason you would do so is to retain the possibility of earning a higher rate of return than what can be achieved with safe alternatives, and/or the possibility of retaining access to more of your principal.

Note   A guaranteed outcome requires more financial capital to achieve your desired level of retirement income.

Index fund portfolios are simply another tool, and like any tool, when used correctly they can be quite effective. They give you the potential for the returns in the 4.0% and 6.5% columns, but not the certainty of achieving them. The key is making sure you go about building your index fund portfolio correctly using multiple asset classes, as shown in prior examples. If you're not going to do it right, you're better off sticking with a low-risk, safe alternative.

Some people choose to use only safe, guaranteed options, the type that are more expensive but provide a known outcome (usually CDs and bonds). Others prefer investments without guarantees (usually stocks and stock funds) hoping to achieve a higher real rate of return. For most people a combination of these choices is the best solution. The question is: how do you combine them?

Asset Allocation Based on Risk Management

You can use your Social Security decision as part of a plan along with laddered bonds, income annuities, and a more traditional investment portfolio of stock index funds to manage the different types of risk you have in retirement.

Each choice helps manage a different type of risk.

- Your Social Security decision (as to when to begin benefits) can provide protection against inflation risk, longevity risk, overspending risk, and sequence risk. It's an important decision.

- Laddered bonds guarantee a specified amount is available in a specified year and may help minimize the impact of sequence risk.

- An income annuity insures against longevity risk, overspending risk, and sequence risk.

- When you build a traditional portfolio of stocks, you diversify to minimize market risk with the goal of achieving a rate of return higher than a safer investment. This part of your portfolio may allow you to spend more and enjoy a higher standard of living than if you choose a 100% guaranteed approach.

Using a combination of these options allows you to diversify against multiple types of risk. Let's take a look at how all this works for Wally and Sally.

Using Your Coverage Ratio

Wally and Sally want to line things up now so they don't have to worry later. They want to know their fixed expenses are secured as they age. With the future secure, they feel they can enjoy traveling and spending more in their first ten years of retirement without worrying about their financial security in their later years.

They agree to follow their suggested Social Security claiming plan and the withdrawal strategy using Option C. They are now trying to figure out how to build the portfolio to match up with their withdrawal needs. Figure 5-5 shows a summary of their annual incoming cash flow and the expenses it will be used for. I intentionally excluded data from 2016 to focus on the years they are retired.

To see how secure their later years look, Wally and Sally determine what portion of their expenses are covered by guaranteed income sources. This is shown in Figure 5-5 in the column "% Living Expenses Covered by Fixed Sources".[95] I refer to this as a "coverage ratio".

In 2025 (the first year Wally and Sally are both age 70 or older for the entire year) Figure 5-5 reveals that 68% of their expected living expenses are covered by Social Security. Research shows cognitive abilities decline as we age.[96] In addition, one spouse often handles the finances. For both these reasons, I think it makes sense to build a plan that provides a higher coverage ratio later. It protects you against a future self that may not be able to make decisions as soundly as you can today, and if you are married, it protects a spouse who may not be as money-savvy as you. (You can also protect your future self and your spouse by hiring a good financial advisor, but I'm an advisor, of course I am going to say that. And I believe it.)

If their projection showed that later in life less than 50% of living expenses were covered by guaranteed income, I would suggest Wally and Sally consider the use of annuities. In this case, Wally and Sally are projected to have more than 50% of their living expenses covered by guaranteed income in their 70s. But that will change when one of them becomes a surviving spouse. As a surviving spouse in 2038, Sally would have about 42% of her projected expenses covered by Social Security.

---

95 This is calculated by taking the total amount of fixed sources of cash flow divided by their living expenses.
96 Michael S. Finke, John Howe, and Sandra J. Huston, "Old Age and the Decline in Financial Literacy," Social Science Research Network (August 2011). Available online at http://papers.ssrn.com/sol3/papers.cfm?abstract_id=1948627.

Figure 5-5
Cash Flow and % Expenses Covered by Fixed Sources

# of Years	Calendar Year	Incoming Cash flow		Outgoing Cash Flow		% Living Expenses Covered by Fixed Sources
		Fixed Income (SS)	Portfolio Withdrawals*	Projected Taxes	Total Living Expenses	
1	2016	-	-	-	-	-
2	2017	$0	$106,477	$14,593	$91,884	0%
3	2018	31,540	64,573	2,686	93,427	34%
4	2019	38,604	53,048	2,580	89,072	43%
5	2020	39,384	53,744	2,151	90,977	43%
6	2021	40,164	55,067	1,601	93,630	43%
7	2022	58,028	36,156	7,425	86,374	67%
8	2023	62,664	34,394	7,846	89,212	70%
9	2024	63,924	36,236	8,012	92,148	69%
10	2025	65,196	38,289	8,300	95,184	68%
11	2026	66,504	40,776	8,954	98,326	68%
12	2027	67,836	43,375	9,636	101,576	67%
13	2028	69,192	46,093	10,347	104,938	66%
14	2029	70,560	48,921	11,064	108,417	65%
15	2030	71,976	51,876	11,835	112,017	64%
16	2031	73,416	54,876	12,550	115,742	63%
17	2032	74,880	58,070	13,352	119,597	63%
18	2033	76,380	61,320	14,113	123,587	62%
19	2034	77,916	64,696	14,895	127,717	61%
20	2035	79,464	68,223	15,695	131,992	60%
21	2036	81,060	71,875	16,518	136,417	59%
22	2037	53,468	103,661	16,131	140,998	38%
23	2038	48,576	94,106	27,871	114,452	42%
24	2039	49,548	97,938	28,806	118,155	42%
25	2040	50,532	101,948	29,732	121,982	41%
26	2041	51,540	106,060	30,598	125,939	41%
27	2042	52,572	110,340	31,431	130,029	40%
28	2043	53,628	114,756	32,201	134,257	40%
29	2044	54,696	119,277	32,843	138,629	39%

*Withdrawal amount shown is net of any amount deposited back into the non-retirement account.

One option: Wally and Sally can agree that upon the death of one spouse the surviving spouse would use a portion of the remaining portfolio assets to buy an immediate annuity to replace the guaranteed income lost due to less Social Security. I like this type of "wait and see" plan, as the pricing on annuities is better for single lives vs. joint lives, and better for those who are older.

Another option is to purchase a deferred income annuity (DIA). A $100,000 DIA purchase would guarantee them $819 a month starting in ten years.[97] This additional $9,828 per year of guaranteed income would mean the portfolio withdrawal column would go down and the fixed income column would go up, resulting in about a 10% increase in the amount of expenses that would be covered by guaranteed income starting in 2025.

Wally and Sally decide not to purchase an annuity right now as they like the "wait and see" approach, and they are comfortable with the portion of their expenses that are covered by guaranteed sources. What they are less comfortable with is what might happen during their first ten years of retirement.

What About the First Ten Years of Retirement

A big concern for Wally and Sally is the first five to ten years of retirement where their planned portfolio withdrawals are large. What happens if the market goes down like it did in 2008/2009?

There is a way to construct portfolios to help reduce the impact of a major market downturn early in retirement. Wally and Sally can arrange their investments so they have bonds or CDs maturing to cover the withdrawals they need in their first few years. Doing this will mean they enter retirement knowing that 100% of their expenses are covered by fixed income sources for the next seven or eight years.

Figure 5-6 shows the withdrawals that Wally and Sally plan to take from each account over the first eight years of their retirement, based on using the Option C withdrawal strategy from Chapter 4 (Figure 4-9).

---

97 Quote run on annuities.direct for joint life, with a 10 year deferral period. Male age 64, female age 62. If balance refund option is chosen monthly guaranteed income drops to $806.

Figure 5-6
Wally and Sally's Withdrawal Strategy

	Non-Retirement	Wally IRA/401(k)	Sally IRA/403(b)	Totals
Starting Balance:	$246,000	$365,000	$546,000	$1,157,000
For Year	Withdrawal Amounts Needed*			
2017	106,477	0	0	106,477
2018	64,573	0	0	64,573
2019	53,048	0	0	53,048
2020	53,744	0	0	53,744
2021	29,299	25,768	0	55,067
2022		10,439	30,000	40,439
2023		10,929	30,000	40,929
2024		11,442	30,000	41,442
Totals:	307,141	58,578	90,000	$455,719

*Gross withdrawals shown - a portion of each year's IRA withdrawal may be deposited into the non-retirement account if all of it was not needed to cover expenses and taxes.

There is one problem with Wally and Sally's planned withdrawal strategy. They have $246,000 in their non-retirement account and they will be adding an additional $21,841, which totals to $267,841. But they need to withdraw $307,141 over their first five years of retirement. The math works in the planning phase because the $246,000 is projected to earn a 5% rate of return. If in fact these non-retirement funds earn a 5% return each year, Wally and Sally will not need to touch their retirement accounts until 2021.

But a 5% return on safe, short-term guaranteed investments is not realistic in today's low interest rate environment. For money that needs to be kept somewhere for use in the next one to seven years a realistic return is 1 – 3%.

When you are planning for distributions in retirement you often need to adjust the rate of return for each account based on how that account will be allocated.

Wally and Sally adjust their numbers to account for this. In their case it means there will not be enough available in their non-retirement accounts to support their original withdrawal strategy; they will need to begin withdrawals from their retirement accounts a year earlier - in 2020. Their revised withdrawal strategy based on the constraints of today's low interest rates is shown in Figure 5-7.

Figure 5-7
Wally and Sally's Revised Withdrawal Strategy

	Non-Retirement	Wally IRA/401(k)	Sally IRA/403(b)	Totals
Starting Balance:	$246,000	$365,000	$546,000	$1,157,000
For Year	Withdrawal Amounts Needed*			
2017	106,477	0	0	106,477
2018	64,573	0	0	64,573
2019	53,048	0	0	53,048
2020	43,743	12,000	0	55,743
2021		60,634	0	60,634
2022		10,439	30,000	40,439
2023		10,929	30,000	40,929
2024		11,442	30,000	41,442
Totals:	267,841	105,444	90,000	$463,285

*Gross withdrawals shown - a portion of each year's IRA withdrawal may be deposited into the non-retirement account if all of it was not needed to cover expenses and taxes.

From this withdrawal strategy a customized asset allocation plan can be developed.

Asset Allocation Plan

When you lay out an allocation plan, the first thing to do is carve out your emergency fund/rainy day money and invest it only in choices that rate a 1 on the 1-5 risk scale. How much should you keep in this category of cash reserves? As with most things, it depends. A standard rule of thumb is six months' worth of living expenses. If you want additional security, bump that number up to 12 months. Wally and Sally did this by excluding their checking, savings, and $48,000 of money market from balances used to fund their withdrawal plan.

Once emergency reserves are set aside, the traditional approach to asset allocation focuses on risk tolerance. One measure of risk that is often used is "standard deviation", the amount by which your return each year varies from its expected average.

For example, an aggressive stock index fund portfolio may have a long-term average return of 10%, but over one year could have a negative return of 40% or a positive return of 60%. This type of portfolio would have a high standard deviation. A selection of CDs would have a consistent return from year to year, and would have a low standard deviation. In fact, if CDs (or bonds) were held to maturity, they would have zero standard deviation in terms of variation from their face value.

In academic papers, typical portfolio construction uses an investment concept called the *efficient frontier* to pick a mix of investments that provide the highest potential for return for any given level of volatility over one year. Based on this research many investment managers use this type of portfolio management approach.

These one-year time horizons are fine for academic research as they allow you to see an apples-to-apples comparison of how different mixes of investments behave. But in the real world, most people have an investing time horizon much longer than one year. Why construct a portfolio around a single year metric that has nothing to do with the long-term goals?

My preference is to construct a portfolio where the investments are chosen to match the point in time where they need to be used. Let's see how this works for Wally and Sally.

If we add up the first eight years of withdrawals from Figure 5-7, we get a total of $463,285. As mentioned, $21,841 of this is going to come from savings accumulated in 2016. That leaves $441,444. Let's assume this portion goes to fixed income (CDs or bonds) chosen so that each matures to match the withdrawals shown in Figure 5-7. The remaining assets, which have a longer time frame, are invested for growth (using stock index funds). That leads to an allocation as shown in Figure 5-8.

Figure 5-8
Wally and Sally's Allocation Plan

	Non-Retirement	Wally IRA/401(k)	Sally IRA/403(b)	Totals
Starting Balance:	$246,000	$365,000	$546,000	$1,157,000
$ to Fixed	246,000	105,444	90,000	441,444
$ to Growth	0	259,556	456,000	715,556
% to Fixed	100%	29%	16%	38%
% to Growth	0%	71%	84%	62%

The $441,444 represents 38% of their starting portfolio value, leaving 62% to be invested in growth. This allocation was not chosen by filling out an abstract risk tolerance questionnaire nor was it chosen by plotting portfolios on an efficient frontier. It was chosen by looking at their specific withdrawal needs by account and determining what approach would best fit those withdrawal needs. Each account has a different allocation. This approach is quite different than what much of the industry does, which is to manage each account to an allocation model rather than manage the household assets toward a goal.

The 62% in equities will be allocated across index funds that fall in the risk level 4 category. A simple approach would be to use a world index fund or global index fund, such as Vanguard's Total World Stock Index fund (symbol VTWSX) or iShares MSCI ACWI Index Fund (All Country World Index, symbol ACWI) exchange-traded fund.

The 38% in bonds can be allocated across investments that fall in the risk level 1 to 3 categories. For those using bonds funds a simple approach would be to use a total bond market fund such as Vanguard's Total Bond Market Index Fund (symbol VBTLX) or iShares Core Total U.S. Bond Market ETF (symbol AGG).

You can achieve additional diversification by using a more complex approach that involves choosing specific funds for each asset class, such as large cap, small cap, international, emerging markets and real estate in an allocation similar to that shown in Table 5-3. With the fixed income investments you could achieve additional specificity by laddering bonds and CDs to meet specific cash flow needs. As a professional, I think additional diversification and specificity have their benefits, and this is the approach I prefer. But for those managing their own investments, a simpler strategy is easier to manage.

Now that they have a starting place, how do Wally and Sally manage the portfolio as they go along? In retirement one of the challenges you'll face is determining which investments to liquidate when you need withdrawals.

Managing Withdrawals

When you are in the withdrawal phase, how you manage withdrawals will depend on how much of your current income is coming from your index fund portfolio.

Here are two common approaches:

- Time segmentation
- Systematic withdrawals

Time Segmentation

In Wally and Sally's situation, you saw that the $441,444 allocated to fixed income was determined by summing up[98] the withdrawals they would need over the first eight years of their retirement. This process of allocating money according to when you need to take withdrawals is often called *time segmentation*.

Time segments can also be broken up into chunks of five years or seven years or any increment you desire, with investments that are specifically chosen to match each individual time segment.

---

98 Rather than summing withdrawals to determine the allocation it is best to choose bonds in the right quantities and maturity amounts so that their cash flows from coupon interest and maturities will match the income stream needed. That math to do this is harder than you might think and usually requires professional help.

If you want to learn more about how you might implement a time-segmented plan, go to the Income for Life Model at www.iflmmovie.com to watch a video presentation that does a fantastic job of explaining the concept. In my practice we use a form of a time-segmented approach much like what has been illustrated for Wally and Sally—something called a *dedicated portfolio*.

With a dedicated portfolio, rather than arbitrarily picking an allocation of say 50% stocks and 50% bonds, you ladder out bonds and CDs in each account to meet your first five to ten years' worth of cash flow needs and invest the remainder of your portfolio in growth-oriented equity index funds. A dedicated portfolio uses a combination of many of the tools discussed in this chapter. The merits and historical success of a dedicated portfolio approach are covered in detail in the book *Asset Dedication* by Stephen J. Huxley and J. Brent Burns (McGraw-Hill, 2004), and this type of portfolio construction is implemented through their company Asset Dedication, LLC.

If you think of your investments in terms of time segments, you realize you will never be in a position where you are forced to sell riskier investments during a market downturn. Thus, even if you have a market-based portfolio, you do not need to be concerned with the daily, weekly, or even monthly gyrations of the stock market. Withdrawals are supported by safe investments that mature each year. When the equity portion is up, you harvest it and sell riskier investments to replenish the safer ones that were used. You need a system in place to help you determine when to do this.

The Critical Path®

Asset Dedication uses a Critical Path® to assess when to sell growth investments and when not to. It plots the path the portfolio should follow if it stayed perfectly on track on a path that would have your assets last for exactly the length of time designated in the financial plan.

This is not an expected path, but rather a worst case scenario. It is a projection of the minimum amount of financial assets you would need to have left each year for your plan to work. Figure 5-9 shows Wally and Sally's Critical Path.

This path stems from the minimum return it would take to get you to life expectancy. For Wally and Sally, that minimum return was calculated to be 3.77%. After paying all fees their financial accounts need to average 3.77% a year or more for them to withdraw their desired amounts each year. If they earn exactly 3.77% their financial account values would follow the path of the dotted line in Figure 5-9.

On occasion I run plans that require a 7% or 8% return. This occurs when the desired level of spending is too high relative to the resources available. I am not comfortable with a plan that requires a return higher than 6%. My preference is to build a plan that works in the worst one third of historical market scenarios. If we get something better, great! That means there is more to spend along the way or more to leave to heirs.

The Critical Path provides a metric to measure against that is related to your goals. During the years where the portfolio is in the safety zone, gains can be taken and put into safe investments to meet future withdrawals.

During years where the portfolio is in the danger zone, you spend the bonds or CDs that are maturing, and leave the remainder of the portfolio alone. During danger zone years you should also forego inflation raises, or cut back on extra "flex" expenses until you are back in the safety zone.

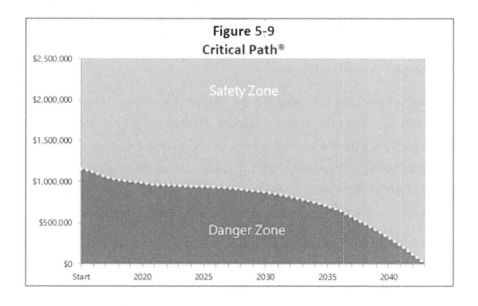

Figure 5-9
Critical Path®

For those of you who build and manage your own withdrawal plans you can use projected account values as a path to measure against, such as what was shown in Figure 4-10. The projected account values assume a 5% rate of return each year and thus are higher than the Critical Path values.

When Wally and Sally's growth portfolio has good years, they will be in the safety zone and will sell growth and buy more bonds. For example, assume in 2016 the $715,556 they have allocated to equites goes up 10% resulting in $71,555 of gains. They would sell at least $44,310 of the gains and buy a bond that matures in Wally's retirement account in 2025 for $12,536 and one in Sally's retirement account for $30,351 to match the withdrawals they have projected for those years.

Using this process each year during retirement they build upon their plan so they can continue to look forward knowing many years of future withdrawals are guaranteed by safe investments. In Mike Zwecher's book, *Retirement Portfolios, Theory Construction and Management* (Wiley, 2010) he refers to this as a "Track Layer". Think of it like laying a railroad track as you go. Wally and Sally start with the first eight "miles" of track built. In 2017 they work on adding mile nine. In 2018, they add mile ten. In 2019, they add mile eleven, and so on.

What happens if the growth portfolio has a year or two when it doesn't grow? They don't do anything. Bad years are to be expected. They simply do not extend their ladder in such years. They allow the market to recover and lift their portfolio back into the safe zone.

If it takes longer than one year for the market to recover, they may allow the bond ladder to go down to a minimum of three years of future coverage. During time periods where equity returns are strong they may sell enough growth investments to extend the bond ladder out to the original length they wanted or even longer - ten or twelve years of future coverage. Each year will require roughly 5% of their overall portfolio with today's interest rates.

Does this process work? Asset Dedication is able to run an historical audit to see exactly how well this withdrawal plan would have held up in the past. Wally and Sally's historical audit is shown in Figure 5-10. Each squiggly line represents a distinct 28-year period of analysis.[99] For example, one line represents the path their financial assets would have taken if they retired in 1927. Another line tracks what would have happened if they had retired in 1928, another in 1929, and so on.

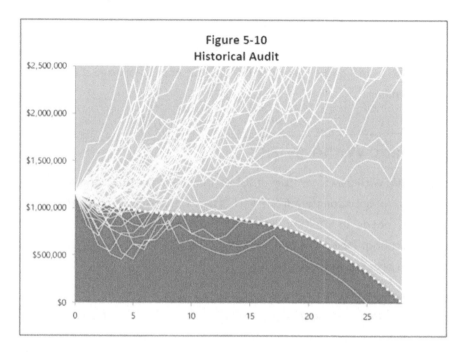

Figure 5-10
Historical Audit

By computing the percentage of times the portfolio ends above the Critical Path, the probability of success can be estimated with this approach. You can see there is one historical time period, which occurred during the Great Depression, where Wally and Sally's portfolio would have been depleted early (the line that ends in the danger zone about year 25). That is what would have happened assuming they made no changes along the way. By measuring and adjusting along the way, small changes, such as foregoing extra travel and not increasing withdrawals with inflation, would have brought even that line back into the safety zone.

---

99 Past performance does not guarantee future performance. This analysis provides historical context of what could have happened. Historical returns do not guarantee future results or success. This analysis is for demonstration purposes to show what could have happened. Future results will vary. The Asset Dedication Critical Path Analysis uses historical index data from a number of providers to create an historical audit of an investor's specific scenario. The dataset range is 1927 to present. The primary sources are: Center for Research in Securities Prices (CRSP), Fama/French Research Database, Dimensional Fund Advisors, MSCI, Ibbotson Associates and Global Financial Data. Some datasets have been extended using multiple regression analysis.

In the past, most of the time, Wally and Sally would have ended up with far more financial capital than they started with. In the future, by using their path to measure against, if this is the way things work out for them they will see this happening and can choose to either spend more or let capital continue to accumulate in order to leave more to heirs.

Most importantly, as they go through retirement, they now have a process they can use to make intelligent decisions about how to manage their portfolio and spending.

Systematic Withdrawals

A systematic withdrawal strategy involves building a portfolio and liquidating investments proportionately from each asset class each year to meet your withdrawal needs. In addition, each year you rebalance to align with your target allocation. Tables 5-3 and 5-4 show the results of using a systematic withdrawal process with rebalancing.

Most mutual fund companies allow you to set up a systematic withdrawal by filling out a minimal amount of paperwork. You tell them what dollar amount of each fund you want liquidated and over what time period. For example, if you have $100,000 in a stock index fund, you might have them liquidate $5,000 a year, but on a monthly basis whereby they send you $416 a month.

If this sounds complicated, you can find a simple solution. Several mutual fund families offer some form of a retirement income fund that builds a balanced portfolio for you and sends you a monthly check. For additional information do research on the following:

- Vanguard Managed Payout Funds

- Fidelity Income Replacement Funds

- Schwab Monthly Income Funds

These types of retirement income funds are designed to provide a stable monthly distribution, which means the fund may be paying out both investment income and principal in order for the fund to achieve its monthly target payout. The fund's ability to maintain its distribution target depends on market conditions and the underlying investment decisions of the fund's management team.

Systematic withdrawals combined with rebalancing makes for an effective strategy as long as you don't withdraw too much. How much is too much? That is something that must be monitored as you go along. If your investments perform well, you may be able to increase withdrawals. If your investments do not achieve your target rate of return, you may need to reduce withdrawals.

Systematic withdrawals are easier to manage than a time segmented approach. Rather than rebalancing based on your withdrawal needs, when you use a systematic withdrawal approach you are rebalancing to a target portfolio allocation such as "60% equities/40% fixed income". This approach can work well if you have only one type of account (the majority of your assets are in a non-retirement account for example), and if you need approximately the same withdrawal amount each year.

You will have to decide what approach you want to take. One thing to consider is your "sleep factor."

By *sleep factor* I mean: how comfortable are you with a given approach? The transition from saving money on a regular basis to taking regular withdrawals is scary. If the market is down, are you losing sleep? If so, maybe you would be better off with a higher allocation to lower-risk approaches. My own belief is that, given a long enough time-horizon (such as "I need this money to last the rest of my life"), a well-engineered market-based portfolio built with index funds, individual bonds, and CDs will not deliver results significantly worse than other approaches and may deliver results that far exceed safer choices. Because this is my belief, I prefer to allocate more toward the market based portfolio because it provides the opportunity for more.[100]

When it comes to monitoring and withdrawing I prefer the time-segmented approach because it is related to your goals - not to an arbitrary benchmark. However, my preferred approach is not an appropriate decision for everyone. Your choices need to be based on your situation.

---

100 For an analysis of various allocation and withdrawal approaches see Reducing Retirement Risk with a Rising Equity Glide Path (September 2013), by Wade D. Pfau and Michael E. Kitces. It is available on Social Science Research Network at: http://papers.ssrn.com/sol3/papers.cfm?abstract_id=2324930.

Your Safe Withdrawal Rate

You may read about something called the *safe withdrawal rate*. This is supposed to be the amount you can withdraw each year from savings without running out of money. The truth is, unless they have a working crystal ball, no one can tell you what your safe withdrawal rate is. Each withdrawal plan needs to be designed based on your situation and monitored based on changing market conditions and tax rates. Even the best research can only give you probabilities of success.

Nevertheless, there are many popular rules of thumb telling you what you should do. If you are examining retirement strategies, you are bound to come across them. One of them is the 4% rule, which says in retirement you should be able to safely withdraw about 4% of your starting portfolio value each year plus the prior year's inflation rate. With a portfolio rebalanced each year to 50% in an intermediate bond fund and 50% in an S&P 500 index fund, you have a reasonable expectation that your portfolio and withdrawals will last for thirty years. This rule is based on historical results using the type of market-based approach illustrated in Tables 5-3 and 5-4.

The problem with this rule is most people don't need to withdraw the same percentage, or same dollar amount, each year. Figure 5-11 shows Wally and Sally's projected account balances, withdrawals and withdrawal rate[101] each year.

Wally and Sally need higher withdrawals early in retirement, lower withdrawals in mid retirement, and higher withdrawals again near the end of their plan.

Based on Wally and Sally's projections, and hundreds of other retirees I have worked with, using a rule of thumb is not the way to go. You need a plan that helps you allocate investments based on the risks you want to manage.

Another popular rule of thumb is the "100 minus age" rule which says you should take 100 less your age and allocate that percentage of your portfolio to stocks. By using this rule, each year you would rebalance your portfolio and decrease your allocation to stocks by 1%. This rule has gotten press primarily because it is easy to remember. It does not address the use of annuities, how to allocate each account, your spending patterns, or anything else.

---

101 Calculated by taking the withdrawal divided by the beginning of year balance.

My advice: don't base your retirement plan on a rule of thumb.

Figure 5-11 Withdrawal Rate			
Calendar Year	BOY Account Balance	Withdrawal Amount*	Withdrawal Rate
2016	$1,157,000	None	-
2017	1,297,968	106,477	8%
2018	1,253,254	64,573	5%
2019	1,249,778	53,048	4%
2020	1,257,931	53,744	4%
2021	1,265,768	55,067	4%
2022	1,272,669	36,156	3%
2023	1,299,148	34,394	3%
2024	1,328,486	36,236	3%
2025	1,357,111	38,289	3%
2026	1,384,831	40,776	3%
2027	1,411,199	43,375	3%
2028	1,436,058	46,093	3%
2029	1,459,240	48,921	3%
2030	1,480,576	51,876	4%
2031	1,499,875	54,876	4%
2032	1,517,026	58,070	4%
2033	1,531,762	61,320	4%
2034	1,543,944	64,696	4%
2035	1,553,365	68,223	4%
2036	1,559,782	71,875	5%
2037	1,562,973	103,661	7%
2038	1,534,426	94,106	6%
2039	1,514,764	97,938	6%
2040	1,490,213	101,948	7%
2041	1,460,351	106,060	7%
2042	1,424,818	110,340	8%
2043	1,383,164	114,756	8%
2044	1,334,953	119,277	9%

*Withdrawal is net any amount deposited back into the non-

Wait, I'm Still Accumulating

If you are still in the accumulation phase and are saving money, the first thing you have to decide is whether you want to take investment risk at all. You can choose only safe options. There is nothing wrong with that.

If you want to build a traditional market-based portfolio, make sure you diversify. Invest 50–80% of your retirement money in risk level 4 funds (closer to 80% if you are younger, closer to 50% if you are nearing retirement), with the remainder spread across risk levels 2 and 3.

Then turn off the TV, ignore current economic news, and continue to save monthly. Unless you are in the investment industry, do not think about your investments. Focus on whatever it is you do well and figure out how to make more money doing it.

Alternative Investments

A former business partner of mine often said, "If you bet on red and win, did that make it a good investment?"[102] There is a difference between speculating and building a portfolio that needs to produce reliable income for you.

You don't need to own any investments other than a combination of safe choices and index funds to achieve your goals. Why complicate things?

If you want to speculate by buying an individual stock or betting on the future price of gold, go right ahead. You might win. But more importantly, you might lose. Psychologists say that the people who win will make sure they tell others, while those who lose generally do not like to talk about it.

Many investment opportunities you'll encounter are designed to appeal to your ego. You may be told they are "exclusive" or previously only available to the super-rich. They may come in the form of a private placement, which is an investment that is not publicly traded. They may be labeled as an "alternative" investment. You need to be able to make a distinction between the commercially packaged alternatives that are gimmicky, and legitimate alternative investments, which for high net worth clients can bring additional diversification to the portfolio.

---

102 David Rosenthal, Wealth Management Solutions, LLC.

In general, don't jump into alternatives unless:

- You have the expertise to thoroughly evaluate the investment.

- You can hire someone who has the expertise to evaluate it for you in an unbiased way.

- You are okay with risk and don't need current income or liquidity from the investment.

In doing research on alternatives I spoke with Joe Seetoo of Morton Capital. Morton Capital is a registered investment advisor in California that specializes in bringing hand-picked alternative investments to their high net worth clients. They receive no compensation from the underlying investments, which puts them in the perfect position to offer an objective opinion and do the research and due diligence that needs to be done.

Joe said some of the key factors they consider when looking at private alternative investments are:

- *Conflicts of interest* – Do the key decision makers have potential conflicts of interest or are their interests aligned with our clients?

- *Transparency* – Are we able to get information from the general partner in a timely manner, and do they provide us access to information in order to conduct proper due diligence?

- *Structure* – Does the partnership have the proper organizational structure and controls to make us feel comfortable (i.e., cash controls, independent auditor, legal counsel, administrator, depth of their team)?

- *"Skin in the game"* – Does the general partner have a significant amount of their personal net worth invested in the strategy they manage? If they have no skin in the game, we will not invest in their strategy.

Another factor to consider is taxes. For many high income, high net worth folks, the after-tax yield on an investment that produces a 9% income stream is 4 – 5%. When comparing the risk-return trade-off on various investment options be sure to look at after-tax results.

If you're looking at alternatives because you want higher yields, consider the level of certainty behind the income stream. I watched the income stream on many such investments dry up in 2008/2009. At the same time, dividends on stock went through a substantial decline.

My personal preference is to build a core portfolio of traditional liquid investments (CDs, bonds, stock index funds) first. The core should be designed to provide a comfortable standard of living for life. Once a core is in place, then for high net worth families with additional capital, alternatives can be considered.

Summary

Your money has a job to do for you. Investing for the purpose of creating life-long income is different than investing with the goal of achieving the highest possible return. It requires looking at risk in a new way.

You can compare choices by using a risk scale of 1-5, benchmarking against what can be achieved by using a risk-free choice, and estimating the price tag of producing $1,000 a month of income. You can then combine options to come up with a plan that manages multiple types of risk.

An income timeline can help show you how much guaranteed income you have, and how much of your expenses it will cover each year. This coverage ratio can be used to help you diagnostically decide if annuities are a good fit in your plan.

You can also use an income timeline to determine when you will need to take withdrawals from savings. You can create alternate income timelines to show you how one strategy compares to another. You can then use your withdrawal strategy to select safe investments for near-term income needs and growth-oriented investments for future income needs.

Chapter 6

Insurance, Life and Disability

Shifting Risk

"Not everything that is faced can be changed. But nothing can be changed until it is faced."

—James Baldwin

Insurance, like any other financial instrument discussed in this book, is a tool.

The primary purpose of the insurance tool is to shift risk. To determine if you need insurance of any kind, follow a four-step process:

1. Identify the probability of the risk.

2. Quantify the risk.

3. Evaluate the needed insurance purchase to shift the risk.

4. Decide to shift risk or retain risk.

This process can be applied to any type of insurance purchase—life insurance, disability, property and casualty, long-term care, and so on. Acquiring the proper types and amounts of insurance represents an investment in your family's financial well-being.

Identify and Quantify Risk

Not all risks are equal. Take the common example of your home burning down. Although unlikely to happen, if it does burn down, the consequences are severe. Therefore, if you own a home, you carry homeowner's insurance.

You choose to pay a reasonable premium to minimize the financial severity of such an event.

Contrast that with death. There is no argument that death is a high-probability event, and the probability goes up as we age. The severity of the event, however, depends on where in your life cycle it occurs and who is financially dependent on you at the time.

If you are young, have many high-earning years ahead of you, and have a non-working spouse or dependent children, the financial consequences of your death are likely to be severe for your family. The probability and severity of a death might fall in quadrant 4 in Figure 6-1.

Figure 6-1. Assessing risk for insurance needs

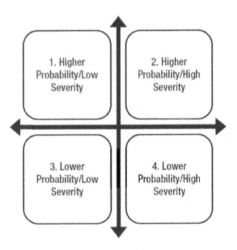

If you are retired, and your spouse will have the same amount of income and resources available regardless of your death, the financial consequences may be minimal. Your situation may fall in quadrant 1 on Figure 6-1.

In the first scenario, you have a need for life insurance. In the second scenario, you don't.

The need for disability insurance might follow a slightly different pattern. The probability of disability is higher than the probability of death when you are younger.

A 50-year-old male is 33% more likely to become disabled than die before age 65, and a 50-year-female is 94% more likely.[103] If you are a working woman between 50 and 60, and you haven't insured your earning power, it's time to give it some thought.

The probability and severity of a disability is likely to start in quadrant 2 in Figure 6-1 and then gravitate toward quadrant 3 the closer you get to retirement.

As you near retirement, all your resources need to work together toward a common goal, including your insurance portfolio. Like other aspects of your financial life, insurance policies need to be reviewed and changed in light of changing exposure to risks.

It can be easy to collect various insurance policies along the way and keep them without giving much thought about whether they are needed or not. It can also be easy to overlook gaps in your coverage.

In this chapter, I provide examples of how I analyze life insurance and disability insurance needs and show how the use of such tools may change as you near retirement.

TYPES OF LIFE INSURANCE

Life insurance can be broken out into two main categories:

1. Term life
2. Permanent life

Term life has only an insurance component. Much like car insurance, you pay a premium, and if an accident happens, it pays. There is no cash value accumulating. If you don't need the insurance any more, you stop paying the premium, and the policy expires.

Permanent life involves a policy that has two components; an insurance component and a cash value component. There are many variations of permanent life policies, such as whole life, universal life, and variable universal life.

The examples in this chapter illustrate the use of both term and permanent policies.

---

103 www.disabilityquotes.com/disability-insurance/death-disability-odds.cfm

Life Insurance in and near Retirement

With life insurance, first and foremost, it is important to establish its purpose. We are, after all, rather attached to our own lives, and sometimes this can make us view life insurance rather emotionally.

I have come across some people who don't like the idea of someone benefiting financially upon their death. It makes them uncomfortable. Others are more than willing to spend money on insurance premiums so that a significant amount of wealth can be passed along. Some are spending far more than they realize on insurance that is no longer necessary.

The primary purpose of life insurance is to provide for someone who is financially dependent on you by replacing income or assets that will become unavailable to them upon your death.

Once retired, you are often in a situation in which children are grown, and if you are married, income remains stable for your spouse. In many cases, there is no more financial dependency. At that point, life insurance policies need to be reviewed. You may not need them anymore.[104]

Let's look at three case studies and see how their existing life insurance holdings were evaluated.

Single Mom

Patricia walked in with seven whole life insurance policies. Her dad had been a life insurance agent; he kept selling them, and she kept buying them. Now, here she was at 58, trying to decide what to do with them.

The total death benefit on all of her policies was $379,000. Patricia had a 15-year-old son, Mark, whose dad had passed away several years prior. Patricia planned to work until 70 to get Mark through college. If she were to pass in the midst of her earning years, the financial severity on Mark would be high. Considering Mark's financial dependency on her and the severity of the situation should she die, Patricia most certainly had a need for life insurance.

---

104 With current estate tax laws (2016), you can pass along an estate of up to $5.45 million, and it would be exempt from federal estate taxes. A married couple could have a $10.9 million estate that would be exempt from federal estate taxes. Life insurance for estate planning purposes is applicable for those who expect their estates to exceed these limits, or for those who own a business.

The first thing I do in such a situation is create a schedule like Figure 6-2, which shows three of Patricia's seven policies. This helps organize the information to see at a glance what we have to work with.

Next, for any policies that have cash value, I request an in-force illustration on the policy based on current interest rate and premium assumptions. This helps determine how the policy is expected to perform if you leave it alone.

For example, many permanent policies were issued with the expectation that the cash value would grow at a much higher rate of return than has actually occurred. In such cases, the policy owner may receive a notice that they either have to pay additional premiums or their policy will lapse. An in-force illustration helps identify many years in advance which policies may have this problem.

Patricia's in-force illustrations showed that all of her policies were in good shape, meaning none were at risk of lapsing. The particular type of policies that Patricia owned had participated in dividends from the company, and the company had done well.

Policies that pay dividends offer you options on what you do with your dividends. Initially, Patricia's dividends were set to purchase additional paid-up insurance; however, Patricia's biggest concern was not her need for more insurance, it was reducing her expenses.

By exploring options with the insurance company, we decided to change her dividend option so that dividends would be used to reduce her annual premiums rather than buy more insurance. With this change, her out-of-pocket costs were reduced while enabling her to keep the insurance coverage she needed.

We also have a future plan for these policies. When Mark is established, and Patricia's need for life insurance is gone, we will look at using these policies for guaranteed income by converting them to an immediate annuity.

Figure 6-2
Patricia's Life Insurance Policy Schedule

Client	Patricia	Patricia	Patricia
Policy #	xx-xxx-xxx	xx-xxx-xxx	xx-xxx-xxx
Company	x	x	x
Date Issued	1998	1992	1988
Type of insurance	Whole	Whole	Whole w/adj term
Owner	Patricia	Patricia	Patricia
Insured	Patricia	Patricia	Patricia
Beneficiary 1	Trust for Mark	Trust for Mark	Trust for Mark
Beneficiary 2			
Death Benefit Amount	$ 50,098	$ 56,133	$ 100,000
Net Death Benefit	$ 50,098	$ 56,133	$ 100,000
A or B Death Benefit			
Premium	$ 1,101	$ 919	$ 558
Premium frequency	annual	annual	annual
Last Dividend	$ 605	$ 660	$ 924
Out of Pocket Premium	$ 496	$ 259	$ -
Cost basis	$ 11,051	$ 11,400	$ 12,782
- as of date:	xxxx	xxxx	xxxx
or taxable inc. on surr.	$ -	$ 6,176	$ 5,819
Cash Value	$ 10,418	$ 17,576	$ 18,601
Surrender Value	$ 10,418	$ 17,576	$ 18,601
Avail to loan at 80%	$ 8,334	$ 14,061	$ 14,881
Outstanding loans:	$ -	$ -	$ -
Loan Rate	8%	8%	8%
Other Expenses 1			
Other Expenses 2			
Div Option	Reduce Premium	Reduce Premium	Reduce Premium
Last in-force illustration	2011	2011	2011

Older Husband/Younger Wife

Matt was a successful surgeon who married a beautiful woman 28 years younger than he. He was 56 when he and his wife Tina came in to see me. They had a three-year-old daughter.

They owned several properties and loved to travel. When we ran their retirement projections, it was sobering. Normally, retirement assets need to provide for a 20- to 35-year life span. In their case, the combined retirement time-horizon was potentially 50 to 60 years. Yikes.

We discussed a combination of all of the following:

- Matt extending his career to 70 or beyond

- Tina building and developing a sustainable career once their daughter reached school age

- Spending less and saving more now

- Using life insurance as a leverage tool

Matt owned three term policies and three permanent insurance policies. Some of his term policies would expire in a few years, and one was a type of policy called *annual renewable term*, which means the premium goes up each year. He was paying $15,000 a year for a combined $1.4 million of life insurance, with the expectation that to keep this amount of insurance the costs would soon go up.

Like many high-wage earners, Matt had bought his life insurance in a haphazard manner over the years. No one had taken the time to structure his insurance properly.

By working with an agent to restructure his insurance, for the same out-of-pocket premium we were able to secure $1.8 million of permanent insurance on Matt with a fixed cost. We used a 1035 tax-free exchange (see sidebar) to transfer his existing permanent policies into a new policy without any tax consequences. Without costing the couple a penny more, we made a significant improvement to their plan both in the amount of insurance and in capping the projected future cost of maintaining this important part of their plan.

THE 1035 TAX-FREE EXCHANGE

Life insurance policies that have a cash value can be exchanged, or transferred into a new life insurance policy, with no tax consequences, through a 1035 exchange. A 1035 exchange can also be used to transfer cash value in life insurance into an annuity. Before cancelling a life insurance policy that has cash value, evaluate your exchange options.

What made insurance such an attractive option for Matt and Tina is the leverage it provided. You can compare owning the insurance to trying to save the equivalent amount of money by calculating the rate of return the insurance provides depending on how long Matt lives.

You use the following data to calculate it.[105]

- *Present Value (PV):* –$61,000 (amount of net cash value in the existing policies they would receive if they cashed them in)

- *Payment (PMT):* –$15,000 (amount of annual premium)

- *Term (n):* 25, 30, 35 (years remaining to Matt's respective ages of 86, 91, and 96)

- *Future Value (FV):* $1,800,000 (death benefit guaranteed to be paid)

You solve for i, the interest rate.

Annualized results are tabulated here:

- *25-year return:* 9.01%

- *30-year return:* 6.78%

- *35-year return:* 5.26%

If Matt lives 25 years to his age 86, slightly longer than the average male life expectancy, the insurance has provided a guaranteed return of 9%.

---

105 I do these calculations on an hp12c calculator that I have downloaded as an app on both my iPhone and iPad.

In Matt and Tina's case, we also had conversations about the risk of spending this much on life insurance. In Matt's case, the risk is that he and Tina should separate or Tina should pass first. In either case, Matt would have a few options. The death benefit on the policies could be reduced, and the beneficiary redirected to a trust for their daughter, or the cash accumulated inside the policies could be used for his own retirement income.

Note   Normally, term policies for a high wage earner make sense; they are a form of low-cost temporary insurance that will replace earnings in the event of death in the midst of a worker's highest-earning years. In Matt and Tina's case, due to the age difference, they have a need for insurance that will extend far past Matt's working years. We needed to know that a death benefit was in place long after the term policies were set to expire. Permanent insurance was therefore a better solution for them.

I'm Retired—What Do I Do With These Policies?

Marvin was 62, and his wife Beth was about to turn 66 when we began working together. Both were still working part-time. Initially Marvin just wanted to pay me hourly to answer some specific questions. One of his first questions for me was what to do with his life insurance policies. My initial response was:

> The first thing to consider when evaluating life insurance is the need for life insurance. Inside every policy, even those with a cash value, there is a cost to the insurance component of the policy.[106] If there is a financial dependency, then this cost becomes worth the benefit. If retirement income and assets are sufficient that either surviving spouse will be financially sound, then the need for life insurance diminishes greatly. This is why it is more difficult to make life insurance recommendations prior to running a retirement income plan.

Financial decisions should not be viewed in isolation, and you ought to be skeptical of anyone who tries to advise you on one piece without having a thorough understanding of your entire financial situation.

---

106 Even with a "paid-up" life insurance policy, there is a still in essence a premium being paid. But this cost is being paid internally with the cash you have accumulated in the policy rather than from a check you write for the premium. If you don't need the insurance, cash might be better used invested elsewhere than inside the insurance policy.

Marvin understood the interaction of the variables. We began working together on a more comprehensive basis and happily discovered that he and Beth had sufficient savings for their retirement income goals, no matter who should be the longest-lived. Marvin had no need for life insurance. There was no financial dependency.

The question of whether to keep the policies or not now became a question of values. They didn't need the cash value in the policies to support their retirement goals, and they could afford the premiums. Paying premiums for life insurance because you want to provide an additional benefit for loved ones is a perfectly acceptable use of cash. Marvin and Beth decided they wanted to keep the policies until they both had stopped working and then re-evaluate.

I had another couple in a similar situation who viewed the cash in their policies as an unexpected windfall, and they cashed in their policies to buy a motorhome. Once you know the policies are not needed, it frees you up to make whatever choices suit you.

Life insurance can also be used to fund the education of future generations. For those retirees who have enough, it may be possible to spend as little as $250 a month to provide up to $100,000 of college costs that would be funded with life insurance and paid upon your death. For example, a policy could be designed to pay off student loans. It all comes down to what is important to you. When you think of life insurance as a tool, you can use it to create wealth for many generations to come.

Blended Families

Some of the most complex situations I encounter are when I work with a couple who is on their second or third marriage and have children from those previous marriages.

Assets need to be used to provide income for the current couple; yet each often has accounts they accumulated before they married, and they want those accounts to go to their respective children.

Life insurance can be a good solution in many of these complex situations. You can use it to make sure a specified amount is left to your children regardless of how you and your current spouse choose to spend the rest. Or you can choose to buy life insurance to provide for your current spouse. The right solution depends on your individual situation.

Business Owners

Business owners most certainly have people who are financially dependent on them; their employees, and for many businesses like mine, their clients. Life insurance can be a much-needed asset in these situations. It is one of the most effective tools to use to make sure the business can continue on if something happens to the owner. The two most common ways business owners use life insurance policies are to:

- Fund buy/sell agreements.

- Provide key man insurance.

With a buy/sell agreement, life insurance can be used to provide cash to an identified buyer so they can purchase the business from the owner's estate upon the owner's death. There are numerous ways to structure this, and working with an experienced life insurance agent[107] and attorney is crucial to making sure everything is set up in a way to minimize conflict.

With key man insurance, the business will own insurance on the owner, partner or key employees to make sure it has cash to cover the operational costs of hiring and replacing this person should something happen.

Every business owner should consider the use of life insurance for business continuity purposes. It may not be needed in every situation, but it should be considered.

---

107 Special thanks to Jeff Carman, the most knowledgeable life insurance agent I've ever worked with. Since 2001 his council on complex insurance cases has been invaluable.

Life Insurance as a Savings Tool

Like any financial instrument, when used appropriately and in the right circumstances, whole life insurance can be an effective vehicle to use for saving for retirement. Unfortunately, too many zealous sales agents have recommended it in the wrong circumstances, and the use of insurance as a savings tool has gotten an undeserved bad reputation.

Wade Pfau, a well-known retirement research academic, did an analysis on a retirement income plan that used only a traditional 401(k) account with no insurance products, one that used the 401(k) with an income annuity at retirement, and one that used the 401(k), the income annuity and whole life insurance. The paper came to the following conclusion,

> We find substantive evidence that an integrated approach with investments, whole life insurance, and income annuities can provide more efficient retirement outcomes than relying on investments alone. Because whole life insurance can play an important role in producing more efficient retirement outcomes, younger individuals planning for both retirement and life insurance needs may view whole life insurance in a new light as a powerful retirement income planning tool. The recent conventional wisdom of "buy term and invest the difference" is less effective than many realize when viewed in terms of the risk management needs of a retirement income plan.[108]

Wade's analysis looked at several factors, such as potential 401(k) values in both good and bad markets, the amount of retirement income available in both good and bad markets, and the remaining wealth available to pass along to heirs under both good and bad market conditions. This scenario was run for both a 35 and a 50 year old. There is no question that the use of annuities and whole life improved the outcomes in almost each scenario.

The key assumption behind this type of research is that someone buys the insurance, keeps it, and faithfully pays the premiums until age 65. My concern for younger folks who pursue this strategy is that a job loss or significant decline in income could cause them to skip premiums, and the projected results would not materialize. For those with high incomes, sufficient emergency reserves, and enough assets to make the premiums as planned for the entire time horizon, I think whole life can be a positive addition to the retirement plan.

---

108 Pfau, W. D. "Optimizing Retirement Income by Combining Actuarial Science and Investments." Retirement Management Journal. Vol. 5, No. 2 (Fall 2015), 15-32.

Analyzing Existing Permanent Life Policies

If you own some form of a permanent life policy, quite a bit of analysis needs to be done before you decide what to do with it. You should look at a few specific things when analyzing an existing permanent policy:

Is the policy at risk? Many permanent policies were issued when interest rates were higher. Your premium was determined based on the expectation of these higher interest rates, which would result in a higher cash value. If the policy has not performed as initially expected, that premium may no longer be sufficient to keep the policy in force. Such situations can be anticipated by requesting something called an *in-force illustration*.

What are the tax consequences of termination? If you terminate a permanent policy while there is cash value, you may have tax consequences that need to be considered before making decisions.

What other options are available? With a permanent policy, you may be able to lower the death benefit, exchange the policy for an annuity, or change the dividend option to use it to either buy more insurance or to reduce the premium you owe. You should consider all options before deciding what to do with an existing policy.

Life Insurance Reviews

To my dismay, I have met very few life insurance agents who offer unbiased and comprehensive reviews of their clients' insurance policies. It seems too many agents contact their clients only to sell them more insurance. Many clients I work with have not heard from their agents in over a decade. The insurance industry does not seem to be well designed to incentivize agents to provide such reviews.

A new type of advisor is cropping up to meet the demand for objective advice: the fee-only life insurance advisor. Many of these advisors are former actuaries or insurance agents who now offer unbiased advice on existing life insurance policies for an hourly rate. The hourly rate may seem steep. But for business owners or executives looking at a large life insurance purchase, it can be smart to get an objective analysis before making a decision.

In addition, those who are in the midst of deciding if a large policy is still necessary may want an objective opinion before canceling the policy. You can search your favorite search engine for "fee-only life insurance advisor" to find such a person.

Many fee-only financial advisors also offer analysis and advice on life insurance policies. Some have more knowledge than others. I used to carry insurance licenses and sold both term and permanent life insurance. Although I have prior experience, I would certainly not consider myself an expert.

When making important life insurance decisions, I seek advice from people who know life insurance inside and out—I rely on the counsel of experienced agents. A knowledgeable agent brings valuable expertise to the table, and when an agent works as a team with an advisor who is looking at your entire financial picture, I think you get solid advice.

Whether it is a review or a new purchase, look for advisors or agents who:

- *View insurance in light of your entire financial situation.*

- *Have experience.* Yes, new agents have to get started somewhere, but as you near retirement, you cannot afford to make mistakes. Work with people who have been in the industry for quite some time.

- *Are objective.* Someone should be willing to tell you when you no longer need a policy, even if they are the person who sold it to you.

Disability Insurance

I figure that unless I sustain brain damage, I can pretty much do what I do for a living. I could lose a limb, an eye, or become paralyzed, and still I would be able to write and think and help people sort through complex financial decisions.

Despite the fact that I consider the odds that a disability would seriously impair my income to be rather small, I still carry disability insurance. God forbid something should happen; I do not want to become a burden to my family or a ward of the state.

It's a good thing I carry disability insurance, because my own view of my odds of a chronic disability is naïve. To calculate the odds that a disability would affect you, you can use the online Personal Disability Quotient calculator[109] at www.whatsmypdq.org.

When I put my information in, it tells me that my odds of being injured or becoming ill and unable to work for three months or longer are 13%. It also tells me if I do fall into the 13%, there is a 43% chance my disability could last for five years or longer. These odds are much higher than I would have guessed.

The first step in any insurance decision is getting a realistic idea of the probability the event will occur. Most people, like me, underestimate the risk of a disability:

- Prior to age 60, you have a higher probability of disability than death.

- Women are at greater risk for disability than men.

- Risk varies by occupation.

- The severity of a long disability is high. You can lose years of income.

- The cost to cover such a loss might be lower than you would guess. Once you estimate costs, you decide whether you want to retain the risk or pay the insurance company a premium and shift the risk to them.

You can typically insure somewhere between 50–70% of your gross income with a policy that would provide income through your age 65. You can also purchase policies that will provide income replacement for a specific time period, such as five or ten years, which could make sense if you are in your peak earning years and expect that you will retire in five to ten years at an early age—say 55 or 60.

109 This calculator is sponsored by the Council For Disability Awareness, a non-profit organization. It appears most of the members of this nonprofit are large insurance companies. Of course, they have an incentive to sell more insurance. Regardless of what the incentive may be, I find the calculator useful, and the information they provide at www.disabilitycanhappen.org is quite informative.

ADDITIONAL RESOURCES FROM THE COUNCIL OF DISABILITY AWARENESS

Disability statistics:
www.disabilitycanhappen.org/chances_disability/disability_stats.asp

Disability awareness quiz:
http://www.disabilitycanhappen.org/chances_disability/quiz.asp

Personal disability quotient calculator:
http://www.disabilitycanhappen.org/chances_disability/pdq.asp

---

Purchasing Disability Insurance

If you still have many earning years ahead of you, you have several ways to go about protecting your earning power:

- Rely on Social Security disability

- Explore all benefits offered by your employer

- Evaluate buying your own coverage from an independent agent

Social Security Disability

It is beyond the scope of this book to go into details about Social Security disability. I will simply say that if you are taking the time to read this book, and you are getting serious about your retirement planning, Social Security disability is unlikely to provide benefits in an amount sufficient for what you will need.

Just as Social Security retirement benefits were not designed to provide anything more than a basic amount of income in retirement, Social Security disability benefits are not designed to do anything other than provide a barebones amount of income should something unfortunate happen. If you make a decent living, you should look into coverage that provides benefits in addition to any provided by Social Security disability.

Employer Plans and Individual Policies

If your employer offers disability insurance, that is likely going to be the most cost-efficient way for you to secure coverage. But beware: many employers offer only short-term disability coverage. If you're 50, what you need is coverage that would pay benefits until you reach age 65.

Small business owners and professionals such as CPAs, attorneys, and doctors need to look at purchasing their own policies. Great coverage is often available through professional associations, such as the AICPA (American Institute of CPAs) for CPAs, the AMA (American Medical Association) for doctors, and the ADA (American Dental Association) for dentists.

In my case, I obtained coverage in a group policy offered through the Financial Planning Association. If you are a member of a professional group or trade association, start there to see what group benefits are offered.

If you need to find an agent to assist you, start with the National Association of Health Underwriters and use their online find-an-agent tool at www.nahu.org/consumer/findagent2.cfm.

MORE ON WHAT TO LOOK FOR WHEN BUYING A DISABILITY POLICY

Both of the following articles provide additional details about what you need to look for in a disability policy.

"Do You Need Disability Insurance?" (AARP): http://www.aarp.org/health/health-insurance/info-08-2012/disability-insurance-do-you-need-it.html

"The Disability Insurance Maze: How to Select and Purchase a Policy" (Get Rich Slowly): http://www.getrichslowly.org/blog/2008/02/27/the-disability-insurance-maze-how-to-select-and-purchase-a-policy/

Reviewing Existing Coverage

When reviewing disability policies, I rely on agents who specialize in disability. They are skilled at determining which policies, benefits, and riders are best for which professions.

Interestingly enough, with disability insurance, I have yet to encounter a single case where an existing policy needed to be replaced.

Instead, if additional coverage is needed, we buy a new policy to stack on top of the old one, or we exercise options within the client's existing policy to purchase additional benefits.

Because most of the clients I work with are only a few years away from retirement, the situation I frequently encounter is determining when disability policies should be terminated.

For example, some policies pay benefits only to age 65. The policy may have a 90- or 180-day waiting period before benefits begin. If you're 64, does it make sense to keep a policy that might, at most, pay out six months of benefits? Perhaps not.

You may be phasing into retirement. If a disability forced you from part-time work to full retirement a few years earlier than anticipated, it may not result in a severe financial hardship. Missing a few years of part-time income is not going to have the impact that missing ten years of your highest earning years will have.

I went back into the Personal Disability Quotient and put in figures for a 62-year-old, relatively healthy male[110], who does mostly office work and makes $85,000 a year:

- The odds of being injured or becoming ill and unable to work for 3 months or longer were 5%.

- Assuming 3% raises, the amount of income at risk is $355,608 (if he planned to work to 66).

- The odds for the same male at age 50 are 13%, and it jumps to 44% factoring in an unhealthy lifestyle, more physical work,

---

110 Used height of 5'9", weight of 180, non-tobacco user.

and any chronic conditions such as diabetes, high blood pressure, chronic back pain, anxiety or depression.

- At 50, the amount of income at risk is $1,713,335.

For a female age 62 with the same income and health status:[111]

- The odds of disability before an age 66 retirement are also 3%.

- For that same female at age 50, the odds of disability are 12%, and jump to 34% with the presence of an unhealthy lifestyle, more physical work and any of the chronic issues named earlier.

Ladies, if you are a working woman as I am, make sure you look into disability insurance.

As you near retirement, both the probability and financial severity of a disability go down. The closer you get to retirement, the more important it is to review your existing coverage and make sure it is still needed.

If you are near retirement and have limited cash flow, disability premiums may need to be repositioned to purchase long-term care insurance. I discuss long-term care insurance in Chapter 10.

Summary

Insurance, like any financial instrument, is a tool. It ought to be used when appropriate by determining the probability and severity of a given risk. Then you determine whether you want to retain the risk or shift it to an insurance company.

Life and disability insurance needs should be evaluated within the scope of your entire financial situation. Look at how these products can protect you and your family against risks that can derail your retirement security.

All insurance should be reviewed on a periodic basis in light of changing risks and changing financial circumstances.

---

111 Used height of 5'4", weight of 135, non-tobacco user.

Chapter 7

Using Your Company Benefits

401(k)s, Pensions, and Rollovers, Oh My

"Our lives bear almost no resemblance, in hardship, pain, or danger, to the lives of our grandparents."

—*Jacob Ward, Editor in Chief, Popular Science*

Company benefits used to be rather simple. Our grandparents, and in some cases our parents, worked for the same company for 25 or 30 years and retired with a gold watch and a pension.

They did not have to manage their company benefits. They did not have to decide how to invest their 401(k) money, when to make their deferred compensation elections, whether they should participate in the voluntary group universal life policy offered, or when to exercise their incentive stock options.

As the quote that begins the chapter says, the hardship, pain, and danger we are exposed to are significantly less cumbersome than that of our grandparents; nevertheless, the company benefits decisions that must be made are infinitely more complex.

Although I would like to, it is impossible for me to delve into the nuances of all the different types of benefit plans you may encounter, so I will stick with a few basics: 401(k) plans, pensions, company stock and stock options, and deferred compensation plans. Let's discuss the most important aspects of these plans and the decisions you need to make as you near retirement.

Your 401(k)

Not all 401(k) plans are created equal. Some have only three or four invest-ment options. Others have so many choices, trying to sort through them all is overwhelming. Some employers offer matching contributions. Others don't. Some 401(k) plans allow loans. Others don't.

Despite their differences, all 401(k) plans do have several rules in common.

Creditor Protection

Your 401(k) assets are creditor protected, even in the event of bankruptcy. I can't tell you how many people get themselves in financial trouble and cash in a 401(k) plan because they think that is their best option. I hope you are reading this book because you are not anywhere near that kind of financial trouble. But trouble is bound to find a few of you.

Maybe you have a great business idea. You decide to use 401(k) money to get your business started rather than take out a bank loan. Bad idea. If your business doesn't work out, your 401(k) money is gone. If you use a bank loan instead to fund your business, and your business doesn't work out, the worst case is that you file for bankruptcy—your 401(k) assets are protected and still available for your retirement.

In recent years, many people faced with a job loss have used 401(k) money to try to keep their homes. Making objective decisions about one's home can be difficult, but as difficult as it may be, you need to look at the long-term consequences of any financial decision. You may spend a substantial amount of retirement money trying to keep a home that you end up losing anyway. One lady I spoke with said, "The stupidest thing I ever did was cash out my 401(k) plan to try to keep that house." The quality of such decisions often becomes clear only in hindsight.

Your 401(k) money is for retirement. That's it. I don't advise you use it for any other purpose—particularly if you are in financial trouble. I think using your 401(k) money before retirement voids a valuable form of protection available to you.

IRA CREDITOR PROTECTION

You will likely end up rolling 401(k) money to an IRA. IRA money is also creditor protected in several ways:

As of 2016, up to $1,283,025 of IRA assets are protected from bankruptcy under federal law if you contributed directly to the account (meaning this protection may not be extended to an inherited IRA account). This limit is indexed to inflation.

The entire IRA account balance is protected if the money was rolled over into an IRA from a company plan.

State laws determine whether IRA assets are sheltered from creditor claims other than bankruptcy, and laws vary widely from state to state.

Age-Related 401(k) Rules

401(k) plans have some interesting age-related rules that differ from the rules that apply to IRAs. You should know these rules before you decide whether to move money out of a 401(k) plan into an IRA.

Age 55

If you withdraw IRA money prior to age 59½, your withdrawals are subject to a 10% early-withdrawal penalty tax in addition to ordinary income taxes. Many 401(k) plans have a rule that may allow you to access funds a few years earlier—at age 55 instead of 59½. This early access to funds applies if you

- Terminate employment no earlier than the year in which you turn age 55, but before age 59½.

- Leave your funds in the 401(k) plan to access them penalty-free.

Tip	If you have a job that ends when you're between ages 55 and 59½, think twice before you roll your retirement funds into an IRA or your new employer's 401(k) because if you do, you can't access the money without paying a penalty until you're 59½. If you don't, you can access the money now.

Age 59½

You can access funds from an old 401(k) plan once you reach age 59½. ("Old 401(k)" here means you no longer work for that company.) But if you want access to 401(k) money at a company you are still working for, you may not be able to get your hands on it, even if you are 59½.

If you are still working and have a 401(k) plan with your current employer, you will have to check with your 401(k) plan administrator to see whether your plan allows what is called an *in-service* withdrawal at age 59½. Some 401(k) plans allow this, and others do not.

Age 70½

Employer plans as well as IRAs require you to start taking withdrawals at age 70½.

If you are still working at age 70½, and you are not a 5% owner of the company, you may be able to delay your required minimum distributions (RMDs) from your current employer plan until April 1 of the year after you retire. Check with your plan to see whether you may do this. (In such a situation you would still be required to take distributions from other retirement plans, just not the one from your current employer.)

In general, plan on starting your RMDs from any and all retirement accounts by age 70½ (with the exception of Roth IRAs, which don't have RMDs).

Aligning Your 401(k) with Your Retirement Goals

Something happens as people near retirement. They wake up one day and look at this collection of accounts they have and think "Now what do I do?" That's usually when I hear from them. The sooner you ask yourself that question, the better off you will be.

With a 401(k), you need to answer several questions before you can appropriately decide how to invest it.

For example, do you invest it as if it were in isolation, or do you invest it after seeing how it fits in with other investments you have? Will you need to begin to use the money at age 55 because it will be more tax-efficient for you to do so, or does your plan work best if you don't touch the funds until age 70?

If you only have a single 401(k) and no other accounts, the answer is relatively easy. You thoughtfully decide how to allocate your money across the funds in your plan by investing according to risk and choosing the funds with the lowest fees in each risk category. If you don't need to touch the funds until age 70, you might choose a more aggressive allocation than if you start withdrawing at 55.

It might even be easier than that. Most 401(k)s offer model portfolios that are already built for you, or something called a *target date fund*. Pick the model that fits your comfort level with investment risk, or the target date fund that is the closest match to your expected year of retirement, and you are done.

If you have multiple accounts outside your 401(k), and/or your spouse also has a 401(k), there might be a better way than allocating each account as if it were its own isolated entity. In this case you look at your investments as a household rather than on an individual account basis.

Investing as a Household

Most people collect investment accounts over time without aligning them toward a common goal. Although it takes work to view investments across a household, this work can pay off. Sometimes the household view can increase your after-tax return. You saw an example of how this works in Chapter 5 with the concept of asset location. Sometimes a household view can be used to lower the total investment fees you pay. The second situation was the case for John and Mary.

John and Mary

John is an architect, and Mary is a nurse at a large hospital. Both had 401(k) plans with about $300,000 each. After discussing investment risk, John and

Mary determined that they wanted their investment allocation to be approximately 50% fixed income (bond funds and other low-risk options) and 50% equities, which were to be divided equally among U.S. and international equities. Mary's 401(k) plan had hundreds of mutual funds as well as a "fixed account" option[112] that was currently paying a 5% fixed rate. The mutual fund choices were actively managed and had internal expenses that ranged from about .55% on the U.S. equity funds to 1.23% on the international funds.

John's 401(k) plan offered eight equity index mutual funds and four bond index funds. The internal expenses on the equity funds in John's plan ranged from about .15% on the U.S. funds to about .35% on the international funds.

We chose to allocate John's account 50% to U.S. large-cap equity and 50% to international because these fund choices had substantially lower fees than the equivalent choices in Mary's account.

We allocated Mary's entire 401(k) to the fixed account, because this was a unique option that did not have the volatility that bond funds have, and something equivalent was not offered in John's 401(k) plan.

By allocating their accounts this way, we were able to reduce their investment expenses by over $1,500 a year—and as you have learned, the best consistent predictor of future fund performance has proven to be lower expenses.

Viewed independently, when equity markets are down, Mary's 401(k) will look great. When equity markets are going up, John's 401(k) will look great. When viewed together, John and Mary have an appropriately allocated investment plan.

When allocating across a household, you cannot compare one account's performance to another. They are designed to work in unison. In John and Mary's case, they were about the same age, so this allocation plan worked for them. If one of them had been substantially younger, we might have taken a different approach.

In many cases, I recommend intentionally planning to draw on an older spouse's retirement accounts first, leaving the younger spouse's accounts to accumulate until required distributions start at their age 70.

---

112 These fixed account options may come in the form of a stable value fund, or are sometimes called guaranteed interest, investment, or insurance contracts (GICs). A GIC is typically a contract issued by an insurance company to a qualified retirement plan.

In these situations, it sometimes makes sense to allocate the younger spouse's accounts more aggressively. If the younger spouse is 50, and the account will not be tapped until 70, there is no need to worry about the day-to-day or even year-to-year fluctuations in account values. In such cases, you want to design an investment approach to maximize the account value twenty years from now, not one that protects the account's value one year from now.

Tip   It's usually best to view your retirement investments across your household. Doing so offers more choices and more ways to reduce risk.

To Roll Over, or Not to Roll Over

I regularly meet people who have the mistaken belief that any time they move funds out of their company plan, they will have to pay taxes. That isn't true.

Once you terminate employment with an employer, you are permitted to move funds that were in the company retirement plan into your own IRA through a process called a *rollover*. As long as you do it correctly, a rollover is not a taxable transaction.

If you take the money out of the company plan and spend it, put it in an account other than your IRA, or fail to deposit the funds in your IRA within the allotted 60 days, then the rollover rules do not apply, and the money withdrawn is considered taxable.

In most cases, if you left an employer prior to reaching age 55 and have an old 401(k) plan still hanging out there, I think you are best off rolling your company retirement accounts to an IRA for the following reasons:

- *Ease of administration:* Your employer may change 401(k) providers at any time. Each time it does so, the investments offered change, and you have to take a fresh look at the fund choices and fees. In addition, you need to remember to update your old 401(k) plans with changes to your address or beneficiary designations.

- *Wider array of investment choices:* In an IRA, you can build a great portfolio using low-fee index funds. You can also use CDs and individual bonds. Such choices may not be available in your 401(k) plan.

- *Better beneficiary options:* 401(k) plans differ in their distribution requirements. They may offer all the options allowed under current law, but they don't have to. Some plans offer a limited set of distribution options to a beneficiary, in which case your beneficiary would have more options with an IRA.

- *Easier-to-handle required minimum distributions:* Once you are required to take distributions, it is going to be easier to manage the process if you have consolidated retirement accounts. In addition, many plans require you to take distributions once per year as a lump sum. With an IRA you can set up a monthly direct deposit which can make it easier to manage cash flow.

If you are lucky enough to accumulate a large retirement account balance at a young age, one other advantage to having the funds in an IRA is the ability to access funds early, penalty-free, via the use of 72(t) payments. This is a special provision of the tax code that allows you to take money out of an IRA before age 59½ and avoid the 10% early withdrawal penalty tax.

In order to use 72(t) payments, also called *SEPP* payments (Substantially Equal Periodic Payments), you must withdraw the money according to a specific schedule. The IRS gives you three different methods to choose from to calculate your specific payment schedule. You must stick with the payment schedule for five years or until you reach age 59½, whichever comes later (this 5 year rule is waived if the IRA owner is disabled or dies). If you deviate from your schedule before the appropriate amount of time has passed, the penalty tax can be imposed on all amounts withdrawn up to that point.

This option may be beneficial in the following situations:

- For tax reasons it makes sense for you to use retirement withdrawals early in your plan and other assets later on.

- You have a large illiquid asset that will become available to you later, such as proceeds from the sale of a business, real estate asset, or known inheritance.

If you think this option would be useful, try one of these two online calculators to calculate the three IRS approved payment schedules:

- 72(t) Calculator by CalcXML at: http://www.calcxml.com/calculators/72t.

- 72(t) Calculator by Bankrate® at: http://www.bankrate.com/calculators/retirement/72-t-distribution-calculator.aspx.

Rollover Rules to Take Note Of

Watch out for mandatory tax withholding. If an eligible rollover distribution is paid directly to your new IRA or 401(k) custodian, no tax withholding is required. If the check is payable to you, your employer-sponsored plan must withhold 20% of the rollover amount for mandatory federal tax withholding. They send this tax withholding directly to the IRS on your behalf.

In such a case, you have 60 days to get the full amount of the distribution into your IRA.[113] This means you have to come up with cash to contribute to your IRA to replace the 20% that was withheld for taxes. If you do so, the full amount of the distribution would be considered to be rolled over, and no taxes would be owed. When you file your tax return, you get a refund for any excess taxes that were automatically withheld and are now owed back to you.

You can avoid tax withholding by choosing a direct rollover option, where the check is payable directly to your new IRA trustee or custodian. This is highly advisable.

IRA rollovers are not an all-or-nothing proposition. You can use an IRA rollover to move a portion of your company retirement account to an IRA. I can think of two reasons you might do this:

- If you left your employer after age 55 but before 59½ and wanted to leave some funds in your 401(k) plan for potential penalty-free access.

- You may want to allocate a portion of your account to a particular investment choice offered in your company plan, but allocate the remainder among a broader array of investment choices that aren't available in the plan.

---

113 Starting January 1, 2015 you are only allowed to do one 60 day IRA rollover (where funds come to you) within each 12 month period. IRS regulations can be found at: https://www.irs.gov/retirement-plans/ira-one-rollover-per-year-rule.

INHERITED 401(k)s

If you inherit an IRA or 401(k) plan from a spouse, you can roll the funds into your own IRA, and it is not a taxable event. But that isn't always the best choice. You may want to structure the account as an inherited IRA, which is subject to slightly different required minimum distribution rules than if you roll the funds into your own IRA. I have written two online articles that go into greater depth on the choices available when you inherit an IRA or 401(k):

"I Inherited an IRA—Now What?" http://moneyover55.about.com/od/iras/a/I-Inherited-An-Ira-Now-What.htm

"401k Beneficiary—When and How You Can Take Money Out" http://moneyover55.about.com/od/RetirementAccountWithdrawals/a/401k-Beneficiary-Inherited-401k-When-And-How-You-Can-Take-Money-Out.htm

---

IRA rollovers are reported on your tax return as a non-taxable transaction. Even if you correctly execute an IRA rollover, on occasion your plan trustee or custodian will report it incorrectly on the tax form 1099-R it issues to you and to the IRS.

Typically, people hand off tax forms like a 1099-R to their tax preparer without looking too closely. Not to worry—the return can be amended if the error is caught, but not incurring the error in the first place is best.

Be sure to carefully explain any IRA rollover or transfer transactions to your tax preparer or double-check all documentation if you prepare your own return.

When a Rollover May Not Be the Best Idea

If you left your employer after you turned 55 but before age 59½, moving your 401(k) plan before age 59½ will void your ability to access your funds penalty-free between ages 55 and 59½. If you won't need the money during that time, this won't be relevant. But if there's a chance you might need to take withdrawals, you may want to wait until age 59½ before you proceed with the rollover.

If your 401(k) plan offers a unique fixed income or guaranteed account option, that might warrant keeping funds in the plan. For example, some plans offer something called a *guaranteed insurance contract* (GIC) that pays an attractive fixed rate of return. Other plans, such as the options offered to many in the public education system through TIAA-CREF, offer a fixed account that usually pays a competitive rate. This type of investment option is not easily replicated outside of the plan.

Pension Choices

When it comes to your pension, you have important, irrevocable decisions to make. Single or married, your decisions today will have a big impact on the 82-year-old you. If you're married, your decision affects your spouse.

Your pension decision can be grouped into three main categories:

- Whether to take a lump sum or annuity

- What survivor option to choose

- When to start your pension

Let's look at two case studies to see how these pension options can be analyzed. The first case is Helen, a single woman about to turn 55.

Helen: Lump Sum or Annuity

Helen was just finalizing her plans to leave corporate America at the age of 55. She had the option of taking her pension plan as a lump sum distribution and rolling it over to an IRA—with no taxes due at the time of the rollover—or taking a lifetime annuity payment of $28,322 a year.

The spreadsheet in Figure 7-1 illustrates how long Helen's money would last if she took the lump sum, and then withdrew the same amount each year that the annuity was guaranteed to provide her.

Figure 7-1
Helen's Pension: Annuity vs Lump Sum

Single Life Annuity			Lump Sum of $341,000 Earning Return of:			
Age	Year	Starting @ 55	4%	5%	6%	7%
			Year End Balances After Withdrawal			
55	1	28,322	326,318	329,728	333,138	336,548
56	2	28,322	311,049	317,892	324,804	331,784
57	3	28,322	295,169	305,465	315,971	326,687
58	4	28,322	278,653	292,416	306,607	321,233
59	5	28,322	261,478	278,715	296,681	315,398
60	6	28,322	243,615	264,329	286,160	309,154
61	7	28,322	225,037	249,223	275,008	302,472
62	8	28,322	205,717	233,362	263,186	295,323
63	9	28,322	185,623	216,709	250,655	287,674
64	10	28,322	164,726	199,222	237,373	279,489
65	11	28,322	142,993	180,861	223,293	270,731
66	12	28,322	120,391	161,582	208,369	261,361
67	13	28,322	96,885	141,339	192,549	251,334
68	14	28,322	72,438	120,084	175,780	240,605
69	15	28,322	47,014	97,766	158,004	229,126
70	16	28,322	20,572	74,333	139,163	216,842
71	17	28,322	(6,927)	49,727	119,190	203,699
72	18	28,322	(35,526)	23,892	98,020	189,636
73	19	28,322	(65,269)	(3,236)	75,579	174,589
74	20	28,322	(96,202)	(31,719)	51,792	158,488
75	21	28,322	(128,372)	(61,627)	26,577	141,260
76	22	28,322	(161,829)	(93,031)	(150)	122,826
77	23	28,322	(196,624)	(126,004)	(28,481)	103,102
78	24	28,322	(232,811)	(160,627)	(58,512)	81,997
79	25	28,322	(270,445)	(196,980)	(90,345)	59,415
80	26	28,322	(309,585)	(235,151)	(124,087)	35,252
81	27	28,322	(350,290)	(275,230)	(159,855)	9,398
82	28	28,322	(392,624)	(317,314)	(197,768)	(18,266)
83	29	28,322	(436,651)	(361,502)	(237,956)	(47,867)
84	30	28,322	(482,439)	(407,899)	(280,555)	(79,539)
85	31	28,322	(530,059)	(456,616)	(325,711)	(113,429)
86	32	28,322	(579,583)	(507,768)	(373,575)	(149,691)
87	33	28,322	(631,088)	(561,479)	(424,312)	(188,492)
88	34	28,322	(684,654)	(617,875)	(478,093)	(230,008)
89	35	28,322	(740,362)	(677,091)	(535,100)	(274,431)
90	36	28,322	(798,298)	(739,267)	(595,528)	(321,963)

If she could be assured of earning a 6% rate of return (net of all fees), the lump sum would provide the equivalent income as the annuity until about age 76. At a 7% rate of return, it would last until about age 81. Contrast that with the annuity payments, which are guaranteed to pay out for Helen's entire life. I advised that Helen take the annuity option, which she did.

If Helen had any health concerns that would lead her to believe she might have a shortened life expectancy, the recommendation may have been different.

Eric and Julie: Pension Survivor Options

Eric was retiring at age 60. His pension plan did not offer a lump sum distribution option, but it did offer numerous choices regarding when he could take his pension and what survivor benefit options would be available to a spouse.

He and his wife Julie had a substantial amount of savings in IRAs and company retirement plans. Although he was retiring at 60, if it was more beneficial for him to wait until 65 to begin his pension, he could use other savings to supplement his income for those five years.

He needed help deciding when to begin his pension and whether he should choose an option that provided ongoing income to Julie if he died first. With a single life option, his pension payments would stop upon his death. With a 100% joint and survivor pension option, he would receive less annual income, but the payments were guaranteed to continue for Julie's life span as well as his own.

Here is a summary of four of Eric's pension choices:

- *Single life at age 60: $19,536 a year*

- *Joint and survivor at age 60: $15,888*

- *Single life at age 65: $34,128*

- *Joint and survivor at age 65: $26,568*

First let's discuss the single life choices versus the 100% joint and survivor choice. If Eric chooses the single life and dies a year later, the benefits end. Julie misses out on $15,888 a year for potentially 30 years or more—what she would have received had he chosen the 100% joint and survivor option. The present value of $15,888 a year, for 30 years and assuming a 4% return, is about $275,000.

The annual difference between the two choices is $3,648 at Eric's age 60 and $7,560 at age 65. He and Julie are the same age.

So, at age 60, the question is: can Eric buy $275,000 of life insurance that has an annual premium of less than $3,648 a year? If so, he might choose the single life option and buy a life insurance policy. The advantage to this option is if Julie were to die first, the life insurance policy could be dropped. The disadvantage to this option is that as people age, they can become forgetful. I have seen older couples inadvertently miss insurance premium payments, causing policies to lapse.

Tip   One problem with buying life insurance to protect family income in the case of your demise is that you could become forgetful as you age. You may miss payments and lose the policy. It's better to lock in guaranteed income that will continue, no matter your state of mind.

If Eric waits until age 65, the present value of 25 remaining years of $26,568 in income for Julie would be $415,000 (again at 4%). Would he be able to buy $415,000 of life insurance for less than $7,560 a year? Perhaps, depending on his health situation.

In Eric's situation, some health conditions ruled out life insurance as an option. He and Julie both agreed that the joint and survivor option was best for them.

The next question was when to start the pension—at age 60 or 65?

Eric: When to Start Pension Benefits

Figure 7-2 shows a comparison of the two pension options. The "Annuity @ 60" column shows the annual joint life payout Eric can receive if he starts his pension early. The "Annuity @ 65" column shows the annual joint life payout Eric will receive if he waits until age 65 to begin his pension.

To understand Figure 7-2, assume that Eric and Julie are going to spend $26,568 a year whether they start Eric's pension at his age 60 or at 65. If they start the pension at 60, they will receive $15,888 from the pension and will need to withdraw $10,680 a year from savings and investments each year to have the $25,568 of income. You see this withdrawal in column A. If they wait and start the pension at his age 65, they will need to withdraw the full $25,568 for five years and nothing thereafter. You see this withdrawal in column B.

Figure 7-2
Eric - Take Pension at 60 or 65

	Joint Life		A	B	C	D	E
					\$150,000 invested at		
					4% after respective		
	Annuity	Annuity	Withdrawals needed		withdrawals in		
Age	@ 60	@ 65	to have \$26,568		columns A and B		Difference
60	15,888		10,680	26,568	145,320	129,432	(15,888)
61	15,888	0	10,680	26,568	140,453	108,041	(32,412)
62	15,888	0	10,680	26,568	135,391	85,795	(49,596)
63	15,888	0	10,680	26,568	130,127	62,659	(67,468)
64	15,888	0	10,680	26,568	124,652	38,597	(86,055)
65	15,888	26,568	10,680	0	118,958	40,141	(78,817)
66	15,888	26,568	10,680	0	113,036	41,747	(71,289)
67	15,888	26,568	10,680	0	106,877	43,416	(63,461)
68	15,888	26,568	10,680	0	100,473	45,153	(55,319)
69	15,888	26,568	10,680	0	93,811	46,959	(46,852)
70	15,888	26,568	10,680	0	86,884	48,838	(38,046)
71	15,888	26,568	10,680	0	79,679	50,791	(28,888)
72	15,888	26,568	10,680	0	72,186	52,823	(19,364)
73	15,888	26,568	10,680	0	64,394	54,936	(9,458)
74	15,888	26,568	10,680	0	56,290	57,133	843
75	15,888	26,568	10,680	0	47,861	59,418	11,557
76	15,888	26,568	10,680	0	39,096	61,795	22,700
77	15,888	26,568	10,680	0	29,979	64,267	34,288
78	15,888	26,568	10,680	0	20,499	66,838	46,339
79	15,888	26,568	10,680	0	10,639	69,511	58,873
80	15,888	26,568	10,680	0	384	72,292	71,907
81	15,888	26,568	10,680	0	(10,280)	75,183	85,464
82	15,888	26,568	10,680	0	(21,372)	78,191	99,562
83	15,888	26,568	10,680	0	(32,907)	81,318	114,225
84	15,888	26,568	10,680	0	(44,903)	84,571	129,474
85	15,888	26,568	10,680	0	(57,379)	87,954	145,333
86	15,888	26,568	10,680	0	(70,354)	91,472	161,826
87	15,888	26,568	10,680	0	(83,848)	95,131	178,979
88	15,888	26,568	10,680	0	(97,882)	98,936	196,818
89	15,888	26,568	10,680	0	(112,478)	102,893	215,371
90	15,888	26,568	10,680	0	(127,657)	107,009	234,666

Assume they have $150,000 in savings earning 4% (shown at the top of Columns C and D). They take the needed withdrawals from this account. In column C, you see that if they take the pension early and use the $10,680 annual withdrawal, they run out of money at Eric's age 81. In column D, you see that if they delay the start of the pension, take the $25,568 withdrawal for five years and then nothing thereafter, it leaves them with more assets. They could use these assets to generate additional income or to pass along more to heirs. The break-even age on this decision is Eric's age 74.

If he or Julie lives longer than 74, the delayed start date will end up providing more—by age 90, $234,666 more (shown in column D), assuming their spending in both scenarios is the same. In lieu of accumulating more assets, they could choose to spend more along the way.

Not all pension plans offer more annual income for delaying. I have seen many plans where beginning the pension as soon as possible is the better decision. A one-size-fits-all rule does not work. Each pension must be analyzed based on the terms being offered.

WHAT RATE OF RETURN TO USE

When running an analysis on how a lump sum compares to an annuity, or which age it might be best to start the annuity, what rate of return should you use? You need to use something that at least has somewhat of an equivalent risk level as the pension. The pension is guaranteed. The investment portfolio most likely is not. It's great if you think you can earn 8% a year in your investments (net of fees), but know you are not comparing apples to apples. Although interest rates are currently quite low, I think 4% is an appropriate proxy for what you might get in long-term guaranteed choices like CDs and fixed annuities. That's why I use 4% as a starting place when doing a pension analysis.

Pension Choice Mistakes

The single biggest mistake I see people make with their pension is assuming that they can secure a better outcome by taking a lump sum and investing the funds themselves. If you could be assured of an 8% return or higher (net of fees), the lump sum option will usually look more attractive. Even in a good market, achieving an 8% return would require a high allocation to equities, and the sequence of returns can have a serious impact on the outcome. I do not think such returns are something you can be assured of.

Another big mistake is made when pension survivor options are chosen. One widow was referred to me shortly after her husband had passed. He had only been retired for one year. He had a $6,500 a month pension, and when he elected his pension benefit he decided that since it was a second marriage and most of his working career they had not been together, he would choose the single life pension option so they could receive more monthly income now.

He was not trying to leave his wife in a bad situation – he made her the beneficiary of his retirement accounts worth $1,000,000. He also had two sons from a previous marriage. Because of the way things were structured, they ended up not receiving much inheritance. All parties would have been better off if he would have chosen a pension option that provided life-long income to his wife, which would have allowed him to leave some of his retirement account assets directly to his sons.

Pension annuities provide a floor of guaranteed income and can be a valuable benefit to offset longevity risk. Don't be too quick to make choices about your benefits without doing a thorough analysis.

IS YOUR PENSION SAFE?

Pension plan benefits are insured by the Pension Benefit Guarantee Corporation (PBGC). If your company participates in the PBGC, it is likely that at least a portion of your pension benefit is insured.

The amount of your pension benefits that is insured depends on your age and is subject to a cap.

In 2016, for a pension recipient age 65, the maximum monthly insured benefit is as follows:

- $4,510 per month for a joint life payout with 50% that would be paid to a survivor

- $5,011 per month for a single life payout

Important: The maximum monthly insured amount of pension benefits is reduced if you are not yet age 65. See full schedule at http://www.pbgc.gov/wr/benefits/guaranteed-benefits/maximum-guarantee.html#2016.

Employee Stock

I worked as a team with a few CPA firms throughout the Phoenix area. Intel has a location in Chandler, Arizona, and so we did a fair amount of work with Intel execs and employees. In August of 2000, Intel stock was at $73 a share. In August 2001, when I moved to the area, it was about $31 a share, which is where it remains in 2016 at the time of writing this.

I was reading through a client file, preparing for an upcoming meeting with an Intel executive who owned 150,000 shares of stock. At $73 a share, that stock had been worth nearly $11 million. He needed to diversify, but the CPA had not been successful at getting him to do so. At the time of our meeting, his shares were worth about $4.5 million. He was convinced the stock would come back, and I also was unsuccessful at convincing him to diversify. Had his stock been sold and invested in a conservative, diversified portfolio of index funds, his portfolio would be worth somewhere in the $7–8 million range today. Diversification would have served him well, but he refused.

If you are an employee of any kind, I hope you are proud of the company you work for, and I hope you wholeheartedly believe in the products and services you produce. But don't confuse that pride with making prudent personal financial decisions.

Employee stock accumulates in numerous ways:

- *Employee stock purchase plan (ESPP):* With this type of plan, employees can purchase company stock at a discount from its fair market value.

- *Employee stock ownership plan (ESOP):* With this type of plan, employees are given an ownership interest in the company. Shares are held in trust and sold when the employee leaves the company or retires.

- *Restricted stock unit (RSU):* This type of compensation is typically in the form of stock grants given to executives with restrictions on when the stock can be sold or transferred.

- *Non-qualified stock option (NQSO):* This type of option grants the employee the right to buy shares at a specified price but has no preferential tax treatment.

- *Incentive stock option (ISO):* This type of option grants the employee the right to buy shares at a specified price and has preferential tax treatment.

Many people mistakenly think that if they part with company stock it reflects a lack of faith in the success of the company. The success of the company is dependent on numerous factors outside of your control. Your personal financial success is dependent on factors within your control.

You can and should take great pride in your work and at the same time be able to make prudent decisions about diversifying financial risks that you and your family are exposed to. Having a large portion of your financial assets, as well as your income and benefits, tied to a single company represents a large financial risk. Do what you can to reduce this risk by setting up a systematic plan to reduce your holding of company stock as it accumulates.

For those with large company stock positions, it is natural to not want to dump the stock all at once. A smart exit strategy can be developed by using covered call options[114] strategies to generate additional income from the stock, while slowly selling shares at an agreed upon price point.

---

114 With a covered call you collect a premium (income) for selling someone an option that gives them the right to buy a specified number of shares, at an agreed upon price, by a defined date in the future.

Remember   Don't pile up company stock in your portfolio, even if it's an excellent company. Even excellent companies can get in legal trouble, and the stock price can quickly go tumbling down.

Taxation of Non-Qualified Stock Options

When you exercise non-qualified stock options, the difference between the market price of the stock and the grant price (called the *spread*) is counted as ordinary earned income, even if you exercise your options and continue to hold the stock.

Earned income is subject to payroll taxes (Social Security and Medicare), as well as regular income taxes at your applicable tax rate.

You pay two types of payroll taxes:

- *OASDI or Social Security* - which is 6.2% on earnings up to the Social Security benefit base, which is $118,500 in 2016

- *HI or Medicare* - which is 1.45% on all earned income; even amounts that exceed the benefit base

If your earned income for the year already exceeds the benefit base, then your payroll taxes on gains from exercising non-qualified stock options will be only the 1.45% attributable to Medicare.

If your year-to-date earned income is not already in excess of the benefit base, then when you exercise non-qualified stock options you will pay a total of 7.65% on gain amounts up until your earned income reaches the benefit base, then 1.45% on earnings over the benefit base.

You should not exercise employee stock options strictly based on tax decisions, however, if you exercise non-qualified stock options in a year where you have little other earned income, you will pay more payroll taxes than you'll pay if you exercise them in a year where your earned income already exceeds the benefit base.

In addition to payroll taxes, all income from the spread is subject to ordinary income taxes. If you hold the stock after exercise, and additional gains beyond the spread are achieved, the additional gains are taxed as a capital gain (or as a capital loss if the stock went down). At Fairmark.com's Tax Guide for Investors (http://www.fairmark.com/execcomp/nqoexer.htm) you can find additional details on taxes that apply when you exercise non-qualified stock options.

Taxation of Incentive Stock Options

Unlike non-qualified stock options, gain on incentive stock options is not subject to payroll taxes, however it is of course subject to tax, and it is a preference item for the AMT (alternative minimum tax) calculation.

When you exercise an incentive stock option there are several different tax possibilities. Here are two of them:

- *You exercise the incentive stock options and immediately sell the stock in one transaction.* In this case you pay tax on the difference between the market price at sale and the grant price at your ordinary income tax rate.

- *You exercise the incentive stock options but hold the stock for at least one year.* In this situation the difference between the grant price and the market price then becomes an AMT preference item, so exercising incentive stock options might mean you'll pay AMT. You can get a credit for excess AMT tax paid, but it may take many years to use up this credit. If you hold the shares for one year from your exercise date (two years from the grant date of the option) then the difference between grant price and market price when you sell the options is taxed as long-term gain rather than ordinary income, and if your ordinary tax rate exceeds your AMT tax rate you may get to use some of the previously accumulated AMT credit. For high income earners, holding the stock for the required time period can mean paying tax on the gain at 15% versus 35%, however there are risks to this strategy that must be carefully evaluated. (I am simplifying the rules here. If you have ISOs I would highly advise you work with a tax professional.)

The tax implications of selling stock and exercising options vary widely from plan to plan. In some cases you may be able to minimize tax consequences by selling stock over 13 months but across three calendar years by selling some in December, some in January, and some the following January. Options could be exercised in the same way. This approach allows you to diversify rapidly and yet spread the taxes out over three filing years. Taxes should be considered when selling stock, but they should not be the only consideration. Minimizing risk should be the primary objective.

Deferred Compensation Plans

There is a special type of deferred compensation plan that works quite differently than the salary deferral option in a 401(k) plan. These types of plans may be called *top hat plans*, *SERPS* (supplemental executive retirement plans), *excess benefit plans* or *benefit equalization plans*.

With this type of plan, you elect to defer a portion of your compensation, and at the time you make this election you must choose when the money is to be paid back out to you.

Most of the time this is an irrevocable election (meaning you cannot change it later), and the earliest the first payout is typically allowed to occur is three years from the year you put the money into the plan.

- *Lump sum* - Some plans only offer a lump sum distribution option. For example, you might elect a lump sum to payout five years, seven years, or ten years from the year you defer the income.

- *Installment payouts* - Some plans offer the option for the funds to be paid out in an installment – for example over a ten-year period of time which will begin five years from today.

You make a payout election for each year of contributions to the plan.

With some plans you can elect different payout options for different types of contributions; for example, an installment payout out on your own deferred amounts and a lump sum payout on employer contributed amounts.

Changing Your Payout Election

Although payout elections may be considered irrevocable, in many cases you can in fact change them – but your ability to make changes will come with restrictions.

For example, here is how one major deferred comp plan describes it, "You can postpone your payout date but must give notice 12 months prior to the previously scheduled distribution date. And the new date must be at least 5 years after the previous scheduled date."

In addition, certain events may trigger a distribution that will occur differently than what you have elected. In your plan document this may be referred to as a "triggering event", or "triggering distribution".

Your plan document will explain how funds will be paid out depending on the type of triggering event. Things that may trigger distributions are:

- Retirement
- Termination
- Death
- Emergency or disability distributions
- Change of control

As an example, if you are terminated your plan may distribute the vested balance within 60 days. Or upon retirement, your elected annual installment payouts may automatically start even though they weren't scheduled to start for another five years.

Each plan sets its own terms so you must refer to your document to see how your plan works.

If you map out a timeline of your future projected retirement income before you elect your deferred comp payout dates, then you may be able to choose payout dates that are likely to occur in years where other sources of taxable income are lower.

For example, suppose you have a large 401(k) balance. When you reach age $70\frac{1}{2}$ you will have to take required minimum distributions, and this will result in extra taxable income. If your plan allows it you may want your deferred comp to payout in ten year installment payments from age 60 to 70. When your deferred comp payout ends, then your required distributions would begin.

Many people choose to have their payouts occur as a lump sum, and that extra income bumps them into a higher tax bracket in that calendar year. If they had chosen an installment payout they may have been able to reduce their tax liability on the payouts by 10 or 15%. Taxes, however, are not the only factor. The financial status of the company should also be considered. If you are concerned about the company's future, a lump sum may be the best option despite taxes.

Consolidating Retirement Assets

Most tax-deferred retirement accounts that belong to the same individual can be combined into one IRA account for that individual. (Spouses cannot combine retirement accounts.)

The following is a list of all the types of retirement accounts that can be consolidated into one IRA at or near retirement:

- SEP IRAs
- SIMPLE IRAs
- Traditional IRAs
- Non-deductible IRAs (but you need to keep track of the amount of any non-deductible contributions)
- 401(k)s
- 403(b)s
- 457(b)s
- Profit-sharing accounts
- Money purchase
- Defined benefit plans (if the plan allows you to take a lump sum distribution option)

- Other qualified plans. Your employer may offer a plan that uses a different name but is still considered a qualified plan. If it is a qualified plan with pre-tax dollars in it, you can roll the funds into an IRA.

If your employer offers a designated Roth account, it cannot be rolled into a traditional IRA, but it can be rolled into a Roth IRA.

In an ideal retirement situation, you would consolidate your accounts so you have one IRA, possibly one Roth IRA and one after-tax investment account.

Consolidating accounts can help reduce fees, makes it easier to design and maintain an appropriate investment allocation, and makes it far easier to manage withdrawals and cash flow. It also reduces the amount of paperwork you have to deal with each month and the number of institutions your beneficiaries will eventually have to deal with.

Once your accounts are consolidated, you can structure how much money should come from each type of account (based on your plan and what is most tax-efficient for you). You can then set up a direct deposit into your working checking account, essentially replacing your monthly paycheck.

Setting up regular withdrawals in a system designed to replicate your paycheck makes it easy to monitor, compare results to your plan, and systematically decide if and when it is appropriate to increase your withdrawals by the rate of inflation.

The alternative is dipping into accounts ad hoc as needed. This is not advisable, because it makes it too easy to spend more than is prudent based on your plan.

Consolidating accounts near retirement makes sense. I can think of no meaningful reason not to do so.

Summary

When it comes to company benefits, you need to use them based on your overall plan after viewing your plan at a household level.

With a 401(k) plan, while working you need to take into account when you expect to draw on the funds, how investment options differ from plan to plan, and what the expenses are on the investments inside the plan.

As you near retirement, you want to begin consolidating IRAs and employer plans to make your withdrawal phase easier to manage and more cost efficient.

With pensions, you need to do careful analysis before you determine what pension option to take. Don't be too quick to take a lump sum; people routinely underestimate how long they think they'll live, and it can be difficult to achieve a rate of return required to provide the same income that many pension annuity options provide.

Speaking of annuities, maybe your company doesn't offer any form of pension or annuity option, and you're thinking of buying one. Should you? I cover that in Chapter 8.

Chapter 8

Should You Buy an Annuity?

Buy Them for the Income

"It's paradoxical that the idea of living a long life appeals to everyone, but the idea of getting old doesn't appeal to anyone."

—Andy Rooney

Some people walk into my office with a definite opinion.

"Annuity? Oh no, I don't want one of those."

I reply, "Oh, which kind do you want to avoid? Fixed annuities, variable annuities, immediate annuities, deferred annuities or indexed annuities?"

The same response applies to those who walk in and declare, "I want an annuity." (Yes, people do this.)

"Oh, which kind do you want? A fixed annuity, variable annuity, immediate annuity, deferred annuities, or an indexed annuity?"

Most of the time the person is not sure. This is understandable because a considerable amount of conflicting information on annuities is out there, and many articles do not clarify which type of annuity they are talking about. Sometimes I receive a call from someone who is trying to make an urgent decision. A salesperson has shown them a fancy brochure about an annuity product that must be bought by the end of the month. That is not the way to buy an annuity.

As with any investment, buying an annuity should be a thoughtful choice that fits into your plan. To be objective about annuities, you need to know about the many different types. Sometimes people read an article or have a bad experience and conclude that all annuities are bad. All annuities are not alike, and certainly all annuities are not bad, so before forming a conclusion, you have to specify what you are talking about. I think many planning objectives can be accomplished without the use of annuities, yet, like any tool, they ought to be considered and used when appropriate.

Let's take a look at the four main types of annuities you might encounter—immediate annuities, fixed annuities, indexed annuities, and variable annuities—and see if and when they are appropriate savings or income vehicles.

Immediate Annuities

All annuities are contracts with an insurance company. With an immediate annuity you enter a contract to buy a stream of income. If you buy a ten-year term certain annuity, you are buying a stream of income for ten years. If you recall the cookie jar analogy from Chapter 5, you'll remember that when you buy a life-only immediate annuity, you are buying income that is guaranteed for as long as you live. You hand over the jar of cookies (a lump sum of money), and in return the insurance company gives you back a cookie each year. If the jar runs empty, they keep providing cookies out of their own jar. If you pass away before the jar is empty, they keep any remaining cookies.

You can buy life annuities that also have a death benefit feature. Death benefit features increase the cost of the annuity. From the insurance company's viewpoint, if they must pay you a life-long income and provide a death benefit to a beneficiary, that represents additional risk than only being obligated to provide life-long income.

You would consider an immediate annuity for two primary reasons:

- It protects against longevity risk (outliving your income).
- It protects against overspending risk.

Let's see how an immediate annuity can be used to accomplish your retirement income goals.

As you near retirement, you often have two competing goals. Goal one is having adequate inflation-adjusted spending money for your lifetime. In pursuit of this goal, many come to me and say, "I want to die with a dollar in the bank."

An immediate annuity, also called a *single premium immediate annuity* (SPIA), can help you accomplish this, because it converts your assets into a guaranteed income stream.

Goal two is preserving financial assets for unexpected expenses and to pass along to heirs. A SPIA does not meet this goal.

One of my favorite fellow retirement-income geeks, Wade Pfau, has done quite a bit of research on how you might combine the use of an immediate annuity with a portfolio of stock index funds to meet these two competing goals.

His work shows that rather than the traditional allocation of stocks and bonds, a retiree may consider an allocation of stocks and immediate annuities. In his paper, "An Efficient Frontier for Retirement Income," he says:

> [T]he evidence suggests that optimal product allocations consist of stocks and fixed SPIAs, and clients need not bother with bonds, inflation-adjusted SPIAs, or VA/GLWBs.[115] Though SPIAs do not offer liquidity, they provide mortality credits and generate bond-like income without any maturity date, and they support a higher stock allocation for remaining financial assets. Altogether, this allows a client to better meet both retirement financial objectives.[116]

Most people I know would not be comfortable with a portfolio that was entirely immediate annuities and stocks, but the research does shed light on the fact that an immediate annuity, when used as part of a plan, can help you achieve the dual goals of maximum current spending along with preservation of assets.

THOSE WHO REALLY NEED IMMEDIATE ANNUITIES

I strive to offer as objective an opinion as possible, recognizing that we are all different, and we all perceive risk differently.

I have run immediate annuity quotes and longevity insurance quotes on many clients and have looked at how such a vehicle might add value to their plans.

---

115 VA/GLWBs stands for variable annuity/guaranteed living withdrawal benefits, discussed later in this chapter.

116 Wade D. Pfau, "An Efficient Frontier for Retirement Income," National Graduate Institute for Policy Studies (September 24, 2012).

Most will not buy these products because they do not want to give up control of their assets. These types usually feel confident in their ability to stick with a diversified portfolio and adjust spending down later if needed. It is not that they are ignoring longevity risk; instead, they have a plan in place to manage it.

There are a few, though, who I think need an annuity to protect them from themselves. These clients are either overspenders or are prone to making rather random and irrational investment decisions. Unfortunately, despite my efforts, these are often the ones who won't implement such a strategy.

It seems those who need annuities the most are often those who won't buy them.

Immediate annuities might fit into your plan if:

- Your or your spouse's family and health history indicates you might live longer than average.

- You have trouble sticking within your spending limits.

- You have trouble sticking with an investment plan and allocation model.

- You have no pension or sources of guaranteed income other than Social Security.

What to Watch Out For

Immediate annuities often publish what is called their *payout rate*. This is not equivalent to yield or rate of return. If a life-only immediate annuity has a published payout rate of 7%, and you invest $100,000, yes, you get $7,000 a year for as long as you live. If you live 30 years, that would be equivalent to about a 5.75% rate of return[117]. If you live only five years, you received a total of $35,000 in income, and nothing more gets paid out, so your actual return would be negative. You buy annuities to manage risk, not for the rate of return. If an immediate annuity fits in with your plan, there are a few strategies to consider.

---

117 If you calculate the return as an annual payout instead of monthly, you get 5.65%.

Stagger Your Purchases

Immediate annuity payouts vary by interest rate and with your age. If an immediate annuity fits into your plan, consider buying your guaranteed income in increments by staggering your purchases over several years.

Staggering your purchases may allow you to lock in a higher payout rate a few years later, because payouts increase with age. Considering today's low interest rates, higher future rates may also increase the payout.

This strategy also allows you to spread your purchases over several different insurance carriers so your benefits fall within state guaranty limits.

HOW GOOD ARE INSURANCE COMPANY GUARANTEES?

Insurance company guarantees are only as good as the claims-paying ability of the insurance company that issues the contract. In the event the insurance company fails, limited guarantees are provided by each state's insurance guaranty association.

State insurance guaranty associations protect policyholders (and beneficiaries) of policies issued by a life or health insurance company in the event the insurance company must file bankruptcy. If you want to make sure the full amount of your investment is covered, learn your state's guaranty limits, and don't invest more than the maximum coverage amount in any single policy with the same insurer. In addition, each state may have a maximum amount of benefits that can be covered across all lines of insurance, and different coverage limits may apply to different types of policies.

Guaranteed coverage amounts typically vary from $100,000–$500,000 in benefits, but you will need to check with your state insurance guaranty association to see what amounts are covered for which types of benefits in your state.

For additional information visit the National Organization of Life & Health Insurance Guaranty Associations at www.nolhga.com/factsandfigures/main.cfm/location/stateinfo.

Take a Wait-and-See Approach

With immediate annuities, you get more income for single lives than for joint lives. For marrieds, a wait-and-see approach involves implementing an immediate annuity strategy if you become a surviving spouse, or if you reach a particular age.

For example, a couple might allocate a portion of their investments to something that was low on the risk scale, with the intention of annuitizing this at the earlier of the time one became a surviving spouse or when the first reaches age 85.

Deferred Annuities

An immediate annuity is not the only way to provide guaranteed income. There is something called a *deferred income annuity* (DIA), sometimes referred to as longevity insurance, which is also a viable option. If using IRA or retirement funds to purchase a DIA, income must start by your age 70½ to meet the Required Minimum Distribution rules.

Longevity insurance options have received more press in the last few years, as the Treasury passed new regulations in July 2014 to clear up confusion about how such annuity types may be purchased and used inside IRAs and other qualified retirement accounts. These regulations use the term Qualified Longevity Annuity Contract (QLAC), and you may see annuities marketed using this terminology. With a QLAC you can defer the start date of income past age 70½. The maximum QLAC purchase amount is 25% of the total qualified account balances or $125,000, whichever is less. If you want to dig into the nuances of QLACs, get Stan the Annuity Man's book *QLAC Owner's Manual*.

In general, with longevity insurance and QLACs, you set aside a relatively small sum today that will provide income starting much later (usually at age 80 or 85). It is a way of insuring that even if you spend everything else you have, a guaranteed income will be available for you later. If you think in terms of a probability curve, the majority of people will live to about life expectancy, with some living short and some living long. Those who live short and those who live long are said to fall into the tail of the probability curve. Longevity insurance reduces this tail risk of not having enough income if you live long.

If you want to design a retirement income plan that is 100% guaranteed, you could use longevity insurance in combination with a laddered bond strategy. As an example, let's look at a strategy designed to produce $25,000 a year of guaranteed income by combining a bond ladder with longevity insurance.

First you would set aside $500,000 in laddered bonds, with $25,000 to be redeemed each year for the next 20 years.

Next you would buy a deferred-income annuity that will provide income starting in twenty years. At a 3% inflation rate, in 20 years it will take about $45,000 of income to buy what $25,000 buys today. You then need to know what it costs to buy $45,000 a year of income starting at age 85.

The cost of a deferred income annuity depends on your age at purchase and what death benefit and survivor options are chosen. Based on quotes I ran for Wally and Sally, age 64 and 62 today, it would cost about $177,000 to buy $45,000 a year of income scheduled to begin in twenty years and guaranteed for their joint lives.

For Sally at age 62, it would cost about $140,000 to buy $45,000 a year of future income starting at her age 82 (assuming no death benefit option).

Add this to the $500,000 set aside for the bond ladder, and you have a total cost of about $640,000 for a single woman, or $677,000 for a couple, to guarantee approximately $25,000 a year of life-long income.

Deferred annuities might fit into your plan if:

- Your or your spouse's family and health history indicates you might live longer than average.

- You are in your 50s planning for income to begin at age 65 or 70.

- You have no pension or sources of guaranteed income other than Social Security.

WHAT DOES ANNUITIZE MEAN?

Annuitize is a term that is frequently used with deferred annuities. You may have an annuity that is in the accumulation phase, and you have not yet "turned on" the income phase.

You are said to annuitize at the point where you trade in a lump sum of money for a guaranteed income stream.

Fixed Annuities

A fixed annuity is a contract with the insurance company in which they provide you a guaranteed interest rate on your investment. Think of a fixed annuity as a CD in a tax-deferred wrapper. Instead of the bank guaranteeing your interest rate, the insurance company is providing the guarantee. The interest accumulates tax-deferred, as it does in an IRA, until you take withdrawals. Interest withdrawn prior to age 59½ is subject to a 10% early-withdrawal penalty tax as well as ordinary income taxes.

The interest-rate guarantees typically run for about one to ten years, at which point you can continue the annuity at whatever rate is then offered, exchange it for a different type of annuity, or (like a CD) cash it in and decide to invest the funds elsewhere. (If you cash it in, you will owe taxes on the accumulated tax-deferred interest.)

The interest rate might be:

- Fixed for the life of the annuity.

- Fixed at a higher rate the first year and then at a lower fixed rate for remaining years.

- Fixed at a higher rate the first year and then at a variable rate for subsequent years with a minimum rate guarantee.

With a fixed annuity, no investment fees are debited out of the account. The fees are embedded in the product, so, as with a CD, the rate you are quoted is the rate you will receive. There are, however, surrender charges, and they can be quite hefty. The insurance company can only guarantee you the rate if they know they have your money for the full length of the contract. A surrender penalty is imposed to provide an incentive for you to leave your funds there for the full term. It also functions as a way for the insurance company to recoup its up-front costs if you change your mind and cancel the contract early.

Tip	Annuity FYI offers a comparison of current fixed annuity rates at http://www.annuityfyi.com/fixed-annuities/fixed-top-picks/.

If you are looking for a safe investment that provides a guaranteed interest rate, you might compare a fixed annuity to CDs and municipal bonds to decide which is most appropriate for you. In some cases fixed annuities pay a higher interest rate than CDs, and the interest is tax-deferred. With a CD you must pay taxes on the interest earned each year (unless you own the CD in an IRA, in which case the interest would be tax-deferred).

What to watch out for: Some fixed annuities lure you in with a high initial year rate, but the blended rate over the life of the contract may end up being quite low. Look for the "yield to surrender" to determine what the rate would be over the life of the annuity.

Example of how a fixed annuity might fit into a plan: Suppose you are age 55 and receive an inheritance. You plan on retiring at 65, and your planning shows you are likely to be in either the same or a lower tax bracket in retirement. Your planning also shows that you need only a 4% rate of return to achieve your goals. You find a ten-year fixed annuity that pays 4%.[118] In this case a fixed annuity would fit nicely into your plan.

AGE 59 1/2 AND FIXED, VARIABLE, AND INDEX ANNUITIES

When you place money in a fixed or variable deferred annuity (deferred meaning the income phase is being deferred until later), you do not have to pay taxes on the gain in the annuity until you take withdrawals. Like most retirement vehicles that offer tax deferral, if you take withdrawals prior to age 59½, any gain withdrawn is taxed at your ordinary income tax rate and is subject to a 10% penalty tax. In a non-qualified deferred annuity (one not owned by an IRA, Roth IRA, or other tax-deferred retirement vehicle), gain is considered to be withdrawn first.

---

118 At the time of writing this (May 2016) the highest yield-to-surrender I am seeing on a 10-year fixed annuity is 3.5%.

Indexed Annuities

An indexed annuity is a type of fixed annuity that is often called a *fixed indexed annuity* (FIA) or an *equity-indexed annuity*. With this type of annuity, the insurance company offers a minimum guaranteed return with the potential for additional returns by using a formula that ties the increases in your investment to a stock market index.

For example, assume you buy a fixed indexed annuity that is tied to the S&P 500 index. It might allow you to participate in 80% of any increases in the stock market index as measured from January 1 to December 31, with a 3% minimum guaranteed interest rate. You might have a 10% cap on the return. In this situation here are a few possible outcomes:

- The S&P 500 index goes up 10%. Your return is 8% because you participate in 80% of what the index does.

- The S&P 500 goes up 20%. Your return is 10% because the annuity contract has a cap on your maximum return.

- The S&P 500 goes down 10%. Your return is 3% because the contract provides a minimum guaranteed 3% interest rate.

In writing about this product, Scott Stolz, president of Raymond James Insurance Group says, "The entire point of an indexed annuity is to get a long-term rate of return that is 1.5–3.0 percent above prevailing CD rates without putting principal at risk."[119] This is a great description of the purpose of this product. The question is, do they accomplish this goal?

A preliminary analysis of existing equity index contracts suggests that sometimes they do, and sometimes they don't. In a paper titled "Real-World Index Annuity Returns," the authors analyze existing FIA contracts to determine how well they have performed over various five-year time periods in relation to stock and bond funds. The authors conclude, "Our rather modest conclusion is that some index annuities have produced returns that are competitive with other asset classes, such as equities and equity/T-bill combinations."[120] I

---

119 Article available online at: http://www.thinkadvisor.com/2010/10/01/do-living-benefits-on-indexed-annuities-make-sense

120 Geoffrey Vander Pal, Jack Marrion, and David F. Babbel, Ph.D., "Real-World Index Annuity Returns," *Journal of Financial Planning* (March 2011).

took the returns published in their article and in Table 8-1 compare them to the comparable five-year CD returns[121] for the same time period.

Table 8-1. Fixed Index Annuity Returns vs. CD Returns

5-Year Time Periods	FIA Avg. Return (%)	5-Year Average CD Rates (%)
1997–2002	9.19	6.76
1998–2003	5.46	6.19
1999–2004	4.69	6.36
2000–2005	4.33	7.6
2001–2006	4.36	5.56
2002–2007	6.12	4.99
2003–2008	6.05	3.85
2004–2009	4.19	4.41
2005–2010	3.89	4.96

You can see that in some five-year periods, the FIA outperformed the CD, and in some time periods it did not.

Today, many indexed annuities come with income riders that guarantee the amount you will be able to withdraw for life depending on the age you begin using the benefit. When used appropriately, as part of a plan, this product can increase a retiree's coverage ratio later in life and have a positive impact on the plan.

What to watch out for: Indexed annuities have complex features such as participation rates and cap rates that spell out the formulas for how your returns are calculated. Compare such features side by side when looking at this type of product. In addition, consider this product as a CD alternative, not as an equity alternative. If someone proposes it to you as an equity alternative, think twice.

Example of how a fixed index annuity might fit into a plan: For a risk-averse investor, a combination of CDs and indexed annuities might be the perfect solution.

121 Source: Jumbo CD Investments, at: www.jumbocdinvestments.com/historicalcdrates.htm.

Tip   For comparing annuities and learning more about the different features and riders, I have found Stan the Annuity Man's site to be the
most valued resource I can find. If you're considering any type of
annuity, it's a great place to start your search:
www.stantheannuityman.com.

Variable Annuities

A variable annuity is a contract with an insurance company in which you
get to choose how the funds inside the contract are invested. The insurance
company provides a list of funds (called *sub-accounts*) to choose from. It is
called a *variable* annuity because the returns you earn will vary depending on
the underlying investments you choose. Contrast this with the fixed annuity,
where the insurance company is contractually providing you with a guaranteed interest rate.

Investments inside a variable annuity grow tax-deferred, so, just as within an
IRA account, you can exchange between investments without paying capital
gains taxes.

For the variable annuity to qualify as an insurance contract, guarantees must
be provided. The standard death benefit guarantee that comes with a variable
annuity simply guarantees the greater of the current contract value or the full
amount of your contributions (minus any withdrawals) as a death benefit. For
example, if you invested $100,000, and the investments went down in value
to $90,000, and you passed away at that time, the contract would pay out
$100,000 to your named beneficiary. If the investments had gone up in value
and were worth $110,000, the contract would pay out $110,000.

Today's variable annuities come with additional death benefit guarantees and
living benefit guarantees that make them one of the most complex consumer
financial products I have ever seen. From what I can see, most of the represen-
tatives who sell these products don't really understand them, so how the heck
is the average person supposed to? I'll do my best to simplify this product into
its most relevant features.

First, you would consider a variable annuity for one of two reasons:

• Tax deferral

- Income guarantees

Let's take a look at how a variable annuity provides tax deferral and income guarantees.

Tax Deferral

The traditional variable annuity offers a series of mutual-fund-like separate accounts inside a tax-deferred wrapper. If you are a taxpayer in a higher tax bracket, the advantage is that inside a variable annuity you can invest in a portfolio of stock and bond accounts and defer the income (interest, dividends, and capital gains) until retirement, when you may be in a lower tax bracket.

When the Bush tax cuts were implemented in 2001, the lower capital gains, qualified dividend, and ordinary income tax rates took effect, and the tax benefits of traditional variable annuities were diminished.

With the 2013 tax rate changes, capital gains and qualified dividend rates remain significantly lower than ordinary income tax rates. For this reason, I do not see a compelling reason to hold traditional stock funds inside a variable annuity. Let me explain why.

Inside the variable annuity, when you take withdrawals, gain is considered to be withdrawn first, and all gain withdrawn is taxed at your ordinary income rate. If you owned stock funds that were not in the variable annuity, the long-term gains and qualified dividends would be taxed at long-term capital gains tax rates, which are lower than ordinary income tax rates. Once you tuck those stock investments into the variable annuity, you lose the preferential tax treatment on long-term gains and dividends.

In addition, when heirs inherit a stock or stock fund, they receive a step-up in cost basis. That means the value at your date of death becomes their basis for tax purposes. For example, suppose you own a stock or stock index fund that has a current value of $100,000. You paid $50,000 for it many years ago. This means you have $50,000 of unrealized gains. If your heir inherits this, their basis for tax purposes is "stepped up" to the $100,000 value, and they pay no taxes on the $50,000 of gain. If this same situation occurs inside the variable annuity, the heir would owe tax on the $50,000 gain at their ordinary income tax rate.

When you put all this together, I don't think it makes sense to own stock funds in a variable annuity. But I can see why you might want to own taxable bond funds inside a variable annuity. Bond funds generate interest income that is taxed at your ordinary income tax rate, and they are unlikely to offer significant unrealized gains. By tucking taxable bond funds into a variable annuity, you are gaining tax deferral on the interest income and you are not losing any form of preferential tax treatment.

If tax deferral fits into your plan, there is one variable product worth considering: Jefferson National's Flat Fee Variable Annuity.[122] It charges a flat fee of $20 a month. There are over 380 investment options to choose from.

Tip   Never forget—fees matter. A 4% annual charge for investment expenses, over time, takes a big bite. If you are buying an annuity just for tax deferral, look for annuities whose underlying fees are 1% a year or less.

Example of how a variable annuity for tax deferral might fit into your plan: I can see two scenarios where a low-cost, variable annuity for tax deferral makes sense:

- *High tax bracket/Lots of after-tax investments:* If you are in a high tax bracket and have a large conservative portfolio that is not inside any type of retirement account, a flat-fee variable annuity might be an attractive option for you. Rather than buying CDs, you could build a portfolio of bond funds inside the variable annuity. All interest income would be tax-deferred.

- *Existing high-fee annuity:* If you already own a high-fee variable annuity with non-IRA money, you could use a 1035 exchange to transfer your high-fee annuity to one with lower fees and continue to defer the taxes on any gains. You would do this if you have a low cost basis in your current annuity, which means if you cashed it in instead of exchanging it, you would have to pay taxes on the gain at your ordinary income tax rate.

---

122 Product details available online at www.jeffnat.com.

IRA-OWNED ANNUITIES

Many people use IRA money to buy an annuity. In such a case, if you no longer want the annuity, you can use an IRA rollover or IRA transfer to move your money out of the annuity and into a regular IRA account where you can buy index funds (or any other type of investment). This kind of transfer is not a taxable event. Of course, you want to inquire about any surrender charges before you cancel any annuity contract.

What to watch out for: One of the concerns I have with variable annuities is the substantial fees they can come with. Many variable annuities are saddled with all of the following expenses:

- *Mortality expenses (M&E):* With a variable annuity, the mortality and expense fee is charged to provide you with some form of a death benefit. This is often a simple guarantee to pay out to your beneficiaries at least the amount of money you contributed. This mortality and expense fee can range from .50–1.5% of the policy value per year.

- *Administrative expenses:* Most variable annuities charge some form of administrative expense, which ranges from .10 to .30% of the policy value per year. Sometimes this expense is included in the mortality and expense fee and sometimes it is separate.

- *Investment expense ratio:* Inside a variable annuity, the sub-accounts, have an investment management fee or expense ratio just as mutual funds do. The expense ratios on the underlying sub-accounts typically range from .25–2.00% per year.

- *Surrender charges:* Many investment and insurance products pay an up-front commission to the agent or representative who sells the product to you. The fees inside the product are designed to slowly reimburse the company for their up-front costs. Surrender charges are usually structured on a decreasing scale from about

4 to 15 years, with most broker-sold annuities having a surrender charge schedule of about 7 years. With a typical surrender charge schedule, if you terminate the annuity within one year of purchase, you will be charged 7% of your invested amount, 6% in year two, 5% in year three, and so on.

- *Additional cost of riders:* Variable annuities today come with all kinds of optional guarantees called *riders*. The most common features are guaranteed living benefit riders, guaranteed withdrawal benefit riders, and guaranteed death benefit riders. Each rider can cost anywhere from .40–1.50% of the policy value per year.

Income Guarantees

Variable annuities and indexed annuities offer numerous types of income guarantees which are broadly classified as guaranteed living benefits (GLBs). They are often an optional benefit that you can add on to the policy and are referred to as riders. The income riders all have a similar function: you pay an annual fee to insure the amount of future income you can withdraw from your portfolio. Much like the cookie jar analogy used earlier, with an income rider the insurance company is providing a guarantee that if your cookie jar runs empty, they'll keep providing cookies out of their jar.

Living benefit riders are referred to by various terms such as lifetime withdrawal benefits (LWBs) or guaranteed minimum withdrawal benefits (GM-WBs).

The typical income guarantee has two phases: the deferral phase and the income phase.

Deferral Phase

The deferral phase of an annuity is the time period where you are not drawing out income. Many variable annuities with income riders have a five- or ten-year deferral phase, meaning you need to own the product for five or ten years before the income guarantee features can be utilized.

During the deferral phase, there is often a guarantee that creates a hypothetical "income base" that will grow at a specific rate of return, such as 5% (or with older contracts, possibly 6%), and usually for a specific time period, such as ten years, or up until a specific age, such as 80.

With contracts that come with an income base feature, think of it as having two wallets of money. In wallet one is your actual account value, which is going up and down based on whatever the underlying investments are doing. In wallet two is a hypothetical income base based on the contractual guarantees offered.

Wallet one is real money. If you cash in the annuity, that's what you get.

Wallet two is a little different. The amount in wallet two is simply an accounting entry used to calculate the amount of guaranteed withdrawals you can take when you enter the income phase. Once income begins, the value of wallet two becomes irrelevant; its only purpose is to calculate the amount of the guaranteed lifetime income. The typical income guarantee allows you to take about 4–6% (the older you are when you start the withdrawals, the higher the percentage) of the wallet two value each year for as long as you live.

INDUSTRY EXPERT COMMENT

After reviewing this chapter Scott Stolz offered this additional comment, which I thought appropriate to include:

"Unfortunately, by insisting on putting a "$" sign before the wallet two value on every client statement, the insurance companies add to the confusion about what wallet two is and what it isn't. The $ sign implies that it is real money. It is not. Always remember that it is only used to calculate your allowable annual income."

Income Phase

When you turn the rider "on" or reach the income phase of the contract, most income riders guarantee that you can withdraw a specific percentage, such as 5%, of the income base for life.

When you take a withdrawal, it reduces the amount in wallet one. This means until wallet one is empty, withdrawals are simply a return of your money.

The advantage is that even if wallet one is emptied out, you continue to receive the guaranteed income amount specified in the calculations based on wallet two.

Many of these income riders offer an additional feature, called a *step-up* in the income base. Such a feature says that if the underlying investments in wallet one perform well and are worth more than the income base, then the value of the income base (wallet two) will be stepped up so it matches the higher value of wallet one. This allows you to lock in a higher income base if markets do well.

I see the primary function of these income riders as protecting you against sequence risk. If markets go down right around the time you retire, or returns are poor during the first ten years of your retirement, these policies ensure that you will at least have a minimum known amount of income and that you'll never run out of it.

Note   Fixed annuities guarantee the interest rate you earn on your investment. Income riders on variable annuities function more like immediate annuities - they guarantee the amount of monthly income you can withdraw.

What to watch out for: There are three things to watch out for when it comes to variable annuities with income riders:

- *The income base is hypothetical:* Many people who buy these annuities with income riders think the income base is real money. It is not. It is a hypothetical figure used only to calculate the amount of your guaranteed withdrawal. If you cash in the annuity, you get the contract value, not the income base.

- *Not using them for income:* Variable annuities with income riders are often presented as offering the best of both worlds: potential for growth if the underlying investments do well, while providing a lifetime income feature much like an immediate annuity, but with any remaining principal getting passed along at death. When you look under the hood of these products, in many cases the hefty fees will in fact make it almost impossible in any but the best market conditions for the investment portfolio value (wallet one) to ever exceed that of the income base (wallet two). The fee structure may force you to rely on the guarantees the product provides. If you are not going to use the guaranteed income feature in this type of product, don't buy it. If you are going to buy a variable annuity with an income rider, find one with reasonable fees, buy it for the guaranteed income feature, and use it for income.

- *Death benefits:* I have seen these products presented as an attractive way for someone to meet the goal of passing along assets to heirs. I disagree. In one variable annuity case I reviewed, when compared to a similar portfolio of index funds, over 20 years in normal market conditions, the variable annuity was likely to pass along $500,000 less to heirs because of the effect of fees. The more bells and whistles the contract offers, the higher the fees. The higher the fees, the lower the investment performance. Don't buy these products for their death benefits.

Most of the annuities that offer an income rider place some restrictions on how you allocate the funds inside the annuity. Why do they do this? To limit their risk. That should tell you something. They think investing by following a diversified portfolio model means that you're unlikely to ever have to use the guarantees they provide.

Other buying considerations: For tax reasons, under current tax law, I think these products are best owned inside an IRA.

THE ACADEMIC VIEW

One of the big challenges faced by both financial advisors and consumers alike is sorting through all the product choices and figuring out which ones actually add value to your situation and which ones are just smoke and mirrors.

As more people near retirement age, academic interest in analyzing retirement income products has greatly increased, and more and more research is becoming available that offers an objective analysis.

If you want to dig into the academic research on annuities, do a search for articles and research papers written by Moshe Milevsky or Wade Pfau.

How Fees on Income Riders Are Calculated

In variable annuities with living benefit riders, many of the asset-based fees can be charged on the income base rather than on your actual contract value. This means you can be paying fees based on an amount of money that you don't actually have. Strange, but true.

When you add all this up, it is not uncommon to see variable annuities with annual fees in excess of 4% a year.

Let's think about these fees with some common sense. Inside the annuity you have the same stuff to invest in as you do outside the annuity: stocks, bonds, and cash.

If you take a typical mix of stock and bond funds, saddle it with a 4% fee, and then fast-forward 20 years and compare it to the same mix of stock and bond index funds with fees of less than 1% a year, which is going to be worth more money?

Fees matter. I describe many of these products as facilitating the slow and smooth transfer of your family's wealth right into the hands of the insurance company.

The key to understanding the fees is to know what value you are getting. If you are paying for an income guarantee that is important to you, just as with any type of insurance, you can look at it as if you are paying a premium to shift risk to the insurance company.

Example of how an income rider *might* **fit into a plan:** I can think of two specific situations where an income rider might be appropriate.

The first is for someone 5 to 15 years away from their target retirement date. Suppose you have IRA money or an old 401(k) plan that needs to be rolled into an IRA. A contract with an income rider that guarantees a specific growth rate on your income base would allow you to lock in market upside and protect your income against a sudden drop in your portfolio right as you neared your retirement date.

The second situation is someone who is about to retire, needs to take income, and wants to maintain a high equity allocation. A contract with an income rider that guarantees a 5% withdrawal rate would protect your income level.

There is one last point to address about variable annuities: the psychological benefits of having guarantees. When the investment markets go down, emotions can usurp logic, and many people are known to liquidate holdings at an inopportune time. Having a safety net can give you the courage to stay invested during these times. Just remember, you pay for this courage in the form of annual expenses.

STAND-ALONE LIVING BENEFITS

There is one additional solution that is rather new: the standalone living benefit (SALB). You use the SALB to wrap an insurance guarantee around a portfolio of index funds. The benefit terms will be slightly different than what is offered in an annuity, but the premise is the same—you are insuring a floor or baseline of income that will be available to you. With an SALB, the underlying investments maintain their natural tax treatment. Capital gains and dividends are taxed as such. This could make an SALB an appropriate alternative for insuring income from a non-retirement account. **For a detailed analysis of this new insurance solution, read Wade Pfau's thoughts in his Advisor Perspectives article titled "The Next Generation of Income Guarantee Riders: Part 1—The Deferral Phase" available online at http:// advisorperspectives.com/newsletters12/The_Next_ Generation_of_Income_Guarantee_Riders.php.**

Existing Variable Annuities

I can't tell you how many times a new client comes in to see me wondering what to do with an annuity they already own. They don't know whether they should keep it, when they should take withdrawals, or how it fits into their plan. There are several things to consider in evaluating an existing contract:

Death benefits. Many current variable annuity contracts are underwater— the contract value is less than the death benefit.

For example, Bernard came in to see me with an annuity that has a death benefit of $410,000. But the actual contract value, if he cashed it in today, is $280,000. He is married and in his mid-70s. He has no need to take withdrawals from the policy. We decided at his current age, it makes the most sense for him to keep this policy because of the death benefit.

Although I don't think you should buy a variable annuity for its death benefit features, if you already own one, consider the current death benefit it is providing before terminating a contract.

Income guarantees. Many current variable annuity contracts have an income base that is much higher than the contract value.

For example, Kathy came in with an annuity bought in 2003. She had invested $200,000. The contract value was $251,000, the death benefit was $348,000, and the income base (wallet two—remember?) was $348,000, which would provide a guaranteed withdrawal of $1,570 a month for her and her husband's joint life.

Currently Kathy is 63 and getting ready to retire. If she cashes in the annuity, she gets $251,000. A $1,570 monthly withdrawal ($18,840 a year) would be a 7.5% withdrawal rate, which is not sustainable in any but the very best market conditions. If she cashes in the contract, it will be impossible for her to replicate the income stream the annuity will guarantee.

I recommended that Kathy keep the contact and turn on the income stream. If she lives just 20 years, she'll have received $376,800 of income. Also, I must note, total fees in Kathy's contract were 3.6% a year. In her case, due to the timing of when she invested and the guarantees provided, high fees or not, the contact is providing a valuable benefit.

Fees and taxes. Other things to consider in evaluating an existing contract are surrender charges, fees, and taxes. Sometimes high-fee contracts can be surrendered or exchanged for lower-fee alternatives. This should not be done without examining all the aspects of the contract.

Features you can no longer buy. You may have an annuity issued several years ago that offers unique features or benefits that are no longer available. For example, fixed annuities used to come with 3% minimum interest rate guarantees, something that is hard to find today. Variable annuities used to offer additional investment flexibility and more attractive death benefit and living benefit calculations than those typically offered today. Someone trying to sell you a new annuity may not be forthright in giving you an objective opinion of your current annuity. Make sure you do a careful analysis before abandoning an existing contract.

Over the years, I have found many opportunities to exit out of an annuity contract altogether, many opportunities to exchange a contract for one with lower fees, and many times where keeping the existing annuity was the right solution. Each situation is unique, and there is no way to provide a one-size-fits-all answer on what to do with an existing annuity.

Summary

An annuity is an insurance product. The first question to ask when considering an annuity is: what are you trying to insure?

Here are the primary reasons you would consider each type of annuity:

- Want to insure you won't outlive your money? Consider an immediate annuity to protect against longevity risk and overspending risk.

- Want to insure safety of principal? Consider a fixed annuity or equity index annuity for safety.

- Want to insure tax deferral on interest income? Consider owning bond funds inside a flat-fee variable annuity.

- Want to insure your future retirement income against market fluctuations? Consider a deferred income annuity, or possibly a variable annuity or indexed annuity with an income rider, to protect against sequence risk.

As with any form of insurance, compare outcomes against non-insured alternatives and decide whether you want to retain the risk or shift it. If you want to shift the risk, shop carefully and spend time figuring out whether the product fits into your plan. To do that, look at when the income stream would begin and what account you should own it in based on the most favorable potential tax treatment.

Chapter 9

Real Estate and Mortgages

All Part of the Plan

"Real estate cannot be lost or stolen, nor can it be carried away. Purchased with common sense, paid for in full, and managed with reasonable care, it is about the safest investment in the world."

—Franklin D. Roosevelt

Several years back, I was having a conversation with a woman who I considered to be successful and intelligent. She was asking me questions about what I do, and in the midst of our conversation she said, "Well, stocks are a much better investment than real estate, right? You're a financial planner, so of course that's what you tell your clients."

I was speechless. She went on. "After all, if you had put all your money in Google when it came out with its IPO, you'd be set now, right?"

I thought, *Absolutely. And if I had put my money in a hundred other stocks I could name off, right now I'd be broke.* I'm not sure why I didn't say this out loud. I should have.

A good planner plans. Planning encompasses all aspects of one's financial life, including real estate and mortgages. It would be irresponsible for a planner to make a statement such as "stocks are better than real estate."

Many of the financially independent people I know achieved their independence through investing in real estate. On the flip side, many people I know have gone through bankruptcy and foreclosure by stretching their real estate investments too far. Real estate can be quite a profitable investment if you know what you are doing, and a disaster if you don't.

When nearing retirement, all aspects of your financial situation need to align toward a common goal: generating a reliable source of income. That means real estate and mortgages need to be evaluated as carefully as anything else. Let's start by taking a look at when investment property might fit into a retirement income plan.

Investment Property

For those looking for a steady source of retirement income, rental real estate may look like the right solution. I've seen people reach age 50, 55, or 60 and, after spending a lifetime in whatever their current profession is, they decide the foundation of their retirement plan is going to be a portfolio of rental real estate. With no experience or training, they head out and buy a property. If they're lucky, it works out. Many aren't so lucky. Investing in real estate is a profession in and of itself, and it is not to be embarked upon without careful consideration.

Whether it's an apartment building, duplex, residential rental, or commercial property, real estate comes with expenses. Following are some of the expenses you incur with investment property:

- Property taxes
- Repairs and upkeep
- Advertising and marketing (to get tenants)
- Legal costs (if you have to evict someone)
- Insurance

As with any profession, to make money doing it, you have to know what you are doing. You can turn real estate investing into a profession that allows you a lot of free time, but it takes patience, knowledge, and a decent sense of intuition. You need to plan on doing plenty of reading and learning before you head down this path.

Tip   Think twice or three times before you invest in real estate. The field is vast, and there are a lot of sharks in the business.

If you are interested in getting into real estate, where do you start your education? You may see numerous seminars on how to invest in real estate.

Some are decent, and some are just going to cost you thousands of dollars for a lot of pretty binders.

If I were starting out in real estate, I'd skip the seminars and instead I'd get my hands on all of John T. Reed's books on real estate investing. Start with *How to Get Started in Real Estate Investing*. His material is not just full of fluff; it provides you with the nuts and bolts of what it really takes to be successful. You can buy his books through his website at www.johntreed.com. He has over 20 books on real estate investing as well as a web page where he ranks other real estate "gurus".

Whether you want to invest in real estate or not, the guru rankings make for fascinating reading. There are plenty of people willing to put together some form of a "get rich quick" packet of information, whether it's on stocks, trading options, real estate, or network marketing. Apparently, plenty of people are willing to buy this information. Reading these guru rankings will provide you with a healthy dose of skepticism about the next "proven" way to riches that you see advertised.

If your career up until this point has not been related to real estate, please think twice before embarking on a real estate investment. I've watched people lose millions in real estate partnerships they thought were a "sure thing". I've watched people pour thousands into rental income properties that were supposed to generate cash flow and instead turned into giant money pits. In nearly every situation that turned out poorly, the person had no experience and did not go through a rigorous learning curriculum before they dove into their new venture. I'm all for real estate as an investment for those who are going to treat it with the respect that any serious profession deserves.

ADJUSTING YOUR PLAN AROUND YOUR REAL ESTATE

Gary and Susan were about to turn 70 when they first came in to visit me. Gary had just retired from his medical practice. He owned part of the medical building, which produced monthly income. In addition they owned two homes, one in New Mexico and one in California. The New Mexico home was paid off, and the California home still had a mortgage on it.

When I completed their plan, I had to be the bearer of bad news. With their desired level of spending, it was not going to be possible to maintain both homes. I suggested they sell one.

They asked whether they might sell the medical building instead. I had already considered this. However, it didn't make sense. If they sold their share of the medical building and invested what they would receive after taxes, it would not be possible to deliver the same level of income that the building was providing. Selling one of their homes delivered gain that was tax-free; the gain on the medical building was subject to taxes.

Interestingly enough, their solution was for Gary to continue working. He chose to work locum tenens (as a substitute for other physicians) for about two weeks a month, and has continued to do so for years. He enjoys it, and it allows the couple to continue the lifestyle they desire. This was not their only solution, but it was the one that fit their values.

Your Home

Plenty of finance writers insist that your home is not an investment. If I were to plot my thoughts on a scale of one to ten, with one being your home is absolutely not an investment, and ten being you should only buy one if it can be profitable, I would say I'm at a three.

A portion of the value of your home may need to become part of your retirement income plan at some point. Knowing this, it makes sense to put thought into your home purchase, how you finance it, and figure out how that fits into your plan.

Note	Your home is neither purely an investment nor purely a noninvestment. It may not seem like an investment—until you need its equity or potential income to live to a happy old age.

For example, one way you can protect yourself against inflation is to choose a home that has ample access to public transportation, make your home as energy-efficient as possible, and make sure it has a garden or other area conducive to growing your own food. In addition, you can choose an area that is tax-friendly for retirees. If you're willing to do the research to secure such a location and then move, your home may offer a substantial contribution to stretching your retirement dollars.

Of course, the values side of the decision must also come into play. You may want to be near family or choose a location that fits your hobbies and lifestyle, or you may be in a home that you've been in for years and you have no desire to move.

Another option is to rent a room in your home, or buy a home that has space that can be converted into a rental. For a large portion of my adult life I had roommates. Financially, it helped cover the mortgage. For me, of even more importance, it provided me with a built-in pet sitter. When I traveled for work or to see family, I never had to kennel my dogs. This saved me quite a bit of money over the years.

Today, online options allow you to rent out your home, or a room in it, on a temporary basis to travelers. If you think this option could help you generate income see how it works by visiting:

- Airbnb.com (www.airbnb.com)

- Vacationrentals.com (www.vacationrentals.com)

- VRBO.com (www.vrbo.com)

If your plan shows you have ample assets to support your retirement lifestyle, then think of your home as an asset you use for enjoyment. If your plan shows you are constrained, meaning your assets may leave you short of the retirement income you desire, then spend more time analyzing your home choice and see if making some changes could improve your plan.

I've worked with retirees who choose to downsize so they could travel more. Others prefer that people come visit them, and so they choose to invest in a beautiful living space that facilitates having company. Either choice involves understanding your values and making financial decisions that support those values.

I can't tell you what your values are. I can analyze numbers and show you how the cost of one home choice versus another affects your plan. Both factors, values and the analytical side, also affect the decision about when to pay off a mortgage.

Paying Off the Mortgage: Sometimes an Easy Savings Plan

Jackie and Bob wanted to retire early. Each time they came in to review their plan I would explain to them what they needed to be saving in order to make that happen.

Six months or a year later, they would come back, and their savings had not increased. They had the income to save more, but it just wasn't happening.

Next time they came in, I decided to try a different approach. In their situation, the extra amount they needed to save by retirement was about equivalent to the dollar amount needed to pay off their mortgage. I suggested they make extra payments on their mortgage and told them as soon as their mortgage was paid off they could retire.

Suddenly they began making progress! Seeing the mortgage balance go down was tangible. They could measure their progress toward a goal they wanted to achieve. Accumulating money in their investment accounts, where the value would fluctuate so much from month to month, did not have this same effect for them.

Their case had two sides to the "should we pay down the mortgage?" question. There was the analytical side, which can be determined by running numbers through a spreadsheet, and there was the psychological or values side, which varies from person to person.

Let's take a look at their numbers first.

Jackie and Bob owed $150,000 on their mortgage. The principal and interest portion of their payment was $1,205 a month. Their mortgage rate was 5%. They were in the 25% federal tax bracket. They were able to itemize deductions, so their mortgage interest of about $7,500 in the current year was reducing their income taxes owed by about $2,100. With their current payment, their mortgage would be paid off in 15 years.

They had an extra $500 a month available to save. If they applied the extra $500 to the mortgage, it would be paid off in about nine years.

Jackie and Bob were already maxing out their tax-deductible retirement plan contributions, so they could either apply the extra $500 to the mortgage or contribute it to a savings/investment account.

Net of fees, if they could earn the same return on savings and investments as the rate they were paying on their mortgage, at the end of their mortgage term, they would end up in an identical place regardless of how they applied the extra $500 a month.

Even if they earned only 4% on their savings, prepaying the mortgage was to their benefit by only $3,578. At a 6% return, investing over paying extra on the mortgage added only $1,063 to their net worth over 15 years.

If there were a chance of earning a lower return on savings/investments than the cost of the mortgage, they would be in a more secure situation by applying extra savings toward paying down the mortgage.

For Jackie and Bob, the conclusion was they would need to be assured of earning a return higher than 6%, net of all investment fees, to make investing their monthly savings a wise decision.

Even if Jackie and Bob earned a 7% return (net of fees), in 15 years the choice of investing versus paying extra on the mortgage added only about $3,550 to their net worth. From a risk/return standpoint, an additional $3,550 over 15 years ($236 per year) did not add up to sufficient compensation for taking on the additional level of investment risk required in an attempt to earn 7% returns net of investment fees.

AFTER-TAX RETURNS VS. PRE-TAX RETURN

If you want to use after-tax returns, the 5% mortgage rate is costing them 3.75% (5% × (1−.25)) on an after-tax basis, but the available deduction for the mortgage interest will gradually go down as the mortgage is paid off. Because you must

pay taxes on investment income, if the 5% investment earnings were all taxed as ordinary income, the after-tax return of the investments would also be 3.75%. If you assume some investments have a long-term gain tax treatment, it changes the analysis only slightly more in favor of investing over paying extra on the mortgage (assuming the same gross rate of return).

If they were not maxing out their retirement plan contributions, there would be a slight advantage to applying their extra savings toward a tax-deferred and/or tax-deductible retirement plan. By my calculations, when factoring in the tax deductibility of the $6,000 annual contribution and assuming they then saved/invested the tax savings, funding a deductible retirement plan over paying excess on the mortgage would result in about a $20,000 increase in their net worth after ten years.[123]

In addition, there was a psychological benefit to Jackie and Bob toward applying savings to pay down their mortgage. They could see the results each and every month, and it motivated them to save even more. The result was that, in many months, they applied more than an extra $500 toward their mortgage.

"PAY OFF THE MORTGAGE OR INVEST" CALCULATORS

There are several online calculators you can use to crunch the numbers for you. Here are a few I like.

Hugh's Investment versus Loan Payoff calculator: I don't know who Hugh is, but I like his mortgage payoff calculators. They aren't fancy, but they are transparent, and he provides a clear explanation of the assumptions used. His "payoff vs. borrow" calculator shows you the results over time of either investing a lump sum or using it to pay off a mortgage. It allows you to specify whether mortgage interest is deductible and whether the lump sum you are using is

---

123 SoundMindInvesting.com provides this scenario in great detail. Available online at https://www.soundmindinvesting.com/articles/view/invest-in-your-401k-or-pay-down-your-home-mortgage.

after-tax or tax-deferred dollars. Find it at www.hughchou.org/calc/payoff_v_borrow.cgi.

Hugh's Prepay vs. Investment calculator: This shows you the effects of contributing an extra monthly amount to your mortgage versus investing it. You can specify whether your mortgage interest is deductible or not, and whether your investments are after-tax or tax-deferred. You cannot specify whether your monthly investment would also be tax deductible, such as if contributed to a 401(k) or deductible IRA. Find it at www.hughchou.org/calc/prepay_v_invest.cgi.

MortgageSum.com Pay Down Mortgage or Invest calculator: This calculator seems to be identical to Hugh's Prepay vs. Investment calculator. It allows you to specify the amount of monthly savings available to apply toward the mortgage or toward an investment. It also allows you to specify whether mortgage interest is deductible and whether savings will go into a tax-deferred account. And it lets you choose various rates of return that your savings may earn; but it does not offer enough low-return choices. For example, at the time I tried this calculator, it showed CDs earning 6%. That would be nice, but it is not realistic in today's economic conditions. Find it at

www.mortgagesum.com/mortgagecalculator/mortgage-prepayorinvest.php

---

In its brief "Should You Carry a Mortgage into Retirement?" the Center for Retirement Research concludes that most retirees are better off repaying their mortgage. Specifically, it says:

> The ... analysis indicates that retired households are, in theory, better off repaying their mortgage. In addition to this theoretical conclusion, there is also a very practical argument against borrowing to invest. If a household with a mortgage mismanages its investments, or over-estimates the rate at which it can decumulate those investments, it risks losing the house, its only remaining asset.[124]

The brief "then considers and (for most households) rejects the argument that households should retain their mortgage because they can earn a higher expected return in stocks and other risky assets."

---

124 Anthony Webb, "Should You Carry a Mortgage Into Retirement?" Center for Retirement Research (July 2009) no. 9–16.

I agree with the general conclusions of the brief. I also think that before making a decision, each family needs to look at its individual circumstances. The right answer for you will depend on all of the following:

- Whether you are in the accumulation phase or already retired

- If accumulating, whether you have already maxed out tax-favored retirement plan contributions

- Your sources of income and expected taxes in retirement (for example, will extra IRA withdrawals needed to make mortgage payments make more of your Social Security income taxable?)

- Available mortgage rates

- Your comfort level with investment risk

- Your desired level of liquidity

MORTGAGE PAYOFF ASSUMPTIONS

In this chapter I assume that you have an adequate emergency fund and that you are not carrying high-interest-rate debt, such as credit card debt. Otherwise, both accumulating an ample emergency fund and paying down high interest rate debt should take precedence over making extra mortgage payments.

As I'm writing this chapter (June 2016), Bankrate.com says the current average 30-year mortgage rate is 3.73%, and the 15-year is 2.71%. With mortgage rates currently at all-time lows does it still make sense to pay off a mortgage?

It depends on your individual circumstances and comfort level with investment risk. If any of the following scenarios applies to you, you might think twice before paying down the mortgage:

- You are still accumulating assets and still have room to add savings to tax-favored accounts like IRAs, 401(k)s, or Roth accounts. In particular, if you are not taking full advantage of employer-matching contributions, this is something you should do before applying extra money toward the mortgage.

- You are retired, with all assets in tax-deferred accounts, your other sources of income put you at the point where all Social Security will be taxed at 85% even if you pay off the mortgage and reduce retirement account withdrawals, and you feel comfortable that over time your retirement accounts will earn a return (net of fees) at least equivalent to your mortgage rate.

- You live in a non-recourse state and incur frequent job changes or moves.

- You have locked in a mortgage rate at current historical lows and are comfortable taking on investment risk with your savings by viewing results over the same duration as your mortgage. This means, if you have a 15-year mortgage, you're viewing investment results over a 15-year time horizon and not measuring them on a week-to-week, month-to-month, or even year-to-year basis.

- You are a high net worth household who uses smart debt as a tool to increase your net worth and decrease taxes. See more on how do this in Thomas Anderson's book *The Value of Debt*.

NON-RECOURSE STATES

If you end up in a situation where your home is underwater (home value is less than remaining mortgage balance), in a non-recourse state the lender cannot go after your personal assets for the difference. Such borrowers have the option of pursuing a short sale (lender agrees to sell the home to a third party for an amount less than the remaining mortgage) or letting the home go to foreclosure. Although many homeowners would be reluctant to pursue such options, they are viable financial choices to be considered in such a situation.

Refinancing

With current low interest rates, many people are refinancing to reduce their monthly mortgage payment. Refinancing may or may not be appropriate for you.

For example, suppose you owe $248,671 on your mortgage. You are paying $2,098 a month in principal and interest payments (this does not include real estate taxes and insurance, which may also be part of your monthly payment) and your home will be paid off in about 15 years. You can refinance into a new 30-year mortgage at a 4% rate. You are going to pay $2,500 in closing costs, which you finance into the balance of the new mortgage. Your monthly payment will go down by $898 a month. That sounds good! But over the life of the loan, you will pay $51,471 more in interest.[125] That sounds bad.

So, is it a good or bad decision to refinance? It depends on numerous other factors. If your mortgage payment goes down $898 a month and you were taking IRA withdrawals to cover the mortgage, now you need to take less out of your IRA each month. This might mean less of your Social Security benefits would be subject to income taxes, and it might mean your overall tax rate would be lower. Decisions like this that are made in isolation do not take into account all the factors that affect your long-term outcome.

Tip   The decision to refinance requires both serious thought and number crunching. Get help doing the analysis, if you need it, before you make a decision based solely on monthly payments.

Home Equity Lines of Credit

Unexpected expenses will come up in retirement, just as they do now while you are working. If you have to take a significant extra withdrawal out of an account, it may mess up your investment and tax plan.

For example, say you have matched up your investments so that bonds or CDs mature in each account to match the amount of your anticipated withdrawals. But now you need an extra $25,000 to help an adult child. Where should the money come from? If the growth portion of your portfolio has done well, you

---

125 Numbers calculated using Realtor.com's mortgage refinance calculator at www.realtor. com/home-finance/financial-calculators/mortgage-refinancing-calculator.aspx?source=web

may be able to liquidate some of your long-term holdings to meet your extra cash needs. But what if the market is down?

In addition, what if you only have assets in tax-deferred accounts? An extra withdrawal may be taxed at a higher tax bracket and cause you to pay more tax on your Social Security benefits, or may push you into an income bracket where you pay additional Medicare Part B and D premiums.

A standing home equity line of credit provides liquidity that may come in handy in retirement. It can provide a ready source of cash that buys you time to figure out how to fit unexpected expenses into your plan in a strategic way. In this situation, you could write a check to your child for the $25,000 without it having a major effect on your other plans other than your need to make loan payments until your child can pay you back (anyone who has children knows they may be waiting awhile).

Be careful though. A line of credit is not an extra piggy bank to draw from. I had one recent retiree who was consistently spending more than we had projected. We discussed the dangers of running out of money if the spending level didn't change. He agreed, and we reduced his portfolio withdrawals. Next time we met, he had accumulated a significant amount of debt on his home equity line. "What happened?" I asked. Instead of taking portfolio withdrawals to fund excess spending, he had tapped into his home equity line. This was like taking money out of the left pocket instead of the right pocket. We had some more tough discussions and eventually got him on track. Home equity lines are best used as a reserve strategy, not as an extra source of spending money.

Reverse Mortgages

It is amazing how readily people will take out a mortgage, and how adverse they are to the words reverse mortgage. A reverse mortgage is a financial tool. There should be no adverse reaction to the words.

Years ago, reverse mortgages got a bad rap, and it hasn't entirely gone away. People seem to cling to false beliefs about this financial instrument. Like a regular mortgage, a reverse mortgage is a tool that allows you to access the equity in your home.

Reverse mortgages are non-recourse loans—if the value of the mortgage grows to the point where it exceeds the value of the home, there is only the property as collateral. The bank cannot attach your other assets or those of your heirs.

Reverse mortgage programs are federally mandated through the FHA (Federal Housing Administration). The U.S. Department of Housing and Urban Development provides a thorough overview of reverse mortgages on its website.[126]

With a reverse mortgage, you own the home at all times, not the bank. Your responsibilities are to pay the taxes and maintain the property, the same responsibilities you have with any mortgage.

Note   Despite what you may have read or heard, a reverse mortgage can be a very useful retirement planning tool.

Here are a few key things that make a reverse mortgage attractive in the right situation:

- You can use a reverse mortgage to pay off an existing mortgage.

- Reverse mortgage income is tax-free.

- No minimum credit score is required, and a reverse mortgage does not affect your credit score.

- When you sell your home, just as with any mortgage, the mortgage gets paid off and any additional equity belongs to you or your heirs.

- You own the property at all times.

Let's take a look at how reverse mortgages work, when to use them, and when not to use them.

How They Work

A reverse mortgage allows you to borrow money against the value of your home without entering into a monthly repayment agreement. Instead of mak-

---

126 See "Frequently Asked Questions about HUD's Reverse Mortgages" at http://portal.hud. gov/hudportal/HUD?src=/program_offices/housing/sfh/hecm/rmtopten.

ing monthly payments to repay the amount borrowed, the bank agrees that the loan will be repaid at some point in the future when the house is sold. Thus the balance owed increases each month as interest accumulates.

To be eligible for a reverse mortgage, you:

- Must be age 62.

- Own a home that you live in.

- Have no mortgage or a low mortgage balance that can be paid off at closing with proceeds from the reverse mortgage.

- Agree to participate in a home equity conversion mortgage (HECM) counseling session to learn more about reverse mortgages.

You can receive the proceeds from a reverse mortgage in the following ways:

- As a lump sum

- In the form of life-long monthly payments

- As a line of credit

- In any combination of the above

The amount you receive depends on the following:

- *Age of the borrower:* The younger you are, the less you can receive

- *Value of the property:* But there's a maximum of $625,500

- *Type:* The type of reverse mortgage program you pick

You can use the online reverse mortgage calculator at the National Reverse Mortgage Lender's Association website (www.reversemortgage.org/About/ReverseMortgageCalculator.aspx) to get an estimate of the amount of income or size of lump sum that a reverse mortgage might provide to you.

Using a St. Louis ZIP code of 63017, a couple age 65, and home value of $300,000, the calculator estimated that as of May 2016, they could receive $817 of monthly income for life, or a lump sum of $89,573. (This estimate was run in May 2016.)

Another option would be monthly income of $553 with a $50,000 credit line to be used as needed.

With a reverse mortgage, a lender can foreclose on you if you do not pay your property taxes, insurance, and repairs. I frequently see this mentioned as a caution against reverse mortgages. I find this a silly reason to say reverse mortgages are bad. If you own a home outright with no mortgage and don't pay your property taxes, you can lose your home too.

With a reverse mortgage, the lender also has the right to demand repayment if you don't live in your home for 12 straight months or more. This means if you move in with relatives, or into a care facility, you need to make plans to sell the home if you don't think you'll be returning. Upon sale of the home, any equity is yours. If the mortgage balance exceeds the value of the home, you have no risk.

When to Use Them

I can think of multiple situations in which a reverse mortgage might be a good planning solution. Let's take a look at a few of them.

To Allow You to Defer Your Social Security Start Date

Suppose you are in your mid-60s. You have some savings and a paid off home. You think you are going to have to start Social Security early, but you know you will get more if you can wait to begin benefits until age 70. Proceeds from a reverse mortgage might fill in the gap, allowing you to defer the start date of your Social Security and lock in a higher guaranteed income amount for life.

To Manage Taxes

You might be in a retirement situation where your income puts you on the border of a marginal tax bracket, meaning each time you take extra money out of your IRA, it is taxed at a higher rate. Because reverse mortgage income is tax-free, it may be the perfect solution either as a credit line to be used when additional money is needed for major purchases or repairs, or as a form of monthly income.

To Manage Sequence Risk

When investing in a traditional portfolio of stocks and bonds, you want to avoid liquidating investments during a market downturn. This is typically managed by some form of time segmentation, such as holding cash reserves and lower-risk investments to meet near-term cash needs. There is an opportunity cost to this strategy: to manage risk you must hold more short-term, low-risk investments that earn lower returns. In an article titled "Standby Reverse Mortgages: A Risk Management Tool for Retirement Distributions,"[127] the authors propose using a reverse mortgage to manage this process. Instead of recommending the holding of excess cash reserves, they establish rules that determine when the reverse mortgage should be used for income needs and when portfolio withdrawals should be used. The executive summary concludes: "We find this risk management strategy improves portfolio survival rates by a significant amount."

As Plan B

A reverse mortgage can be a strategy you keep on the shelf only if needed. You might build your plan based on a reasonably conservative set of assumptions about investment returns, longevity, and spending—a plan that works without incorporating the use of your home equity. Then, if investment returns are lower than expected or if it looks like you may outlive your money if you don't implement some changes, you can consider a reverse mortgage as plan B. In several cases where I have recommended a reverse mortgage, it was a combination of overspending and low returns in the first ten years of retirement that put the client's plan in jeopardy. I was happy that a reverse mortgage had not been part of their original plan. If it had been, we would have had no viable Plan B options.

When Not to Use Them

Those who seem to think *reverse mortgage* is a bad word frequently cite fees as one reason to avoid them.

If you look at a reverse mortgage as a long-term solution, the fees, when amortized over the life of the loan, are reasonable. The reverse mortgage

---

127 John Salter, Ph.D., and Harold Evensky, "Standby Reverse Mortgages: A Risk Management Tool for Retirement Distributions," *Journal of Financial Planning* (August 2012).

calculator I used on the St. Louis ZIP code estimates fees. For the scenario I ran, total fees were $7,987 composed of a $5,000 loan origination fee, $1,500 for mortgage insurance and $1,487 of other closing costs. To me this seems quite reasonable when you consider this financial instrument is providing you with guaranteed income for life.

Whether you consider the fees reasonable or not, there are situations where a reverse mortgage might not be the right solution. Here are a few of them:

- *Moving soon:* As with any mortgage, it doesn't make sense to pay refinancing costs and fees if you think you may be moving soon. A reverse mortgage is most appropriate for someone who plans on remaining in their home for quite some time.

- *Overspenders:* If you are an overspender, you ought to get a handle on your overspending before you use a reverse mortgage. You may end up not being able to pay the property taxes one day, and the lender can foreclose on you in that situation. Of course if you spend too much, you're going to have a problem no matter what financial tools you use, unless you choose an immediate annuity.

- *Medicaid-eligible:* If you are eligible for Medicaid, lump-sum proceeds from a reverse mortgage may affect your eligibility. In these situations, a reverse mortgage that provides monthly income may be a better option than one that provides you a lump sum. (In all cases where you receive aid based on your income and asset amounts, check all the rules before making any changes to your financial situation.)

If you need additional income, and your home has equity, your other alternative to using a reverse mortgage is to move. All options should be explored before you make a final decision.

Summary

Your real estate and mortgage decisions should be viewed, as objectively as possible, as part of your retirement income plan.

When it comes to taking on new real estate investments, you should realize that it is a profession unto itself. Do plenty of homework before diving into real estate as a solution to generating your retirement income.

When it comes to your residence, your home choice can have a significant effect on your income needs. Extreme savers and those with constrained plans can find creative home solutions that reduce their spending needs on transportation and energy. Those with ample room in their plan will make values-based decisions, aligning their home choice with their desired retirement lifestyle.

Mortgages are financial tools. If you have the money to pay down the mortgage, and don't do so, what you are effectively doing is borrowing in order to invest. Whether this makes sense or not depends on your individual circumstances.

Reverse mortgages can provide guaranteed income later in your retirement years, or they can serve as an optional cash reserve bucket to draw from as part of your plan. You may not want to count on using one, but don't rule it out on based on hearsay.

Chapter 10

Managing Health Care Costs in Retirement

What? It's Not Free?

"Yet this is health: To have a body functioning so perfectly that when its few simple needs are met it never calls attention to its own existence."

—Bertha Stuart Dyment

In recent years, it seems there's hardly a subject more controversial than health care coverage, except maybe gun control.

Regardless of your personal views on a minimum standard of care that should or should not be available to everyone, as with most things in life, the more money you have, the more health care choices are available to you. You have choices about how much you spend, and some choose to spend quite a bit more than others.

The purpose of this chapter is to provide a broad outline of those choices and to give you tools you can use to estimate health care expenses and incorporate them into your retirement income plan.

Total Medical Costs in Retirement

A couple age 65 can expect to spend anywhere from $245,000–$266,000 on health care in retirement.[128] This big number may sound scary. I like to put it in perspective. The cost of raising a child is estimated to be in the same price

---

128 "Don't freak out about health care costs in retirement," CNN Money (December 30, 2015). Available online at http://money.cnn.com/2015/12/30/retirement/retirement-health-care-costs/.

range, about $245,000.[129] Despite this scary price tag, people do find a way to finance the cost of raising their children. You take it one year at a time, and often a health care or child care expense replaces some other discretionary item.

For example, I am not sure what you do when you are ill, but I stay in bed, drink tea, and sip chicken soup. When I am not feeling well, I am not likely to be out shopping, traveling, or eating out. In the latter part of your retirement years, as spending on health care increases, it is often not an additional cost in the budget. It replaces other items.

That doesn't mean you shouldn't take the expense seriously. If there is one item that is nearly always missing from a retirement budget, it is the adequate accounting of health care costs. You want to do your homework and estimate this expense as accurately as possible, but you also want to keep a healthy perspective on it. It is likely that when excess health care expenses come up, they will displace other flexible items in your budget, just as they do now while you are working—with one exception.

The one exception is end-of-life care. Some types of health plans do not cover extended hospital stays, which are those most likely to occur during one's last year of life. Such expenses can cause a serious dent in the amount one leaves to heirs or leave a loved one saddled with debt.

To do your best to account for such costs, you want to gain an understanding of how the system works and develop a basic estimate of how much you can expect to spend on health care. Of course, that depends on numerous factors such as where you live, when you retire, what medications you take, and whether you are self-insured or have an employer that provides retiree medical benefits.

Considering these variables, I break planning for health care expenses into four segments: early retirement (pre-age 65), Medicare-age health care (age 65+), long-term care, and saving for health care.

---

129 "Average cost of raising a child hits $245,000" CNN Money (August 18, 2014). Available online at http://money.cnn.com/2014/08/18/pf/child-cost/.

Early Retirement and Health Insurance

Doug worked for a construction firm and had planned on working until age 65. He was forced into retirement a few years early, at 62, when the economy took a dive. His wife, Beth, was about eight years younger, and had no plans to retire in the near future.

With a little rearranging, and through Doug's use of extended unemployment benefits, their plan absorbed the change in Doug's retirement date fairly well. To my surprise, a year later they came in to see if they might find a way for Beth to retire as soon as possible.

Beth explained that her take-home pay was only about $1,450 a month and that if she started her pension at 55 it would be $1,247 per month. "What was the point of continuing to work?" she asked.

On the surface, her logic made sense, until I explained to them the cost of health insurance. Beth was paying only $54 a month for health coverage; her employer was paying the rest of the premium. Once retired, as neither was yet Medicare age, equivalent health insurance for the two of them would run $1,400 a month. When we factored in benefits, Beth's job was paying her nearly twice what she had thought.

If your employer provides some type of group health plan, it is likely subsidizing the cost, and you may have no idea how expensive it can be if you leave the workforce.

Estimating Health Care Costs pre-65

If you plan on transitioning to self-employment or leaving the work force early (before age 65), you must factor the expense of health care into your plan.

Because of the provisions of the Affordable Health Care Act that went into effect January 2014, you no longer have to worry about pre-existing conditions. You are guaranteed to get coverage, and your premium cannot be higher due to health conditions. This is the good news.

The bad news is that coverage can still be expensive.

You can start your search on healthcare.gov. To get a general overview of prices go to the "Get Coverage" section and then find the section that says "See plans and prices". This is what I used to get the costs that were used in

Chapter 2 for Wally and Sally's health insurance for their pre-65 years. Costs vary by location, age, and the type of plan you choose. The least expensive plan we found for Wally would run about $591 per month; the most expensive came in at $1,078. For Sally the least expensive was $479 and the most expensive was $916.[130]

If you are a healthy individual out shopping for insurance, you can start your search with a health insurance broker[131] or by visiting one of the large health insurance company websites that provide online tools to help you find a plan that fits your needs. Here are five health insurer websites you may want to check out:

- *Aetna*: www.aetna.com

- *Blue Cross Blue Shield*: www.bcbs.com

- *Humana*: www.humana.com

- *United Health Care*: www.uhc.com

- *Cigna*: www.cigna.com

For a healthy individual who is not yet 65, I think one of the most effective ways to compare plans is to look at your maximum out-of-pocket cost, including premiums.

For example, one of the decisions you'll need to make is choosing between a high-deductible plan and a low-deductible plan. Let's walk through an example.

Using the healthcare.gov website, I chose an Arizona ZIP code and examined plans for a female age 62.

The most expensive plan on a monthly premium basis had the following features for in-network services:

- *Deductible*: $1,000

- *Monthly premium*: $916

- *Maximum out-of-pocket*: $5,500

- *Co-pays/Coinsurance*: $15 primary care /$40 specialist

---

130 Pricing was for 2016 plans.
131 For assistance finding an agent, visit the National Association of Health Underwriters website at www.nahu.org and use the Find an Agent tool.

If you add up the costs for a year with no doctor visits, this woman would spend her monthly premium for a total of $10,992 for the year.

If she had a year with maximum expenses, she would spend her monthly premium plus her maximum out-of-pocket amount, for a total of $16,492. If she chooses this plan, she will have to count on the $10,992 per-year cost, and she should expect it to increase a bit each year until she reaches age 65 and becomes eligible for Medicare.

One of the lower cost plans on a monthly premium basis was an HSA-qualified plan[132] and had the following features:

- *Deductible*: $6,450

- *Monthly premium*: $451

- *Maximum out-of-pocket*: $6,450

- *Co-pays*: With these plans you pay all costs up to your deductible, and there is no charge after you meet your deductible.

If you add up the costs for a year with no doctor visits other than preventative care (which was covered) with this plan, she would spend her monthly premiums for a total of $5,412 for the year and use her savings to fund an HSA account to the maximum allowable amount of $4,350 (2016's single person limit of $3,350, plus $1,000 catch-up contribution amount for those age 55 and older).[133] This would put her annual expense at $9,762 although technically much of that would be savings rather than a current-year expense.

If she had a year with maximum expenses, she would spend her monthly premium plus her maximum out-of-pocket amount for a total of $11,862.

For those who are eligible for HSA plans, I think they are a great choice.

Of course, the choices online include all kinds of additional plans offered with various combinations of deductibles, premiums, and coinsurance amounts. I picked these two extremes to give you a sense of the diversity of your options.

If you want an early retirement, the key will be to explore your options based on your health situation, geographic location, and plan choices. Then build the estimated expense into your budget.

---

132 I discussed the tax benefits of Health Savings Accounts in Chapter 4. Additional HSA features are outlined later in the present chapter.

133 Once you reach 65, you are no longer eligible to fund an HSA.

Your choices and expenses will change once you become eligible for Medicare at age 65.

THINGS YOU MUST DO BETWEEN 62 AND 65

Once you hit age 62, it's time to do some Medicare homework to prepare you for reaching age 65. You'll need to do the following:

- Learn Medicare basics.

- Find out how your current plan interacts with Medicare. The earlier you do this the better, so that you have ample time to change plans if you need to.

- Explore your new health insurance options, such as Original Medicare combined with a Medigap/Supplement policy or a Medicare Advantage plan.

- Enroll in Medicare when you turn 65.

Age 65: Medicare Basics

When you reach 65, the health insurance landscape changes. You become eligible for Medicare, the U.S. federal health insurance program for people age 65 and older.[134]

Medicare has four parts, Parts A, B, C and D. Each part covers different items, and overall Medicare does not cover all your health care expenses, so most retirees will want additional coverage in the form of a Medicare Supplement policy or Medicare Advantage plan, as well as some form of long-term care insurance.

Navigating your way through all these choices can be challenging. Consider this comment from HealthView Services in 2012:

> A recent study conducted by the National Council on Aging (NCOA) and United Healthcare reveals that large numbers of seniors don't understand Medicare and are unaware of recent changes. The findings highlight the need for more education regarding Medicare. This

---

134 Medicare also covers certain young people with disabilities and those with End-Stage Renal Disease even if they are not yet 65. See medicare.gov for details.

becomes all the more pertinent as over 10,000 people are turning 65 and becoming eligible daily. In the next twenty years, tens of millions will sign up for Medicare, whether or not they know what they are doing.[135]

You may want to seek professional help as you navigate your way through your health care choices. Here are a few resources you can use:

- Your state's SHIP program (State Health Insurance Program). This is a group of volunteers who offer free counseling on your health benefit choices. Find your state's SHIP program at http://www. seniorsresourceguide.com/directories/National/SHIP/.

- Allsup's Medicare Advisor Plan Selection service. Learn more on their website at https://www.allsup.com/medicare-advisor.

- Using an insurance specialist. In my business, we work with Hank Segal, an amazingly knowledgeable health insurance agent who, in his current semi-retired state, has found he enjoys continuing to assist those referred to him sort through their options. He can be contacted at onwisc021@gmail.com.

Let's take a brief look at what Medicare covers and why additional insurance coverage (and thus additional money) is often needed to cover non-Medicare eligible expenses.

Medicare: Parts A, B, C, and D

Medicare.gov offers a wealth of information. When you near 65, or if you are assisting someone who is Medicare age, I suggest you spend some time on it. It offers this concise overview of what Medicare is all about:

Medicare covers services (like lab tests, surgeries, and doctor visits) and supplies (like wheelchairs and walkers) considered medically necessary to treat a disease or condition.[136]

Of course, it is the definition of *medically necessary* that is so difficult to determine. I'll leave that one alone and instead take a brief look at how Medicare benefits are structured.

---

135 "Baby Boomer Confusions About Medicare Soars as Enrollment Date Looms," HealthView Services (December 19, 2012).
136 Source: Medicare.gov.

Medicare coverage is broken into four parts: Parts A, B, C, and D. The foundation of Medicare is Part A, which is often referred to as *hospital insurance*. If you are eligible for Social Security, you are eligible for Medicare Part A for free.

Medicare Part B, which covers additional services and supplies needed to treat medical conditions as well as some preventative services, is not free. Most benefit recipients pay a monthly premium for Medicare Part B, which is announced annually.

As discussed in Chapter 4, the basic Medicare Part B premium in 2016 is $121.80 per month. Those with modified adjusted gross incomes over $85,000 for single filers or $170,000 for married filers pay more, according to a schedule based on their income; the more income, the higher the premium.[137] Medicare estimates this schedule results in increased premiums for about 5% of the population.

Medicare Parts A and B comprise what is now often referred to as *Original Medicare*. With Original Medicare, as with most other insurance plans, you still have deductibles, co-pays, and coinsurance expenses as well as prescription costs. That's where Medicare Parts C and D come in—offering additional coverage you can purchase.

Medicare Part C is called a *Medicare Advantage Plan*, or *Medicare Health Plan*. It is private insurance that provides coverage in a single plan that includes Medicare Parts A and B, and may also include prescription drug coverage (Part D). Medicare Advantage plans may also include extra covered services like vision, dental, and hearing. These plans may cost less than other options if you do not have frequent medical needs.

Medicare Part D refers to prescription drug coverage that you can add as an a la carte plan to your basic Medicare Part A and B benefits. As with Medicare Part B, high-income recipients pay more for Medicare Part D.

Medigap and Medicare Supplement plans are intended to wrap around Original Medicare. Currently, you must choose between either a Medicare Advantage plan or Original Medicare augmented with Medigap/Medicare Supplement policies.

The right choice for you will depend on your health care needs and location. Not all plans are offered in all states. Some plans provide a significant advan-

---

137 This means-tested premium schedule is provided in Chapter 4.

tage over others, depending on the medications, lab work, and other services you may routinely use.

To help you wade through these choices and see what is offered in your location, Medicare.gov offers an online Plan Finder tool at www.medicare.gov/find-a-plan/questions/home.aspx.

I used the Plan Finder feature with a Brooklyn, New York ZIP code to see what it would come up with. It gave me the option to choose the specific medications I was on, the dosage, and to substitute generic versions. It also asked if I bought from a retail pharmacy or via mail order. I chose "none" for the medications, but my understanding is that this tool can be quite useful when you need to find a plan that covers something specific. The results were categorized as follows:

- *Prescription Drug Plans with Original Medicare:* 20 plans

- *Medicare Health Plans with Drug Coverage:* 36 plans available

- *Medicare Health Plans without Drug Coverage:* 6 plans available

Yikes! How is the average person supposed to wade through all these choices?

Some of the plans listed provided an estimate of annual health and drug costs, which ranged from $1,890–$3,470, but this estimate did not include hearing, vision, or dental. It also did not include Medicare Part B premiums, which would tack on another $1,461 per year for the average person and as much as $4,677 a year for high-income recipients.[138]

The first choice you'll make is deciding between an Original Medicare plan or a Medicare Advantage Plan. Here are three key differences:

- *Choice of provider:* One of the big differentiators between Original Medicare and Medicare Advantage plans is the ability to choose your own provider. You may be able to reduce routine out-of-pocket costs by using a Medicare Advantage plan, but to do so you need to use the plan's in-network providers. If you want complete freedom to choose your provider, and if you travel or go back and forth between states, Original Medicare with a Medigap/Supplement may be your best option.

---

138 Based on 2016 Medicare Part B premium schedules.

- *Extended hospital stay coverage*: Another big differentiator is the extended hospital stay coverage. Medicare Part A pays for the first 60 days of a hospital stay in full. For days 61–90, you pay a portion. For days 91–150 you pay an increased portion, and from day 151 on, the cost is yours to bear. Extended hospital stays are most likely to occur in the last year of life, and Medigap policies provide coverage for this cost. Most Medicare Advantage plans only cover up to the first 90 days.

- *Ancillary benefits*: One more differentiator among plans is the additional benefits that may come with Medicare Advantage plans— things like dental, vision, and hearing. These benefits are not part of the Original Medicare + Medigap type of coverage. Ancillary benefits are not mandated benefits and can be dropped or modified by the insurance company each year.

Note   With prescription drug plans, you have the choice of either picking a plan a la carte (Part D) that complements Original Medicare or choosing a Medicare Advantage plan that incorporates a drug plan. Either way, co-pays and costs for certain drugs may vary widely from plan to plan. It pays to shop around.

Your plan choice needs to be made based on your personal health situation, and it may need to be re-evaluated each year. As your health needs change, a different plan structure may prove to be more economical for you. Each year, you have the opportunity to switch Medicare health plans during an open enrollment period that occurs toward the end of the year. (For the 2017 year the open enrollment period runs October 15, 2016 through December 7, 2016.) Use this open enrollment period to evaluate your plan choice.

QUALIFY FOR MEDICARE

To be eligible for Medicare at no cost, you or your current or former spouse[139] must have:

- Entered the United States lawfully.

- Lived in the U.S. for five years.

- Paid Medicare taxes while working in the United States and have 40 or more quarters of Medicare-covered employment, or would be entitled to Social Security benefits based on your spouse's (or divorced spouse's) work record, and that spouse is at least 62.

- Achieved age 65 (except in limited exceptions explained in footnote 134).

- If you do not qualify based on these criteria, in some cases you can still purchase Medicare by paying a monthly premium. A situation where this might occur would be with an older spouse who is not eligible for Medicare based on his/her own work record and who is married to a younger spouse who will be eligible for Medicare but is not yet 62. I found the following *Consumer Reports* article to be most helpful in reviewing such a situation: http://www.consumerreports.org/cro/news/2011/11/i-m-65-and-have-been-denied-medicare-because-my-husband-is-five-years-younger-help/index.htm.

Medicare Gaps

The biggest misconception I see regarding Medicare is the belief that it will cover all your health care expenses. Perhaps this belief is why so many people do not include an expense line for health insurance premiums and other medical costs in their retirement budgets.

---

139 Rules for eligibility based on a former spouse's work record mirror the rules for eligibility for Social Security based on a former spouse's work record.

290 CHAPTER 10 - MANAGING HEALTH CARE COSTS IN RETIREMENT

According to the Employee Benefit Research Institute, Medicare only covers 51% of health care expenses.[140]

This means the other 49% will be paid by you or by other insurance coverage that you carry.

According to the Kaiser Family Foundation, health expenses accounted for nearly 15 percent of Medicare (age) household budgets in 2010.[141] If you want to create a very simple estimate of your post-65 health care expenses, take your expected retirement income and multiply it by 15 percent. This can give you a starting place, but the number may be too low.

You can use the online tool by HealthView Advisor to come up with your own estimate at http://apps.hvsfinancial.com/hvadvisor/.

Using the HealthView Advisor calculator, I did not check off any of the health conditions and said I was a 65-year-old female. It estimated health care expenses in 2016 (age 65) as ranging from $5,206 to $9,552, depending on income level. For a 65-year-old male, the estimate was $5,095 to $9,441.

This price range included costs for all of the following:

- Medicare B and D premiums
- Medicare Supplement policy premium
- Dental insurance premium
- Hearing and vision
- Out-of-pocket (OOP) costs for hospital visits, doctor and tests
- OOP costs for prescriptions
- OOP costs for dental

Based on this price range, in the expense timeline of your retirement income plan you need to include about $424 to $797 per month on health care starting at age 65. Yes, this is a broad range, but it gives you a starting place. This amount will increase with inflation.

If you want top-notch health care, choice of providers, and long-term care coverage, you'll want to budget more.

---

140 EBRI Issue Brief No. 295 (July 2006).
141 Kaiser Family Foundation Medicare Policy. Available online at
    https://kaiserfamilyfoundation.files.wordpress.com/2013/01/8171-02.pdf.

Applying for Medicare

If you are already receiving Social Security benefits when you reach age 65, you will be automatically enrolled in Medicare. Your Medicare card will be mailed to the address on record with Social Security.

If you are not receiving Social Security benefits, you need to apply online[142], at your local Social Security office, or by phone at 1-800-772-1213. There is a seven-month open enrollment period which starts three months prior to the month you turn 65 and extends three months past the month you turn 65. If you want benefits to begin at 65, make sure you apply before you turn 65.

You should almost always apply even if you still have coverage through a group health plan. If you are still working, most employer-provided health plans will become secondary to Medicare once you reach age 65. If you have private insurance, it may also become secondary to Medicare when you reach 65.

TRANSITIONING TO MEDICARE

If you are covered by a group health plan as you near age 65, read Medicare.gov's Retiree Insurance page at https://www.medicare.gov/supplement-other-insurance/retiree-insurance/retiree-insurance.html.

If you have private insurance, read Medicare.gov's "How Medicare Works with Other Insurance" at https://www.medicare.gov/supplement-other-insurance/how-medicare-works-with-other-insurance/how-medicare-works-with-other-insurance.html.

You may also want to read "Should I Get Part B?" at https://www.medicare.gov/sign-up-change-plans/get-parts-a-and-b/should-you-get-part-b/should-i-get-part-b.html.

---

142 Start your online application process at www.socialsecurity.gov/medicareonly/.

Medicare Part B and Medigap Policies

Medicare Part B enrollment is not mandatory, but the majority of people will want to sign up for Medicare Part B when they enroll in Medicare. However, there are exceptions. The best thing you can do is talk to your current health care provider to determine whether you should enroll in Part B at the same time you enroll in Medicare.

In limited cases, due to the coverage provided by your employer-sponsored plan, it may not be to your benefit to sign up for Part B right away. In such cases, you'll have an open enrollment period where you can sign up for Part B after your employment or employer-sponsored health coverage ends.

Note   If you don't sign up for Part B and Part D when you're first eligible, you may have to pay a penalty to get them later. For additional details, see Understanding Medicare Enrollment Periods at www.medicare.gov/Pubs/pdf/11219.pdf.

You have six months from the time you sign up for Medicare Part B to get a guaranteed-issue[143] Medigap policy. If you wait and apply for a Medigap policy after this six-month window, you may or may not be eligible, because the terms and conditions in most states are determined after this period by the private health insurance company issuing the policy.

This makes for an interesting dilemma. On the Medicare.gov Medigap & Medicare Advantage Plans page,[144] it says:

> Medigap policies can't work with Medicare Advantage Plans. If you have a Medigap policy and join a Medicare Advantage Plan (Part C), you may want to drop your Medigap policy. Your Medigap policy can't be used to pay your Medicare Advantage Plan copayments, deductibles, and premiums.

If you want to cancel your Medigap policy, contact your insurance company. If you leave the Medicare Advantage Plan, you might not be able to get the same Medigap policy back, or in some cases, any Medigap policy unless you have a "trial right."

---

143 Guaranteed issue means you cannot be denied coverage for health reasons.
144 Available online at https://www.medicare.gov/supplement-other-insurance/medigap/medigap-and-medicare-advantage/medigap-and-medicare-advantage-plans.html.

If you have a Medicare Advantage Plan, it's illegal for anyone to sell you a Medigap policy unless you're switching back to Original Medicare.

When you consider that Medigap policies cover extended hospital stays—a benefit which may prove quite valuable much later in life—and Medicare Advantage plans don't, it's almost as if you're forced to roll the dice when you turn 65. Do you want to ensure eligibility for the Medigap policy and pay more to have both plans along the way? Those who have the means to do so may in fact do this to preserve future choices.

One of the things to keep in mind with Medicare is that it does not cover long-term care expenses. This is the final health care cost you should examine as part of your retirement plan.

Long-Term Care

John and Cathy were in their 70s when they were referred to me by their CPA. They had been married over 50 years, and they brought a smile to my face every time they came in, often still holding hands.

About ten years after we met John had a stroke and Kathy was diagnosed with Parkinson's.

I went to visit Cathy numerous times and eventually met all their children. She was weak and frail; I honestly didn't think she'd make it more than a year past John's passing, but slowly a sparkle returned to her eye, and her strength returned. When I go see her now, we sit and have a glass of wine, and I gain the most marvelous insights from this amazing 84-year-old woman.

She shared that she misses John every day and yet at the same time she realizes her opinions and thoughts had been entirely shaped by him. In the era in which she married, that was natural. In her 80s, she is now finding a new kind of independence: an independence of thought as she forms her own opinions on current events and enjoys intellectual conversations with her visitors. It has been an amazing process to watch.

Although Cathy is healthy and alert, she needs assistance around the home. Her long-term care policy covers in-home care, so she has a helper who comes each day from about 10 to 2 to offer whatever help is needed, such as running errands, preparing meals, cleaning, bathing, laundry, and so on. Although we think of long-term care needs as being confined to a nursing home facility, Cathy's situation is quite common, and in-home care is an important feature offered by most long-term care insurance policies today.

Contrast Cathy's situation with that of my grandpa. In 2012, I flew to Des Moines, Iowa for a family reunion put together in honor of my grandpa's 90th birthday. Grandpa's short-term memory loss had started to result in things like the stove being left on and forgotten medications. This was my first time to visit him in the care facility the family had located for him.

It was a nice place with spacious, living room–like gathering areas, and Grandpa expressed that he was quite happy there. There were security codes with a double door system to get in and out, and although I realize they are needed for his protection, it was still odd, as if we start in a playpen and one day end up back in one again.

Grandpa knew who I was, but other parts of his memory were jumbled up a bit. Other than memory loss, he is quite healthy and may be in this care facility for many years. Grandma passed away a number of years ago, so all of Grandpa's income and assets can be used to support this need. If Grandpa still had a spouse at home, though, the financial strain of the situation would be more substantial.

Your Long-Term Care Situation

You do not know what the future may bring. Will you, like John, go quickly of a stroke, never needing any form of long-term care? Will you, like Cathy, need in-home care? Or will you, like my grandpa, need years of a full-care facility? And how will such care needs be financed?

If you want to estimate the odds that you will need long-term care, start with the U.S. Department of Health and Human Services website at www.longtermcare.gov.

Medicare and supplemental health insurance policies cover a minimal amount of care needed after a hospital stay, but they do not cover the cost of extended long-term care needs. If you incur an extended care need, it can eat up your nest egg leaving little, if any, funds to pass along to heirs.

As with any insurance needs, your choices are to retain the risk, and, if needed, you will spend your assets and potentially go on state aid, or shift the risk by buying a long-term care insurance policy.

From my own observations in working with retirees, it seems most people who can afford long-term care insurance policies find having them brings them greater peace of mind.

Types and Terms of Coverage

In the market today there are three long-term care insurance designs:

- Pool-of-funds (traditional long-term care insurance)
- Life insurance based
- Annuity based

The pool-of-funds design comprises about half of policies sold today with the rest a combination of life and annuity based products which are often referred to as either "asset-based" or "hybrids".

Pool-of-funds

Premiums for the traditional pool-of-funds products are designed to be "pay as you go". You pay premiums each year and then apply for benefits when a care need arises. This type of policy is likely to be the least costly insurance solution if you end up needing care. That is because premiums are less costly than with the asset-based design, and all the risk is held by the insurance company. For example, the insurance company could end up paying for many years of care after you had only paid one or two years' worth of premiums. One concern for those of you on a fixed income in retirement; the premiums can increase if a rate increase is requested and approved by a state's insurance commissioner.

One option that can help protect your assets in the event of a lengthy long-term care expense is called a *Partnership* policy. If you use up all your insurance benefit, you must then spend down your own financial assets before Medicaid benefits apply. A Partnership policy protects some of your assets from Medicaid resource reduction requirements. For every dollar that your policy pays for your care, a dollar of your assets is disregarded from Medicaid resource reduction requirements. Two states, Indiana and New York, offer total asset protection if a required level of coverage is purchased. All but five states currently offer or are in the process of offering these policies. Partnership policies only apply to the traditional pool-of-funds products.

Asset-based

The life insurance based products offer a death benefit and allow you to access that death benefit early in the case of a long-term care need (as defined in the policy).

With the annuity based products, you put a lump sum into an annuity contract that will then provide a specified benefit available if you need care.

The majority of the asset-based products (life insurance or annuity) require a significant single premium to create a meaningful long-term care benefit. These products end up being more costly if you end up needing care because you are sharing risk with the insurer. For example, the first 24 to 30 months of care benefits come from the premium you paid to fund the product. This is the portion of the risk you covered, and it is a significant portion. The advantage to these products is premiums are guaranteed not to increase, and if care is not needed premiums that fund the policy are returned either in the form of a death benefit or cash value.

Terms of Coverage

Most policies express their coverage in terms of a daily benefit amount and a number of years. For example, a policy that provides a $200 daily benefit amount for four years would provide you with a pool of $292,000 available for care ($200 × 365 days × 4 years), expressed in today's dollars. If you buy a policy that has an inflation adjustment (this is usually recommended), your daily benefit amount, and thus your pool of available dollars, will increase according to the inflation formula in the policy.

A four-year policy may last far longer than four years, depending on your care needs and how you schedule benefits. What do I mean by that? If your policy will pay up to $200 per day, and you are only spending $100 per day, your policy would last eight years instead of four, using the example in the preceding paragraph. Also, some policies reimburse monthly, and some daily. A monthly reimbursement structure gives you quite a bit more flexibility when it comes to in-home care services.

For example, many people like to bundle their in-home care services. Perhaps they need help bathing and dressing every day. Let's assume the time required is two hours and the cost is $20 per hour, or $40 per day. On Mondays, in addition to help bathing and dressing, they also like to have all the meals prepared for the week and the laundry and cleaning done. These services require eight hours to perform at a cost of $160. With a daily reimbursement of $100 they would exceed their limits on Monday and have to pay out-of-pocket but be under their limits on other days. With a monthly reimbursement policy, this would not be an issue.[145] The carrier would pay up to the monthly maximum of $3,000 per month, covering the higher costs of Mondays and allowing the policyholder greater flexibility in how services are scheduled.

How Much Coverage Do You Need?

How do you determine the amount of long-term care coverage? You could go about it in one of two ways. If you can afford a Cadillac policy, you may just decide that's what you want regardless of cost. If you're working on a limited budget, you'll have to narrow your benefits down a bit. You might go through the following exercise to determine what you need.

First, estimate long-term care costs in your area. Using the online interactive Genworth Financial Cost of Care website www.genworth.com/cost-of-care/landing.html, I looked up the Dallas area and got the following results:

- *Homemaker:* Median hourly rate: $20

- *Home Health Aide:* Median hourly rate: $20

- *Assisted Living Community:* Median monthly cost $3,700

- *Skilled Nursing Home:* Median Semi-private daily cost $151

- *Skilled Nursing Home:* Median private room daily rate $203

Assume you have $60,000 coming in from Social Security and investment income. That's about $164 a day, or about $4,920 a month.

---

145 Special thanks to Nicole Gurley of Gurley Long-Term Care Insurance. Her input, contributions, and knowledge in helping me develop this chapter have been invaluable.

However, all the income is not available for care needs, because you still need income for living expenses in addition to your long-term care costs. And if you have a spouse, they likely need a significant portion of that income to continue their own standard of living.

You may decide that of that $164 a day, $40 of it would be available for long-term care costs. That would cover about two hours a day of non-medical in-home care at $20 an hour.

If you wanted to cover a full eight hours a day of non-medical care, with the goal of enabling you to stay in your home for as long as possible, you would need an additional benefit of $120 a day.

If you decide to protect against a care need of about 3.9 years, then you would buy a policy that had a $120 daily benefit that would provide coverage for three to four years. You would also want an inflation rider so that if and when you needed care (likely 10 to 20 years after purchase of the policy), that $120 per day would have increased to keep pace with the increasing cost of care.

This is just one example of how you might go about purchasing a policy to cover the risks that concern you the most.

Long-Term Care Insurance for Wally and Sally

I asked Nicole Gurley of Gurley Long-Term Care Insurance to put together some policy options for Wally and Sally.

To acquire basic coverage, we looked at pool-of-funds policies[146] that provide a $130 per day benefit or $3,900 per month with a three-year benefit period creating an initial pool of money of $140,400 per person (see Table 10-1). The policies quoted have a shared rider, which gives the couple six years to share between them. This means if Sally needed care, and Wally did not, all six years could be used for Sally (or vice versa). The policies also have a 3% compound inflation rider, so the daily benefit, monthly benefit and total pool of money all increase by that amount every year.

---

146 Policies quoted represent Iowa rates. Rates will vary depending on age, health status, state, and benefits chosen.

Table 10-1. Long Term Care Insurance Quotes for Wally and Sally

	Carrier 1		Carrier 2		Carrier 3	
	Wally	Sally	Wally	Sally	Wally	Sally
Annual Premium	$2,680	$2,460	$3,159	$2,739	$2,015	$2,958
Combined Annual Premium	$5,140		$5,898		$4,973	

The quoted pool-of-funds policies all had the following features:

- *Tax-qualified*: This means that benefits paid are not taxable, and premiums may be deductible depending on how the client files taxes.

- *Underwriting class*: These are all quoted using standard health ratings.

- *Integrated design*: The coverage is applicable to all venues including home care, adult day care, assisted living, skilled nursing and hospice.

- *Facility elimination period*: All plans have a 90-day elimination period for facility care. Policyholders are responsible for the first 90 days of expense if care begins in a facility.

- *Zero-day home care elimination period waiver*: All plans have a 0-day elimination period requirement for home care. The first day of care is covered if care begins at home.

- *Spousal premium waiver*: All plans include a spousal premium waiver. If one spouse/partner goes on claim, neither pays premiums during that specific claim period.

- *Monthly home care*: All plans pay home care on a monthly basis. This provides more flexibility in how services are received.

- *Partnership policies:* All plans qualify as partnership policies which provide added protection from Medicaid resource reduction requirements if policy benefits are exhausted.

If Wally and Sally wanted to purchase a richer policy; one that provided a $150 daily benefit amount for six years each, the maximum offered by most carriers, and 5% compound inflation, their combined premium could reach a whopping $14,420 a year.

In response to how people are reacting to current premiums on long-term care insurance[147], Nicole said, "Today, we ask clients to consider two things as they explore long-term care insurance: 1) how much risk do you really need to offset, and 2) what is a comfortably affordable premium. The new normal is some is better than none. And, it must be comfortably affordable because policyholders may pay premiums for a very long time."

To determine your needs, review family health history and longevity. Then discuss your primary concerns and financial circumstances with a knowledgeable long-term care broker, and let them help you find a policy that fits your needs and your budget. I prefer working with a broker who specializes in long-term care insurance and who can offer a full range of product offerings from a variety of carriers.

The challenge today is figuring out the amount of risk to offset. Unlimited coverage is offered by few carriers today, is quite pricey, and may result in over-insuring for most folks.

---

147 Today 76% of policyholders buy between the ages of 45 and 64 with 55% buying between age 55 and 64. Claims history indicates that 64% of claims occur between the ages of 80 and 85.

WHO HAS THE GREATEST NEED FOR LONG-TERM CARE INSURANCE?

Middle income, married couples typically have the greatest need for long-term care insurance. If one spouse needs care and the other doesn't, income levels are often not sufficient to cover both the cost of care and maintaining a reasonable lifestyle for the healthier spouse. A long-term care policy that provides a few years of benefits can give you a buffer—a period of time where the healthy spouse can assess the situation and, if it looks like the long-term care event will exceed the policy limits, have time to plan. One option in this situation: meet with an elder law attorney to see what options are available to protect your remaining assets and standard of living.

Alternatives to Traditional Long-Term Care Insurance

As the population ages, I expect many care alternatives will become available. One that is gaining popularity is the continuing care retirement community (CCRC).

With this arrangement, you move in while you are healthy and purchase a living space with a lump sum. You also have monthly fees. One of my long-term clients decided to do this at age 88 in Scottsdale, AZ. His home was paid for and worth about $300,000. He sold it and used the proceeds to purchase a beautiful living space in a high-end CCRC. When I visited, honestly, I was inspired. It had the look and feel of resort living with all the amenities. In addition to his $300,000 purchase amount, he pays monthly dues of about $3,000. This arrangement guarantees that he has care available if/when he needs it.

One thing to watch out for; additional care needs may result in additional fees. These arrangements are not necessarily all-inclusive so make sure you have the finances to cover any future expected costs. There are four types of CCRCs, and with each it is very important to carefully read the contract and understand what is provided. With some CCRCs it may be important to continue to keep a long-term care insurance policy; with other types of CCRCs it could be redundant.

Note   Read your CCRC contract carefully. Learn more at Leading Age's What You Need to Know About CCRCs' page at: http://www. leadingage.org/What_You_Need_to_Know_About_CCRCs.aspx.

Another option is to pool resources with like-minded friends. I was reminded of this option with a photo that made its way around Facebook. It depicted two spirited gray-haired women who were obviously best friends and had the caption "Reminder: your girlfriends will probably outlive your husband. So find good ones." I call this the Golden Girls care plan, although it could just as easily include mixed company. By bringing back the roommate concept in later life, you can share costs for services like house cleaning, cooking, etc.

PAYING FOR CARE WHEN YOU DON'T HAVE INSURANCE

What do you do when you or a loved one need care and can't afford it? Here are a few resources that may help you out:

- *Check your state's Medicaid rules:* To be eligible for Medicaid, your income and assets must be under a certain limit, and these limits vary from state to state. Start with your state's Medicaid office to find out your limits: https://www.medicaid.gov/medicaid-chip-program-information/program-information/medicaid-and-chip-eligibility-levels/medicaid-chip-eligibility-levels.html.

- *Contact your local Area Agency on Aging:* This organization can help you locate resources such as elder-abuse programs, counseling, meals on wheels, volunteers who will visit, adult day care services, and so on: http://www.n4a.org/.

- *Visit VeteranAid.org:* See if you or your loved one is eligible for a Veteran's Aid and Attendance Pension that may apply to both veterans and their surviving spouses: www.veteranaid.org/program.php.

- *Visit Eldercare.gov:* This resource can help you locate local services such as home health services, transportation resources, senior housing options, and respite care. It may be able to help you find financial assistance that you could be eligible for: www.eldercare.gov/eldercare.NET/Public/index.aspx.

Saving for Health Care Costs

Winning the lottery would be great, but the odds are not in your favor. If you want to be certain to have the funds you'll need, it is best to save. Health Savings Accounts (HSAs) are a great option. I touched on the tax benefits of these in Chapter 4. I go into a few additional features here.

You can use money in an HSA tax-free for qualified medical expenses. What constitutes a qualified medical expense?

Per IRS guidelines, that includes things like the following:[148]

- Expenses applied to your health plan deductible

- Dental care services

- Vision care services

- Prescription services

- Over-the-counter medications prescribed by your doctor

- Certain medical equipment

Once you reach age 65, you can use HSA money like an IRA—for anything! This makes it an incredibly flexible savings vehicle.

Accessing your HSA funds for medical expenses is easy. I have an HSA account that comes with a debit card. When I incur medical expenses, I could use that debit card to pay for these expenses directly from my HSA account with tax-free dollars. Instead, I pay for expense out-of-pocket so my HSA can accumulate for use in my retirement years.

HSA funds cannot normally cover insurance premiums. However, there are four exceptions:

---

148 http://www.hsabank.com/~/media/files/eligible_medical_expenses

- Premiums for continuation coverage under COBRA or ERISA for the account holder, spouse, or dependents

- Premiums for a tax-qualified long-term care insurance policy

- A health plan maintained while the account holder, spouse, or dependent is receiving unemployment compensation under any federal or state law

- Premiums for those over the age of 65, including Medicare or retirement health benefits provided by a former employer

This means HSA funds can be valuable under almost any circumstance— unemployment, buying long-term care insurance, or to use for living expenses after age 65.

To open an HSA account, you must first have an HSA-qualified health plan. Then you need to find a financial institution that offers HSA accounts.

Note   Once you reach age 65, you can no longer fund HSA accounts.

Some institutions allow you to invest your HSA money in stocks, bonds, and mutual funds. For most people starting an HSA, I don't think this is wise. I'd suggest you take your deductible times five and keep this portion of your HSA in something safe and stable, like risk level 1 and 2 choices (see Chapter 5). If no medical expenses occur, your HSA balance will continue to grow, and as your balance gets larger you may consider investing amounts in excess of five times your deductible in something more aggressive.

Outside of HSA accounts, the wisest thing you can do to plan for health care expenses is build them into your budget, review your insurance coverage annually, live within your means, and do your best to live a healthy lifestyle.

Summary

If your health insurance costs are currently subsidized by your employer, you may be in for a big surprise when you go to build these expenses into your post-retirement budget.

You can break your health care expenses into two tiers: pre-age 65 and post-age 65. You'll likely want to do this when putting together your budget.

When you reach 65, you have important decisions to make about the type of health plan you choose, and the right plan for you will depend on your personal set of health circumstances. Don't be shy about seeking help when navigating through your choices at this point. And remember that your plan may need to be reviewed from year to year during the open enrollment period. As your health needs change, an alternate plan may prove to be more economical for you.

If you are eligible for an HSA-qualified plan, using it in conjunction with fully funding an HSA account each year is one of the most effective health care planning tools currently available.

Chapter 11

Working Before and During Retirement

Using Your Human Capital

"The best Armour of Old Age is a well spent life preceding it; a Life employed in the Pursuit of useful Knowledge, in honourable Actions and the Practice of Virtue; in which he who labours to improve himself from his Youth, will in Age reap the happiest Fruits of them; not only because these never leave a Man, not even in the extremest Old Age; but because a Conscience bearing Witness that our Life was well-spent, together with the Remembrance of past good Actions, yields an unspeakable Comfort to the Soul."

—Cicero

I had a liberating experience in 2010. I figured out what I was good at, and what I wasn't so good at. I stopped trying to be like other people and started being who I was. And a funny thing happened: work no longer felt like work. Instead, each day it felt like I got to go play. Oh sure, there were tasks that I had to do that I didn't love. It wasn't completely Goldilocks. But it was different.

I owe the difference to the Kolbe A Index[149] assessment tool. It helps you identify your natural, instinctive way of approaching problem solving. When you're not using your instincts, you're working against your grain. It's like bicycling against the wind; it takes more effort to get to the same place. Once you understand your instinctive talents and how to use them, the wind is almost always at your back, and work doesn't feel as work-like.

At the time I discovered Kolbe, I was feeling quite frustrated in my business situation. I always had ideas and wanted to figure out how to do things more efficiently and/or more effectively. I liked to follow the latest trends in financial

149 All terms relating to Kolbe products and service are property of Kolbe Corp.

planning and test out new software packages. My associates had more of the "if it ain't broke, don't fix it" mentality. One day, a colleague said something to me along the lines of, "Why can't you just be happy and leave well enough alone?" I thought about that for a while and wondered, "Why can't I? Is something wrong with me?" Then I found Kolbe. Through an assessment process, I discovered my Natural Advantage—a Kolbe term—was that of an entrepreneur.[150] No, nothing was wrong with me. I am supposed to change things, and I am good at it. Instead of fighting myself I went full force ahead into seeing what I could create, and I haven't stopped since. I love it.

Kolbe had such a profound effect on me that, in 2011, I chose to invest in its certification class and become a Kolbe Certified Consultant, simply because I wanted to know more. The more I learned, the more I became convinced that an incredible amount of progress remains to be made in the field of human capital.

USING KOLBE

Many corporations use Kolbe's tools to improve the use of their corporate human capital. Kolbe can be particularly useful in putting together teams of people that function more effectively. I use Kolbe in my business for this purpose, and it has had a significant, positive effect on how we work together and make the most of each other's strengths.

I think one of the most empowering things you can do to improve your human capital results is discovering your natural instincts. You have a unique way of approaching problem solving, and someone is looking for your talents. You can start expanding on the potential of your human capital by going to www.kolbe.com and taking the Kolbe A Index. You can also use the Career MO+ to help you identify careers that most closely match your talents.

150 For those familiar with Kolbe, I'm a 6-5-8-2.

You possess human capital. It is in part your ability to earn a living. You can continue to use that capital in your retirement. You can focus on your human capital and look for ways to use it more effectively, just as you can focus on other assets on your balance sheet. Michael Haubrich of Financial Service Group, Inc., authored a book on this topic, *Career Asset Management*, which offers a plethora of ways to view your career in this way. If you're still in your peak earning years, I'd suggest you read it. And give it to every upcoming college graduate you know. I wish I'd viewed my career as an asset at an earlier age.

When focusing on human capital, you can take a strictly utilitarian approach and figure out how to make the most in the least amount of time. Or you can take a softer approach and make sure your human capital decisions align with your goals. Either way, it starts with knowing yourself.

What Kind of Retirement Is for You?

There are two aspects to retirement you need to figure out. The first is: can you afford it? The second is: will it work for you?

For many people, even those who can afford it, the traditional view of retirement doesn't work. This is well illustrated in the stories of Dr. Barry, Chuck, and Ed.

Dr. Barry

Dr. Barry is 80 and still a practicing physician. He works three days a week, down from four days a week a few years ago. When he and his wife last came in for a review, I asked if he had any thoughts about fully retiring.

He said, "I am a doctor. I've been a doctor my whole life. When I go to the office, staff members are respectful to me. Students in residency come through, ask me questions, and graciously thank me for my time. Every day it's Dr. Barry, Dr. Barry. If I retire, who will I be? I'll be nobody."

Dr. Barry loves—and thrives on—his work. If you are like this, retirement can be an unfulfilling experience.

Part-time work can help ease the transition to retirement, both financially and psychologically. On the psychological side, it allows you to slowly figure out what to do with your newfound leisure time.

On the financial side, part-time work gets you used to the idea of withdrawing money from savings to live on. I have seen many people who are afraid to retire, even though the numbers say they can afford it. The thought of withdrawing money from savings on a regular basis can be frightening. A gradual transition to retirement can help you get comfortable with it.

Chuck

Contrast Dr. Barry with Chuck. Chuck and his wife were excellent savers. When Chuck reached age 55, his company offered an early retirement package. We ran through the numbers and decided that, from a financial perspective, they would be fine if he took it. Chuck was excited. A year later, he came in for a review and told me he was busier than ever. He had always been actively involved in his church and he was having a wonderful time volunteering and contributing in ways he never had the time for before.

Traditional retirement worked well for Chuck. He had activities lined up that he found fulfilling, things he and his wife had planned for years, and they knew their plan was solid financially.

Ed

Ed sidled up to me at a social event. He wasn't my client, but we'd known each other for years, and he knew what I did for a living. He looked around to make sure no one was listening. "Dana, I've got to tell you. I'm having trouble with this." I instantly knew what he was talking about. I'd heard he had sold his business and retired just a few months prior.

"Yes, a lot of people do. Particularly career-oriented people such as professionals and business owners."

He continued. "It's only been a few months. And I'm thinking, is this it? I've got to find something to do."

We talked for a while. Ed had run a successful business for years. He had carefully planned his exit strategy. He had been busy in his first few months of retirement, but it wasn't the right kind of busy. It wasn't satisfying.

Ed was used to leading a team, making decisions, and working toward goals. To be happy in retirement, he needed to find a way to continue to use these skills.

Retirement is a big life transition. It's not for everybody. It may not be for you.

You will need to figure out what type of retirement will work for you. Like Dr. Barry, do you want to find a way to schedule a gradual transition into retirement? If you're like Ed, can you figure out a way to stay involved with an interest of yours so that you can continue to contribute?

If you're married, what does your spouse want? What will you do with your time in retirement? Do you have activities you are excited about pursuing?

The answers to these questions have financial implications, yet that is only one reason to think about them. Retirement may be an opportunity where you can use your talents in a new way.

QUESTIONS TO ASK YOURSELF

Before you retire, ask yourself the following:

- What does retirement mean to me?
- When will I retire?
- What will I do with my time?
- Can I describe my ideal retirement day, or week?

Getting More Out of Your Human Capital

If you earned on average $45,000 a year from age 25 through 65, that would be $1.8 million of earnings. Many people earn far more in their lifetimes but don't stop to think of their earning power as the valuable resource that it is. Your entire perspective can change when you begin to figure out how to get the most out of this resource.

There are several different views on how to effectively use your human capital.

I break them into two approaches:

- The mercenary approach

- Finding work you thrive on

The Mercenary Approach

In their book *Die Broke* (Harper Business, 1998), authors Stephen Pollan and Mark Levine suggest a *mercenary approach* in which you maximize your career potential and offer your work to the highest bidder. You save as much as you can and put much of your savings in immediate annuities to provide guaranteed income in retirement to replace your earned income. I think this approach is interesting and, no doubt, it may work for some.

It means sacrificing current lifestyle while working, or potentially choosing work that is not fulfilling, in order to focus your financial and human capital efforts on the goal of retirement.

This mercenary-like approach can be combined with an extremely downsized lifestyle to reach retirement far more quickly than you may think. This approach is illustrated quite effectively on the website Early Retirement Extreme (see http://earlyretirementextreme.com/about). In the About Me section, author Jacob Lund Fisker says:

> If you're new here, this blog will give you the tools to become financially independent in 5 years. . . . This is not some stupid get rich quick scheme. The method is robust and replicable (no need to win the lottery, sell your business, or win at real estate), but not easy. . . . The key is to save 75%+ of your net income and invest it in income producing assets (bonds and dividend stocks). This is done by running your personal finances much like a business.

If your goal is to get out of traditional work as quickly as possible, I'd suggest you check out the Early Retirement Extreme website. Financial independence can be achieved in a far shorter time period than you may think, but it does require sacrifices. The advantage is that once you reach financial independence, you then have the freedom to choose what type of work you might want to do—if you want to work at all.

Another option is to spend time figuring out what academic programs, credentials, or certifications could help boost your income. Evaluate the financial cost of any program against the potential increase in income you might expect, and make sure you talk to many people in your industry to find out whether they think additional education will actually translate into increased income.

Years ago, I went through this process in considering the CFA (Chartered Financial Analyst) designation. This is a designation that many investment analysts, mutual fund managers, and institutional money managers hold. I am interested in the designation even to this day, but it involves a significant time commitment. The industry leaders I spoke with said that for the career path I was choosing, they did not think it was necessary for me. Instead I have chosen other designations that more directly correlate with the work of a financial advisor who works with individuals and their money decisions.

Finding Work You Thrive On

An alternative to the mercenary approach starts with figuring out what makes you tick and what type of work puts you "in the zone". When you find a niche you thrive in, it changes everything. If you enjoy what you are doing, you are likely to work longer, and it won't feel like work. Career counseling, coaching, and tools like Kolbe can assist you in finding work you thrive on.

A coaching process I have found beneficial is the Rediscover Your Mojo process,[151] designed by executive coach Lisa Stefan. Her process is designed to find that place "where strength meets spirit".

Lisa is one of my best friends, and I went through her process while it was in the design stage. At the time, I was frustrated with the direction of my business. I was looking for answers and hoping she could help me find them. To my surprise, what I got out of the process were valuable insights that have profoundly affected the way I operate on a daily basis and have changed the way I make decisions. I didn't get a nice neat "answer" about a career decision; instead I got tuned in to my internal compass so that it has become far easier for me to find my own answers to tough decisions.

If your retirement income plan calls for working until age 70, and you're currently 50, why wouldn't you spend some time, and perhaps work with a pro-

---

151 www.mojoassociates.com/index.php/services/rediscover_your_mojo/

fessional coach, to figure out what type of work you thrive on? In my opinion, 20 years is too long to do work you don't enjoy.

If you're closer to retirement age but realize that traditional retirement is not for you, you'll also want to do some soul searching. Brainstorm various ways you can use your impending free time to work on something you'll find fulfilling.

Many in the 55–64 age range are choosing to start a business. The Start Your Own Business page at Retired Brains[152] says, "Data from the Kauffman Foundation shows the highest rate of entrepreneurship in America has shifted to the 55–64 age group, with people over 55 almost twice as likely to found successful companies than those between 20 and 34, and individuals between the ages of 54 and 64 represented 22.9% of the entrepreneurs who launched businesses in 2010."

Starting a business isn't easy. I'll attest to that. Yet, if it is work you thrive on, even when it's hard, it is still fulfilling.

Note   The Kauffman Foundation finds that those aged 55–64 now have the highest rates of business formation and are twice as likely to found successful companies as those aged 20–34. If you've always had an urge to try entrepreneurship, don't let age hold you back.

Of course, continuing to work is not always about choice. It is often a matter of necessity. The mother of one of my close friends spent every summer in Alaska working in a dinner theater well into her 70s. In this way, she was able to save enough over the summer to supplement her Social Security throughout the remainder of the year. She had to work, yet she found a solution that got her out of the Arizona heat in the summer and allowed her to earn enough in a few months' time so that, for the rest of the year, her time was her own.

If you must supplement your income, explore every avenue you can think of. Do you have skills, hobbies, or specialized training that can be used to generate income? Can you teach part-time or turn your craft into a salable product?

---

152 www.retiredbrains.com/Home/Start+Your+Own+Business/default.aspx

A few years ago, over the Fourth of July, I stayed at a bed and breakfast in the mountains. The couple who owned it had recently retired, and this home was their retirement dream. They enjoyed people and entertaining. They wanted a beautiful house with a view, and by turning it into a business they found a way to afford it.

The town near their bed and breakfast hosts an annual arts festival. As I walked around talking with the vendors, many of them were retired. They were people who enjoyed traveling and had found a way to support their lifestyle by turning their craft into a source of income, which also enabled them to deduct many of their travel expenses.

There are numerous creative ways to use your human capital. Explore them all, just as you would explore options on how to use your financial resources.

Tip Remember that your human capital—all the skills and insight you've built up over the years—doesn't go away at retirement. You can still put it to use to continue to enjoy life to the fullest and perhaps increase your income.

Working in Retirement

Retirement is a relatively new concept for society. It is easy to forget that. Think about someone who works from age 20 to age 60, then retires and lives to 100. During their 40 years producing goods and services, they need to save enough to support 40 years of consumption. That is not an easy task. To support even a modest lifestyle, many will need to plan on working longer, or working part-time, well into their 70s.

Particularly for people whose plan does not leave a lot of wiggle room, it makes sense to find some way to supplement income.

Whether you work in retirement because you want to or because you have to, there are two areas where retirees get themselves in trouble when they retire and then go back to work. The first often happens to those who have never been self-employed before, and the second to those who are unaware of the Social Security earnings limit.

Self-Employment in Retirement

If you have never been self-employed before and decide to venture down that path, the first thing I recommend you do is get a good accountant. Many newly self-employed people quickly get behind on their taxes. They are used to having taxes withheld from their own paychecks and don't realize that once they are self-employed, they need to do their own withholding, and sometimes it can amount to many more dollars than they thought.

In addition, a good accountant can tell you which expenses you can deduct, which ones you can't, and how to keep accurate records. The last thing you want is tax trouble disrupting your new venture.

Earnings Limit

As discussed in Chapter 3, if you begin receiving Social Security benefits before you reach full retirement age, and you have earnings that are in excess of the Social Security earnings limit, the Social Security Administration will reduce your benefits or ask you to pay back the appropriate amount.

I've seen this cause problems for those forced into early retirement. Perhaps they experience a layoff and begin Social Security benefits because they don't think they should take withdrawals from savings or retirement accounts. Then a new job opportunity presents itself. They begin work and are surprised, or even shocked, when they get a notice that they owe some of their Social Security benefits back.

If you retire before you reach your full retirement age, do a careful analysis into how your plan should be structured. Starting Social Security benefits early is often not the best solution.

Tip	Go back and reread Chapter 3 before you decide to take Social Security at age 62. That decision will have ramifications if you then decide to go back into full-time work.

Aligning Your Plan to Your Potential Retirement Date

You can't always plan out your retirement date just the way you want to. Sometimes life has something else in mind. If you have a plan in place, you'll know what items need to be adjusted if your retirement date gets shifted (often due to health reasons, corporate restructuring, or the economy).

As you learned in Chapter 4, smart tax-planning moves can be designed around periods of time when you will have less earned income. You want to keep this in mind when you make decisions about your human capital.

For example, should your retirement date coincide with the end of the year, so that the following year you have no earned income, or should it occur midyear? Intentionally designing your income plan to work with your intended retirement date can put more dollars back into your pocket.

In addition, if you have a plan and are forced out of your current job earlier than expected, you can quickly revisit the plan to determine whether you must continue to work, and if so, to what extent.

I've seen this occur first-hand many times. Gale and Kurt are a good example. They ran a small business and were thinking of selling it. When we put together their plan, they realized the amount they would receive was not enough to continue their desired retirement lifestyle. They rallied and focused on building the business. A few years later, Kurt passed away, rather unexpectedly. Because we had a framework in place, Gale was able to evaluate her options fairly quickly. She couldn't run the business on her own, so she located a buyer, sold the business, and went to work part-time for a former employer doing something she enjoyed. The decisions were stressful, but the stress was minimized because she and her husband had taken the time to do the planning ahead of time. She knew human capital had to be part of her plan for several more years. It was just a matter of figuring out how that was going to happen.

Summary

The traditional view of retirement is not for everyone. It is also not affordable for everyone. You need to figure out whether you are wired for traditional retirement, and whether you can afford it, and build your retirement plan around the answers.

Human capital—defined as your ability to generate income—can help fill in any gaps. Your human capital is a valuable resource. You can look for ways to make the most of this resource, just as you would look for ways to make the most of your financial resources. Explore ideas now on how to continue to use your human capital even in retirement.

Chapter 12

Whom to Listen To

And How to Avoid Fraud

"If you think it's expensive doing business with a professional, just wait until you do business with an amateur."

—Anonymous

Not everyone needs a financial advisor, but certainly everyone needs smart financial advice. So where do you find it?

The media can be a source of broad, generic advice. However, the media knows nothing about your personal situation. I'll never forget one investor calling me once and asking, "Do you have municipal bonds?"

"Yes," I replied. "Why do you ask?"

"Well," she said, "they told me I needed municipal bonds."

I was a bit confused, as I was her financial advisor, so I apprehensively said, "Do you mind telling me who 'they' is?"

"Oh," she said, "you know—the people on TV."

For numerous reasons, including her tax bracket and the types of accounts she had, other investments were more appropriate for her than municipal bonds. The TV host, however, didn't provide specifics—only an overview of municipal bonds and the fact that they paid tax-free interest.[153] This woman heard "tax-free" and thought it must be something she should pursue. The media doesn't know you. I don't know you either. I have tried throughout this book to show you how smart planning can lead to better decisions. I have

---

153 Municipal bond interest is generally exempt from federal taxes, but some types of municipal bond interest may be subject to AMT (alternative minimum tax). If the bond is issued in the state you reside in, it may also be exempt from state income taxes.

tried to avoid prescribing specific advice because I am well aware that I do not know you. Advice is personal. It is delivered after a process of data gathering and analysis, and it relates to your situation.

You can educate yourself in numerous ways. By all means, use all forms of media to educate yourself; just don't mistake what you read, watch, or hear for advice.

Tip   Take what you hear from TV financial pundits with a grain of salt. They don't know you or your financial situation; the advice may or may not be relevant.

The Financial Advice Industry

In 1995, at age 23, I started my career as a financial advisor. I studied for 60 days and passed an exam. I was granted a Series 6 securities license. I didn't know much, and I didn't know that I didn't know much—but I was a financial advisor. This license granted me the right to sell mutual funds. That meant I could legally collect a commission on sales. I went to work.

As of 2011, there were about 350,000 financial advisors in the United States. About 94 percent of them (330,000) carry some type of insurance or securities license, which means they may legally be compensated in some way or another from selling investment or insurance products.[154] I started my career as part of this 94 percent.

I was earnest, believable, and genuine. I had never owned a home, didn't know anything about taxes, and had absolutely no perspective on what a bear market[155] could or would look like. Yet I was a financial advisor.

I believe a lot of financial advisors are like I was when I started my career: well-intentioned. Many of them are sincere, reliable, smart, and genuinely good people. However, the industry of financial advice still has a long way to go to reach maturity.

---

154 *Journal of Financial Planning* (July 2011), Stat Bank, p.14.
155 A bear market is defined as a period where the stock market goes down 20% or more, from peak to trough. From 1900–2008, bear markets have occurred 32 times, or about 1 out of every 3 years. The average length of a bear market is 367 days.

Take the CPA industry or the medical industry as an example. If you use the services of someone who is a CPA or an MD, you can be assured they have a minimum level of competence. That is currently not the case with the financial planning industry. There is fragmentation in how the industry is regulated, and there are numerous credentials and compensation structures.

As a consumer, your choices will dictate the evolution of this industry. If you demand a higher level of competence and choose to use the services of firms who provide it, then the industry will evolve and become more consumer focused. I look forward to watching this evolution and hope you make choices to help it move that direction.

This chapter covers a few practical steps you can take.

Don't Confuse Products with Advice

An investment product cannot solve a financial-planning problem any more than a drug can solve the problem of an unhealthy lifestyle. The right drug, prescribed after testing and diagnosis, may improve your health situation, and the right financial product, prescribed after testing and diagnosis, may improve your financial situation. But simply moving your money to a new slick investment is not going to accomplish much for you. Financial planning and investment advice are intricately intertwined, but they are not the same.

Many financial advisors—and the media—place far too much emphasis on investment selection and investment products and far too little emphasis on planning.

A 2012 paper by the Center for Retirement Research[156] concludes that financial advice

> [t]ends to focus on financial assets, applying tools that give prominence to the asset allocation decision ... and are often silent on the levers that will have a much larger effect on retirement security for the majority of Americans. These levers include delaying retirement, tapping housing equity through a reverse mortgage, and controlling

---

156 Alicia H. Munnell, Natalia Sergeyevna Orlova, and Anthony Webb, "How Important is Asset Allocation to Financial Security in Retirement?" Center for Retirement Research (April 2012). Available online at http://crr.bc.edu/wp-content/uploads/2012/04/wp-2012-13.pdf.

spending ... for many with substantial assets, these ... levers may be as powerful as asset allocation in attaining retirement security.

If planning decisions (which you can control) can be just as powerful as investment decisions (the results of which are outside of your control), it only makes sense to me that you should start by creating a plan.

A Morningstar paper titled "Alpha, Beta and Now ... Gamma" went to additional lengths to quantify the difference that smart financial planning can make, saying: "We estimate a retiree can expect to generate 29% more income" by "following an efficient financial planning strategy."[157] The efficient financial planning strategy this Morningstar paper goes on to describe encompasses much of what I have discussed in this book.

If you decide to seek professional help in planning your retirement, and the advisor begins by discussing their investment approach, which includes buying an annuity, a real estate investment trust, a life insurance policy, or any financial product, you should quickly recognize that these are product solutions. There is nothing wrong with a product solution if it is the result of smart planning. But if the planning work has not been done, think twice before you buy.

Tip   Make sure you have planned well before you buy any financial product.

You should also understand that when it comes to investment advice, all investment advice is not alike.

The National Bureau of Economic Research (NBER) conducted a research project in which they sent undercover auditors to investigate the type of advice you might receive from a typical advisor. It published the results of its study in a paper titled *The Market for Financial Advice: An Audit Study*.[158] The paper summarizes its purpose and conclusions in an excerpt that states: "We use an audit methodology where trained auditors meet with financial advisers and present different types of portfolios. . . . We document that advisers . . . encourage returns-chasing behavior and push for actively managed funds that have higher fees, even if the client starts with a well-diversified, low-fee

---

157 David Blanchett and Paul Kaplan, "Alpha, Beta and Now ... Gamma," Morningstar (September 8, 2012).
158 Sendhil Mullainathan, Markus Noeth, Antoinette Schoar, The Market for Financial Advice, the National Bureau of Economic Research (March 2012). Available online at http://papers. nber.org/papers/w17929.

portfolio." This NBER study defines the typical advisor as an "advisor whom the average citizen can access via their bank, independent brokerages, or investment advisory firms."

Michael Kitces, an industry expert, took a look at this study and said, "... a look under the hood reveals a significant methodological flaw with the NBER study—simply put, they failed to control for whether the people they sought out for advice actually had the training, education, experience, and regulatory standards to even be deemed advisors in the first place, and in fact appear to have sampled extensively from a pool of salespeople with little or no advisory training or focus."

Or as Wade Pfau put it, this study "tended to investigate brokers who could be better characterized as salespeople rather than advisors."

What stood out to me about the NBER paper's conclusion is that when it comes to investing, there is in fact a definition of "good advice", and as a general rule much of the industry is not delivering it.

Until the industry matures, if you seek professional advice, it is going to take some work on your part to find an advisor who offers meaningful planning advice and takes an investment approach that fits the definition of "good advice."

Before you seek such services, the first question to tackle is do you need an advisor?

Do You Need an Advisor?

I am a financial advisor, and I own a firm that delivers financial advisory services. So I am clearly biased in my opinion on whether someone needs professional assistance with their retirement planning. Thus, I would like to share someone else's thoughts on this question.

I am fan of the online advice website Oblivious Investor (www.obliviousinvestor.com), written by Mike Piper. Mike also has a series of books that he describes as "somewhat akin to Cliffs Notes for personal finance topics." I've read two of his books and recommend them.

In his book *Can I Retire?*, Mike states that "... most investors do not need a financial advisor if they're willing to take the time to learn all the ins and outs."

But he adds that "as an investor gets closer to retirement the usefulness of an advisor increases dramatically."

I agree with this. Not everyone needs an advisor. But I have seen first-hand that when it comes to the permanent and irrevocable decisions you need to make as you near retirement, smart advice can provide results that are measurable in dollars and provide additional retirement security.

Another factor to consider is how you want to spend your time. I know I am perfectly capable of doing my own tax return, yet I don't. I am also capable of cleaning my own home, but I don't. I happily pay for these services and feel like I get a great value for the price. If you hire an advisor, this is the way you should feel about it—that you are getting a service that is worth the price you pay. Let's see how you can come close to ensuring you get the advice you deserve.

How to Find Advisors

How do you find an advisor who has expertise and can provide the type of planning you need? Start by understanding what credentials to look for, what compensation models an advisor may use, and what to look for when you interview an advisor.

Advisor Credentials

Last I looked, there were over 75 possible credentials, or letters, that financial advisors could place after their names. That's like looking for a doctor and having 75 different versions of MD. How do you know which credentials signify that advisors have truly taken steps to further their education and provide exemplary advice?

There are several credentials that stand out. It doesn't mean the rest are bad, but if I were looking for a financial advisor, the following are what I would look for: CFP, PFS, CFA, or RMA.

Certified Financial Planner or CFP®

To earn a CFP designation[159], professionals must pass a two-day comprehensive exam that shows they have knowledge about many areas of financial plan-

---

159 Author disclosure: I have been a CFP since 2003.

ning, including taxes, insurance, retirement planning, investments, and estate planning. To use the CFP designation, they must fulfill three years of relevant financial planning work experience. They must also agree to adhere to the CFP Board's ethics requirements. To keep their designation they must keep up with ongoing continuing education requirements.

HOW TO FIND A CERTIFIED FINANCIAL PLANNER

The Financial Planning Association (FPA)[160] offers a Planner-Search tool on its website that can help you locate an advisor who has a CFP. You can narrow your search by location, compensation method, and area of specialty. To start your search visit: http://www.plannersearch.org/.

Personal Financial Specialist or PFS designation

If you need advanced tax advice, you may want to find an advisor who is a PFS. This designation may only be acquired by a CPA (Certified Public Accountant). To first become a CPA one must have a bachelor's degree, have passed the Uniform CPA Exam, and have two years of general accounting experience supervised by a CPA. Then, to acquire the PFS, the CPA must have an additional 80 hours of personal financial-planning education (across nine defined areas), gain two years of full-time experience in personal financial planning, and pass the six-hour comprehensive PFS exam. (Candidates who already have their CFP are exempt from the exam requirement.)

Chartered Financial Analyst or CFA

This designation is particular to the investment management piece of financial planning. If you have advanced investment-management needs—for example, you may own a big chunk of stock or stock options through your employer, be an officer of a publicly traded company, or have inherited complex investments—then you may want to find someone who either has a CFA or has a

160 Author disclosure: I am a member of FPA and have been since around 2003.

CFA as part of their team. To become a CFA, an advisor must pass three levels of exams, each requiring an estimated 250 hours of study, hold a bachelor's degree or have equivalent work experience, and have four years of acceptable professional work experience.

Searching for professionals with these designations will lead you to the highest-quality advisors. There is one additional designation I would like to mention, because it is near and dear to my heart, and this book would not have come about if I did not have it: the Retirement Management Analyst designation.

Retirement Management Analyst or RMA®

In 2010, the Retirement Income Industry Association (RIIA)[161] began to offer the RMA designation. I immediately signed up, completed the education program, and was in the first class to take the RMA exam. This book would not have come about were it not for what I learned through the RMA educational materials and the presentations I have attended at RIIA conferences. Visit http://riia-usa.org/ to learn more about this organization.

Once you have found an appropriately credentialed advisor, you should take steps to verify your advisor's credentials and check their complaint record.

Verify Credentials and Complaint Record

The world is full of people who are not who they say they are. Taking a few precautionary steps can help you steer clear of them. I would advise you take these steps even if you know someone well. Many prominent cases of fraud take place in close-knit groups of people where trust is automatically given— church groups or country clubs, for example.

First, verify your advisors' credentials. Ask them what regulatory agency oversees their business. If they carry a securities license, the answer will be FINRA (Financial Industry Regulatory Authority). You can use FINRA's online Broker-Check feature to make sure your advisor is listed and make sure there are no complaints on file: www.finra.org/Investors/ToolsCalculators/BrokerCheck/.

If your advisor does not carry any securities licenses, they are probably regulated by the SEC (Securities and Exchange Commission) or a state securities

---

161 Author disclosure: I am a member of RIIA and served as the Chair of its Peer Practitioner Review Committee, which reviews peer-written articles for potential publication in the Retirement Management Journal.

commission. Either way, you can use the Investment Advisor Search feature on the SEC website to check out both advisors and their firms at http://www. adviserinfo.sec.gov/IAPD/default.aspx.

Note   Some advisors are *dually registered*, which means both FINRA and the SEC or a state securities agency have oversight over their business.

If your advisor is a CFP, visit the CFP Board's search feature, type in that person's last name, and verify the advisor has the credential he or she claims to have at www.cfp.net/search/.

There are also specific questions you can ask to determine if your advisor has expertise in the areas that are relevant to your situation. The following questions will help you learn more about your advisor:

- *"Tell me about your ideal client."*: You want someone who has expertise working with someone like you. If you're about to retire, and they tell you they work with young families, maybe this isn't the person for you. Find a financial advisor whose ideal client sounds very similar to your situation in terms of age, stage of life, and asset level.

- *"How long have you been practicing as a financial advisor?"*: If any of your advisors are new to the field, find out if they are part of a team where a more experienced advisor oversees their work.

- *"Can you provide tax-planning advice?"*: Many large brokerage firms and banks limit the topics their advisors may address. If you want someone who is fully aware of the tax implications of their recommendations, make sure this falls within the scope of what they can discuss with you.

Learn About Compensation Structures

Currently, there is no standard pricing model in the financial services industry. As a consumer, that can make it difficult to compare services.

I began my career as an advisor who worked on a commission basis and then transitioned to a fee-based model. When I became a partner in my own firm, I made a commitment to practice as a fee-only advisor. Let's take a look at each of these compensation models and what you might expect.

Commissions

Under a commission structure, when you buy an investment or insurance product, your financial advisor receives a commission for the sale of that product.

Take the case of something called an *A share* mutual fund. You may pay a 5.75% upfront sales load on this type of fund on purchase amounts up to $25,000, with the sales load dropping to 3.5–4% for purchase amounts of $100,000. That means on a $100,000 investment, you just paid $3,500–$4,000. Did you get any meaningful planning work for that fee? Do you receive ongoing tax planning and financial counseling for that fee? Usually the answer is no.

Advisors who are compensated by commissions may have a limited set of investment products to choose from. I have met advisors under this model who sell only variable annuities, only mutual funds, only indexed annuities, or only life insurance. They know their products inside and out, but all too often. they have limited knowledge of the choices available to you outside of their product line.

When I have a need for a specialized product, there are times—usually for the purchase of insurance products—when I refer business to commissioned advisors. If you have already determined the type of investment product you need, the right commissioned advisor may be a great resource to help you sift through the choices in that product line, but they may not be the best resource in helping you design your overall plan.

Fee-Only Methods of Compensation

Fee-only means the financial advisor cannot be compensated by commissions. You may write a check for their services, or they may debit their fees from an account that they manage on your behalf—either way it is clear that they work for you.

You will find various forms of pricing arrangements with fee-only advisors.

Hourly Rate

With an hourly pricing structure, you are paying for your advisor's time. Most advisors who charge hourly will provide you an up-front estimate of the amount of time it may take to deliver the advice you need.

When we encounter complex situations in our firm—for example, a couple who has previous marriages, each with children from previous marriages, numerous properties and/or business interests, and a plethora of investment accounts and holdings—it can easily take 50–100 hours of our time to put together a comprehensive plan.

For a single person with one retirement account and one home, it may take only five to ten hours.

With hourly pricing, much like that of an attorney or CPA, rates vary with the experience level of the advisor. You may expect to pay somewhere between $100 and $300 an hour.

TO FIND AN ADVISOR WHO USES AN HOURLY COMPENSATION STRUCTURE

If you want an advisor who charges hourly, start your search with the Garrett Planning Network (www.garrettplanning-network.com). This is an organization of advisors who charge an hourly rate for their professional services. The website offers a search feature where you can seek a member advisor in your area.

Percentage of Assets

Under this method of compensation, an advisor will handle the opening and management of all your accounts and may also offer financial-planning advice along with investment advice. Their services are charged as a percentage of your account value, which may range from about .5–2% per year. Ask an advisor for their fee schedule, because usually the more assets you have, the lower their rates. Many advisors have minimum account sizes that must be met, so you may also want to inquire about minimums before you meet with an advisor.

There is often a vast difference in services delivered between brokers who want to put you in a fee-based account model (and who often can't provide tax-planning advice) and registered investment advisors,[162] who are typically more focused on holistic wealth management. At my firm we do far more than put an account into a model and rebalance once a year. We update their plan, manage assets at a household level in a way that reduces their annual taxes, provide annual tax projections, and match their investment needs to their retirement cash flow needs. It takes far more hours than most people think, and we keep people from making horrible mistakes with their money. Not everyone is cut out to do their own financial planning and investing. For those who aren't, 1% is cheap.

As you age, you must also consider your spouse. You may be well qualified to manage your finances and investments on your own, but whose hands might your spouse end up in when you are gone? It may be better for you to select the appropriate firm and build a relationship with them rather than leave such a thing up to chance.

Per Plan Pricing

Some advisors charge per financial plan. They quote you a specific price that covers a particular set of services, such as $2,500 for a plan, recommendations, and a defined number of meetings.

Retainer Fees

Many boutique advisory firms charge an annual or quarterly retainer fee that includes unlimited access to them and may also include investment management services. Pricing for this type of service can vary depending on the minimums of the advisor.

---

162 Not sure exactly what a registered investment advisory firm is? See Schwab's RIA Stands For You website to learn more at www.riastandsforyou.com.

FINDING A NO-COMMISSION ADVISOR

Regardless of the pricing structure, to find a fee-only advisor who cannot be compensated from the sale of investment or insurance products, visit NAPFA's (National Association of Personal Financial Advisors) website at www.napfa.org. NAPFA is a member organization of fee-only financial advisors. They require applicants to submit documentation and a written sample of their work before becoming a member. The website offers a search feature where you can seek such a fee-only advisor in your geographic area.[163]

Fee-Based

Many financial advisors currently practice in a structure called *fee-based*, which can be confused with *fee-only*. They are not the same.

A fee-based advisor may charge a percentage of your assets and/or collect a planning fee for putting together a financial plan for you, but may also be able to collect commissions or receive bonuses from their company depending on what type of investments or insurance products they recommend to you.

Many fee-based models have broker-dealers who put together portfolio models that dictate which funds or investments are placed in your account. In addition to the advisor's fee, you need to look at the average expense ratio of any investments that will be used in your account.

Some advisors choose to practice as fee-based rather than fee-only because the fee-based model gives them access to a suite of annuity and life insurance products that may be quite appropriate for their clients, and they can then be compensated for researching and recommending these products.

---

163 Author disclosure: I am a member of NAPFA and have been since 2006.

TO FIND AN ADVISOR WHOSE CREDENTIALS HAVE ALREADY BEEN VERIFIED

The Paladin Registry (www.paladinregistry.com) offers a service which pre-qualifies financial advisors based on a set of specific criteria that they have developed. If an advisor meets the requirements, the Paladin Registry then verifies the advisor's credentials and compliance background. If everything checks out, the advisor becomes eligible to be listed. Advisors in the Paladin Registry are not limited to a particular compensation method, but their compensation structure is fully disclosed in their listing.

Which Compensation Model Is Best?

I have met fabulous advisors who work under all compensation models. Personally, after practicing in all three ways, I am partial to the fee-only model. I feel that it is free of many of the conflicts of interest[164] that come along with other compensation models. Fee-only advisors, however, are not entirely free of biases. Many commissioned advisors accuse fee-only advisors of neglecting to place enough emphasis on solutions like annuities or insurance.

Ultimately, the right advisor and compensation model for you depends on your needs. Yet sorting through various compensation models and comparing services can be challenging.

For example, one advisor may charge you 1.5% of the value of your investment portfolio per year. This price may include making limited financial planning recommendations, such as suggesting you fund a Roth or Traditional IRA. There may be additional underlying expenses in the mutual funds inside your account, so total expenses may be 2–2.5% per year.

---

164 See 2015 study "The Effect of Conflicted Advice on Retirement Savings" at: https://www.whitehouse.gov/sites/default/files/docs/cea_coi_report_final.pdf.

The next advisor may charge 1% a year, use low-fee mutual funds, and include a full suite of financial-planning services in this price. With this advisor, you may be paying less and getting more in terms of meaningful planning advice.

In those two scenarios, clearly advisor number two offers a better value.

The next advisor may charge an hourly rate, but it's up to you to implement their financial-planning and investment recommendations on your own. I have had many frustrating experiences working with clients on an hourly basis, only to discover when they next came to visit me that they did not follow any of my recommendations. If you are the type of person who will follow through and implement the advice that is given, hourly advice might be appropriate.

Pricing models may change over the next few years due to a Department of Labor Conflict of Interest Rule[165] that passed in April 2016, but it will likely take many years to see how this rule impacts the industry and the way it charges for its services.

You must determine what services you want or need, how you want to pay for it, and how much of it you are willing to do yourself.

Note   According to author and consultant Bill Bacharach, "Price is only an issue in the absence of value. You may not necessarily want to say, 'I'm looking for the lowest-cost approach to achieving my dreams and goals.'"

Interviewing Advisors

Once you understand the credentials and compensation models you will encounter, the next step is the interview process.

Traditionally, people look for an advisor in their geographic area so they may meet face-to-face, but with technology today, you can work with an advisor located just about anywhere, as long as they have the proper credentials or licenses to work with people in your state. (It is the advisor's responsibility to make sure they can work with you.)

---

165 https://www.dol.gov/ebsa/regs/conflictsofinterest.html

Two questions can help you gauge the financial advisor's communication and planning style.

"Can you explain [pick a financial concept] to me?"

You want to work with someone who can explain financial concepts to you in language you can understand. If an advisor speaks over your head, or their answer makes no sense and they do not respond well to additional questions, move on. Here are a few concepts you should have learned from this book that you could inquire about:

- What do you think of index funds?

- How do you determine how much of my money should be in stocks versus bonds (or high-risk versus lower-risk investments)?

- How do you help me determine what types of accounts I should contribute to, such as an IRA or Roth IRA?

- What do you think of annuities?

- What is sequence risk and what steps do you take to minimize its effects?

"What assumptions do you use when running retirement planning projections?"

All financial-planning projections are based on assumptions about the rate of return your investments will earn, the pace of inflation, taxes, and your personal spending habits.

If you prefer safer, more conservative investments, and an advisor runs a financial plan projecting your investments will grow at 10% a year, you have a problem. This assumption makes the future look rosy, but it's make-believe. You need realistic projections to make appropriate decisions.

You want to find someone who uses a conservative set of assumptions; after all, you'd rather end up with more than what is on paper, not less.

The following are a set of realistic financial-planning assumptions, which should be adjusted according to your personal circumstances and changes in the general economy:

- *Investment returns:* About 5–7% a year (this is the expected return after all investment fees) on average[166]

- *Inflation rate:* About 3% a year on average

- *Increase in value of real estate assets:* 2–3% a year on average

- *Tax rates:* Based on your income and investment situation. For example, if you have a large sum of money in retirement accounts, you will pay taxes on that money as it is withdrawn. That puts you in a completely different tax situation than someone who has a large sum of money that is not in retirement accounts. This needs to be considered when running financial-planning projections.

In lieu of seeking professional help, you may want to do your own planning and investing. If you are comfortable with numbers and complex financial decisions, you can use Excel to lay out your plan just as I have done throughout this book.

Do It All Yourself

You can do your own planning if you are so inclined. To do it well, you'll either need to subscribe to the same types of software that professionals use or have the ability to build detailed spreadsheet models on your own.

I still find Excel to be the most versatile and useful program ever designed. You have seen samples of Excel worksheets through this book. What I like about Excel is that I can see exactly what is happening and create reports to illustrate the specific information that I think is relevant.

If you build a retirement income model in Excel, the most difficult part will be accurately assessing taxes. You could take your model and ask your accountant or CPA to help you with assessing the tax consequences of various distribution options. They have access to tax-projection software that would be useful for this type of planning.

In our firm, we use three primary tools to run retirement income projections:

---

166 In my firm we run our projections at a 5% return. I want a plan that works based on the worst one-third of historical outcomes, not one that works only if we get average or above average returns.

- *Finance Logix:* Finance Logix offers fantastic tutorials, a dynamic interface that allows you to see the effects of different decisions, and the ability to link your investment accounts to the software so that account balances update in real time whenever you log in to review your plan. Finance Logix also offers Retire Logix, a free downloadable that can be fun to play around with. Visit www.retirelogix.com or www.financelogix.com for details.

- *BNA Tax Planner:* BNA Tax Planner allows us to run detailed tax projections to see whether one course of action might result in a lower tax liability than another. It incorporates all the relevant state tax rules as well as AMT calculations. For additional information visit www.bnasoftware.com/Products/BNA_Income_Tax_Planner/Index.asp.

- *Social Security Timing:* Social Security Timing helps us take a detailed look at someone's potential Social Security claiming decisions. For additional information visit www.socialsecuritytiming.com. (For consumers there are several Social Security software packages you can use to help with this decision. Find one at my Social Security Calculator list on About.com at http://moneyover55.about.com/od/socialsecuritybenefits/tp/Best-Social-Security-Calculators.htm.)

Anyone can subscribe to these various software packages. You will spend several thousand dollars a year to do so, and you will need to spend additional time to learn how to use them effectively.

There are also many free online retirement calculators. I think these are great tools to give you a general sense of how well prepared you may be for retirement. However, the free calculators do not offer the functionality needed to create an accurate retirement income plan.

Regardless of how you do your planning, I do hope you plan.

One additional thing you'll want to plan for is how to detect and avoid fraud.

Avoiding Fraud

People who conduct fraud are often charismatic and engaging and find it easy to gain people's trust. I could fill an entire chapter with the stories of fraud I have personally seen. I will share just a few of them with you and then provide tips you can use to avoid these situations.

The Outright Lie

If you haven't heard of him, Bernie Madoff is the former chairman of the NAS-DAQ stock market and the man who ran what is considered to be the largest financial scam in U.S. history. It came unraveled in December 2008, when he was arrested. Many families lost their entire life savings in this scandal.

These losses could have been avoided by following two simple rules. The first rule has to do with understanding what is and is not realistic.

There was at least one person who understood this rule and tried, unsuccessfully, to get authorities to look into the Madoff situation for many years. His name was Harry Markopolos, and he is often credited as the man who figured out Madoff's scheme.

Markopolos has said, "As we know, markets go up and down, and his only went up. He had very few down months. Only four percent of the months were down months. And that would be equivalent to a baseball player in the major leagues batting .960 for a year. Clearly impossible. You would suspect cheating immediately."[167]

I heard the story of Bernie Madoff and Harry Markopolos at a conference in March of 2012, from a man named Frank Casey. Frank worked closely with Harry Markopolos, and he was speaking at this conference to tell the story that he and Harry detail in their book *No One Would Listen: A True Financial Thriller* (Wiley, 2011). It is really a fascinating story.

As Frank Casey so aptly put it, "How do you compete with a lie?"

I've come up against the lie many times. I have not yet found an effective way to compete against it. It's difficult because it's a lie everyone wants to believe in. I can present all the logic in the world, but when some unscrupulous advi-

---
167 "The Man Who Figured Out Madoff's Scheme," CBS News (March 1, 2009).

sor promises 12% returns with little downside risk, it is often with a sense of helplessness that all I can do is stand by and watch a client lose money. If you understand that no one, no matter how smart, can game the system, you'll be more skeptical of people who claim they can.

The second rule investors can use to avoid the Madoff-type scam is to only use advisors that use third-party custodians. The custodian is the company that generates your account statements. In Madoff's case, he could generate his own account statements, which meant he could make up what they contained. Contrast that with the typical structure of a registered investment advisor that uses a third-party custodian, like Charles Schwab, Fidelity, T.D. Ameritrade, or Pershing. The advisor can direct the investments, but the custodian reports directly to the client. With this structure, an advisor has no ability to make up what the statement says.

Returns That Are Too Good to Be True

The first lie about returns I encountered was in 2007. One of my clients, a railroad engineer, came in to meet with me a month before he retired. He told me he wasn't going to need to withdraw his monthly retirement income from his IRA as we had planned.

"Why?" I asked, rather intrigued. I wondered if he'd changed his mind about retiring.

He replied that he'd invested $100,000 in a currency-trading program that was paying him $5,000 a month. He showed me the checks he had been receiving.

I got a sick feeling in my stomach. I knew the math didn't add up. At $5,000 a month, that's $60,000 a year, on a $100,000 investment. No one can deliver those kinds of returns. But how do you explain this to someone who has checks in their hand?

Within six months, this client's currency trading program was discovered to be a scam, and the perpetrators were arrested. I wasn't surprised.

After netting out the checks he had received, and the tax deduction for the fraud loss, he ended up about $50,000 poorer. Luckily, the rest of his retirement money remained invested in a balanced portfolio of no-load index funds, so his overall retirement security wasn't affected.

Appealing to Your Ego

On another occasion I watched a former client of mine get scammed out of nearly $4 million. The perpetrator did what con artists are good at: they appealed to his ego. They told him he would have access to exclusive investments only available to high net worth individuals. They also told him their firm would handle everything for him: his legal work, accounting, and investments. In hindsight, this makes sense. It keeps other expert eyes from questioning what is being done.

In his case, he moved his investments to this new firm. A few years later, he came back in to see me with a stack of papers in hand, asking me to help him figure out what had happened. I read, and I read some more. I turned white as chalk as I kept reading. Four million dollars—nearly all of his money—was gone. I immediately sent him to see an attorney who specialized in these types of cases.

The Family Friend

Con artists are skilled at finding people who are trusting and vulnerable. You may be savvy, but what about your spouse?

Henrietta's husband Frank passed away when she was 78. They had an impressive collection of original art worth millions.

Sam, a friend of Frank's, reached out to Henrietta after Frank's death. He offered to buy her art collection. Henrietta didn't seek legal counsel because she'd known Sam for a long time. Why would she need an attorney? She trusted him.

They negotiated a purchase price of $3 million to be paid to Henrietta on a schedule of $25,000 a month for the next 10 years.

About a year after this deal was finalized, Henrietta was referred to me by her accountant. I reviewed the documents associated with the art sale. Something wasn't right. The sale agreement lacked professionalism, did not follow basic accounting principles, and was missing important legal clauses. But Henrietta was receiving checks.

A year later, the checks stopped. Sam was nowhere to be found. Henrietta was finally able to track him down, at which time he told her he was going through financial difficulties, and that he would send her money as soon as he could. She waited. A few months later he sent one additional payment. Then nothing more.

It wasn't until she hadn't received a payment for two years that I was able to convince Henrietta to hire an attorney and pursue litigation. She kept telling me that Sam was a friend. She wanted to give him the benefit of the doubt. Henrietta was 82. Of course she didn't want the hassle. Who would expect to have to sue a family friend at 82?

But who would guess a family friend would prey upon a 78-year-old widow, blatantly stealing millions?

What to Look Out For

According to the Center for Retirement Research at Boston College, fraud is on the rise. Its report "The Rise of Financial Fraud,"[168] provides a list of Fraud's Red Flags. If you encounter one of these, just say no. It doesn't matter how nice the person is. Just say no.

Fraud's Red Flags

Investments may be fraudulent if they:

- Look too good to be true.

- Offer a very high or "guaranteed" return at "no risk" to the investor.

- Require an urgent response or cash payment.

---

168 Kimberly Blanton, "The Rise of Financial Fraud: Scams Never Change, but Disguises Do," the Center for Retirement Research (February 2012), No. 12-5. Available online at http://crr.bc.edu/wp-content/uploads/2012/02/IB_12-5-508.pdf. Used with permission.

- Charge a steep up-front fee in return for making more money on an unspecified date.

- Suggest recipients do not tell family members or friends about the offer.

- Lure prospective investors with a "free lunch."

- Come unsolicited over the Internet, are of unknown origin, or come from overseas.

- Instill fear that a failure to act would be very costly.

- Cannot be questioned, inspected, or checked out further.

- Are so complex that they are difficult or impossible to understand.

In addition to protecting yourself from fraud, you may want to keep an eye out for elderly family members and neighbors. The story of one of my own family members illustrates why.

Aunt B

It was mid-summer. Dad called to give me an update on Aunt B. Aunt B, at 94, was a spirited and intelligent woman. She'd had a fulfilling career as a professor, had never married, and had managed to save a significant amount of money.

Over the past few years, her hearing and sight had become impaired, and a medical condition developed which meant Aunt B needed 24-hour-a-day in-home care.

Aunt B did not want to use an agency to provide care. She lived in a small town in a rural area and wanted local help. She found a young woman who said she and two of her friends would be willing to provide in-home care services. They started coming around to stay with Aunt B regularly.

Dad had power of attorney over Aunt B's financial affairs and lived about 15 miles away. The first problem arose when Aunt B decided it would be a great idea to write a $60,000 check to help a local failing business stay afloat. Dad investigated—and overruled. Aunt B was furious. We found out later that the business was owned by the spouse of one of the caregivers.

Dad continued to investigate and soon realized that the three caregivers had managed to drain over $300,000 out of Aunt B's accounts within a matter of months.

When Dad tried to explain the situation to Aunt B, she became angry and adamantly defended the actions of her caregivers.

Dad brought in the police and an attorney. Despite clear explanations, Aunt B insisted that the caregivers were only going through a naughty spell, and that they should be forgiven and rehired.

The attorney, who was familiar with these types of cases, explained to us how these situations develop. Homebound people often forge close bonds with their caregivers. The caregiver becomes the eyes, ears, and primary news source for the homebound person and thus can exert great influence. The caregivers can screen phone calls, mail, and outside information so their patient is only exposed to the information they want them to see.

Aunt B was nearly blind. They would present her with checks for services like lawn care or house cleaning. She would sign the checks, which were often made out directly to the caregivers. They also ordered new appliances, tools, and other household items, all delivered to their own homes, not to Aunt B's.

To perpetrate their fraud, they convinced Aunt B that Dad was out to get her money. Each time he stopped by, they would tell Aunt B that he was only there to look out for his own future inheritance. They had even talked Aunt B into changing her will to make the primary caregiver the main beneficiary (this was later remedied).

The scam would never have been discovered if Dad didn't randomly stop in at Aunt B's, ask questions, and poke around, even when she didn't want him to.

Unfortunately, because this type of crime is not a violent crime, even after law enforcement was brought in and the case went to trial, and despite the fact that the perpetrators were prior felons, they did not go to jail. They received a 15-year suspended sentence, which is like being on probation for 15 years.

The law is interesting when it comes to these things. We were told that if they had robbed a bank for the same amount they took from our aunt, they most certainly would have served time.

We also learned from the attorney general that they likely learned their techniques in prison, as strategies on how to defraud the elderly are passed along among the incarcerated. Apparently the elderly make easy prey, and someone trained to swoop in can do serious damage in a matter of weeks—then disappear.

Numerous people out there are trying to part you from your money. I found one book about them, *Snakes in Suits* by Paul Babiak and Robert D. Hare (HarperBusiness, 2006), to be most insightful in providing tips on how to identify these types of people in advance.

Tip   Keep an eye on your elderly friends and relatives. They can be easy prey for financial predators.

Snakes in Suits

If I mention the word *psychopath*, most likely a known killer such as Ted Bundy comes to mind. We think of psychopaths as deviants who maim and kill others for pleasure. The book *Snakes in Suits* provides insight into a different kind of psychopath—the kind found in the business world. These psychopaths may not be physically violent, but the destruction they cause is just as unthinkable.

According to the book, the psychopath's first goal is "to convince others of their honesty, integrity, and sincerity." Trust is often easy for a con artist to gain because they come across as charismatic, charming, and grandiose. My own experience with someone who was quite grandiose has changed my understanding of the word.

I used to think that if someone made grand claims, there must be some truth to them. After all, how could someone blatantly lie about such things when the truth would come out later? I've since learned that these types of people often lie because it is in their nature—they simply can't help it. They may have some type of mental illness that causes their destructive behavior. They also frequently believe their own lies, which makes it all the harder to detect them.

A good business con artist will appear passionate and give the illusion of having high ethical standards. They may ingratiate themselves with a church group and say they are on a mission, either for God or for the company or industry they work in. They'll often be a newcomer to a community you are involved in. They'll build trust quickly and say and do all the right things. They can make you feel incredibly special, and after they feel they've earned your trust, they may turn on you and question your own morality and values in an attempt to manipulate you. When they get what they want, they leave chaos behind.

How can you recognize them?

Snakes in Suits offers the following insights into the typical behavior of a business con artist:

- When challenged or asked questions about details, "he or she will simply shift gears, subtly change the topic and generally weave an altered tale" that is quite believable.

- They avoid answering direct questions.

- Their banter and dialogue is filled with "jargon, clichés, and flowery phrases" as well as inconsistencies and bad logic.

- They avoid taking responsibility for things that go wrong, always placing blame on something external—other people, circumstances, fate.

- They "spread disinformation in the effort of protecting their scam and furthering their own career" and "seize opportunities to bring harm to others' careers or professional standing."

Con artists are particularly skilled at eliciting emotional reactions in people. If you find yourself experiencing strong emotions around someone new in your life, be wary. Slow things down a bit. Get away from them so you can think clearly.

In addition, if someone you care about seems too quick to place unwarranted trust in someone new in their life, ask questions. If they get defensive, keep investigating.

Summary

Education is good, and I encourage you to learn all you can, but education is not advice. Investment and insurance products are needed solutions, but they in and of themselves are also not advice.

Advice is personal and appropriate to your individual circumstances, including your attitudes about risk. As I have often told my clients, I can have two families with identical financial circumstances, and after going through the same planning process they will make different decisions. That is exactly as it should be.

If you need professional advice, decide what type of advice you need and be sure to do a thorough job of interviewing and selecting the person you will hire. Investigate their credentials and make sure you understand their compensation model.

In addition, take steps to avoid fraud and teach others how to do the same. Scam artists could not get away with their cons if we were all trained to recognize the tell-tale signs.

Finally, however you do it, engage in the planning process. People don't ever plan to fail; instead they simply fail to plan. There is one more step in your planning process. It is a step you take for others more than for yourself. It is your estate plan.

Chapter 13

Estate Planning

Asset Transfer Goals

"What you leave in your children is more important than what you leave for them."

—Jon and Eileen Gallo

Henry had recently been to the doctor to have another outcrop of skin cancer taken care of and had a bandage on the side of his face. He and his wife were sitting in my conference room. He took his wife's hand and said to me, "I'll tell you, Dana, we've had a wonderful life. We have delightful children. We couldn't ask for anything more. But now, we're ready to go. We spend all our time going back and forth to the doctor's office. It's no fun. The only question I have now is "Why are we still here?""

In that moment I could feel what he felt, and it was something I had never experienced before. It was peace and contentment and acceptance all wrapped together. It was the first time I understood that there is a point in time where we may feel ready to go.

When you do go, I believe one of the best gifts you can leave your loved ones is the gift of having your affairs in order. I've had the experience of having many clients pass, and I can tell you it is a tremendous amount of work for those of us still here. A little planning can go a long way toward ensuring things go smoothly. It is also a gift to yourself - when things are in order you are free to feel calm and peaceful.

Estate planning doesn't have to be as cumbersome as you may think. Many people assume that estate planning means having a will (and possibly a trust) and that will take care of everything.

I've seen many errors arise out of this misconception that "estate planning = wills & trusts". The most common error I've seen is the belief that because you have a will and trust that everything is in order. This is far from the truth. In fact, for many of you, a will may be the least important part of your plan. It all depends on your family structure and what it is you want to accomplish.

Purpose

The idea of "having your affairs in order" sounds pretty simple. And it may be if you are still in your first marriage and only have children from this marriage. In this situation your goal is usually, "I want everything to go to my spouse and upon their passing, to my children in equal shares."

As your family situation gets more complex, the goals get more complex, and the necessary planning gets more complex.

The primary purpose of estate planning is leaving your assets according to your wishes, but within that broader purpose there are many other things you may want to accomplish such as:

- Eliminating or reducing estate taxes (doesn't apply to most of you)

- Avoiding probate (may not be as big a deal as it used to be)

- Reducing fees (some costs are inevitable)

- Maintaining privacy (probate files are public court records; other forms of asset transfer are not public)

- Making things easy for those who are wrapping up your affairs (requires having your documents, account registrations, asset titles, and beneficiary designations in order)

- Being fair (one family member may need more financial assistance than another)

- Maintaining control (especially regarding health care decisions and minor children)

- Making it easy for someone to pay your bills and household expenses if you are ill or incapacitated (this is really life planning not estate planning, but I'm including it here)

- Avoiding conflict (if you have a troublemaker in the family, there may be no way to avoid conflict regardless of the steps you take)

- Leaving a legacy (perhaps an annual scholarship given in your name or a charitable bequest)

- Protecting assets from your heirs' creditors (requires a certain type of trust)

- Providing for a special needs family member (requires a certain type of trust)

Once you know what you want to accomplish you can figure out the level of complexity that is needed.

Many of the estate planning goals on this list can be accomplished by properly structuring your account registrations, asset titles, and beneficiary designations.

Other goals may only be accomplished by working with a knowledgeable estate planning attorney to establish the proper types of legal documents and trusts.

By the end of this chapter you'll have a pretty good idea of the level of advice and complexity you may need in this area.

Nothing in this chapter is to be considered personal legal advice. What I am going to cover are the things that apply to most people, and the areas where I see the biggest mistakes occur. Here is what we'll be talking about:

- The estate planning you engage in without knowing you're doing it: account registrations, asset titles, and beneficiary designations

- Taxes

- Trusts

- Second marriages

- Other documents and things

The Estate Planning You Engage in Without Knowing You're Doing It

Each time you open an account, name a beneficiary on a retirement plan, or buy a car, you have engaged in some form of estate planning. I see more mistakes made here than anywhere else.

Many estate planning objectives can be accomplished by using these three things appropriately:

- Account registrations

- Property titles

- Beneficiary designations

The account registration determines how your property passes along. Many people do not realize that an account registration takes precedence over a will or trust. Let me explain.

Note   The terms "account registration" and "account title" may be used interchangeably. I am going to refer to "registration" as applying to financial accounts and "title" as applying to real property like real estate and vehicles.

Example

Let's assume you add your daughter as a joint tenant on your bank account. Your will (or trust) specifies that your money should be split evenly between your children. At death, what happens?

Legally that entire bank account belongs to your daughter regardless of what the will (or trust) says. A financial institution must pass assets along according to how the account is registered. Here are a few guidelines:

- If you register an account in a trust, then the terms of the trust control how the account is disbursed.

- If the account is registered only in your name, and you have a will, then the will controls how the account is disbursed.

- If you add a joint tenant, or some other formal account registration such as tenants in common, transfer on death, or payable on death, then that account registration takes precedence over the will or trust.

Types of Account Registrations

Here are a few examples of how accounts can be registered:[169]

- Your name (account will go through probate)

- Your estate (this occurs when you don't name a beneficiary on an account or life insurance policy, or when you name the beneficiary to "the estate of _____". This will mean the asset has to go through probate.)

- Joint tenants (with joint tenants both parties own the property equally)

- Joint tenants with rights of survivorship (JTWROS) (account automatically belongs to remaining joint tenant)

- Tenants in common (ownership does not have to be equal, upon your death your share will go through probate, other tenant's share continues to be owned by them)

- Community property[170] (applies to married couples in certain states)

- Transfer on death (TOD)/Payable on death (POD) (accounts pass directly to named beneficiaries at your death)

- Registered in the name of a trust that you have established

---

169 Note: IRAs, HSAs, and other retirement accounts cannot be titled in these ways. They must have one owner and will pass according to the beneficiary designation on file.

170 As of 2016, community property states are Arizona, California, Idaho, Nevada, New Mexico, Texas, Washington, Wisconsin, and in Alaska married couples may elect community property treatment.

Can't I Just Add My Son or Daughter to My Account?

As you get older, it is tempting to simply add someone as a joint tenant to your bank accounts and real estate. This may be fine if it is a small checking account. It can be problematic if it is a large investment account or if you are adding them to the title of your home or other piece of real estate.

Here are some things to consider before you add a joint tenant to an account or asset title:

- They can access and use the funds now, if they so choose.

- It is difficult to remove them if the nature of the relationship changes.

- Should they end up in an adverse financial situation their creditors can go after the asset.

- If the asset has capital gains (such as a home, mutual fund, or stock) the heir may not get a full step-up in cost basis upon your death (because they were a joint owner prior to your death). Step-up in cost basis is covered later in this chapter.

If your goal is to pass the asset along at death, for simple situations where you know exactly who you want the account (or house) to go to there is a great alternative to joint tenancy. It is called a "transfer on death" (TOD) or "payable on death" (POD) registration.

When Joint Tenancy is Fine

In practice, many older single people add a trusted family member or friend as a joint tenant to their household checking account (account used to pay bills and such). The advantage is that if you are ill, this person can pay bills and manage your household expenses, and can continue to do so after your death while affairs are being wrapped up. This is often the easiest, simplest solution as long as you are aware of the potential pitfalls already discussed.

LET THE RESPONSIBLE CHILD DIVVY THINGS UP

Every few years I meet a parent who thinks it will be easier to leave one of their accounts (or their home) to one child and let that child divvy it up among the other siblings. They tell me they have the kind of daughter (or son) who will do the right thing and divide the account equally. That may be so, but legally the account now belongs to that child so you are putting them in a position where they must now gift the appropriate portion to the other siblings. Depending on the value of the asset, they may run into trouble with both gifting limits and income taxes. Don't put an heir in this situation. Take the time to structure things so they pass directly to your intended beneficiaries.

POD/TOD/Designated Beneficiary

If your goal is for an asset to pass directly to someone (or to multiple people) there is a better way to accomplish this than adding them as a joint tenant. Financial institutions offer a *POD* (payable on death) or *TOD* (transfer on death) registration option.[171]

With this type of account registration, you are naming the specific beneficiaries that are to receive the asset. In this way, the asset passes directly to the named people upon your death, but while you are living you own the asset and retain control of it.

This type of registration:

- Avoids probate

- Preserves your heirs' ability to get a step-up in cost basis if that applies

- Leaves you in control of the asset while you are alive

---

171 Some financial institutions may have their own terminology for this type of account. Schwab, for example, calls it a "designated beneficiary" registration.

A couple can jointly own an account and still have designated beneficiaries on file.

For example, an account registration for a couple might look like this:

> Wally and Sally Sample, Designated Beneficiary Plan, TOD to John Sample and Suzy Sample.

In this case they would have designated that upon the death of the last joint tenant, John was to receive 50% of the account and Suzy was to receive 50% of the account.

This type of account registration does not allow someone to pay your bills or make decisions about the account if you are ill or incapacitated. If you want someone to have this capacity, options include a durable power of attorney, trust, or, in many cases, something simpler like a designated signer.

Designated Signer Accounts

Another alternative to joint tenant registration is to add a *designated signer* to your accounts. This person can write checks on the account, but they are not a co-owner. This means their creditors cannot go after the asset. It also means it is easy to remove them if that becomes necessary.

The designated signer registration doesn't spell out what happens to the account upon your death, but it does allow someone other than you to pay bills and write checks on the account while you are alive.

If You Have a Trust

We'll discuss trusts later in the chapter, but if you have one, unless your attorney advises otherwise, it is most likely that your financial accounts and real property need to be titled in the trust. More to come on this in the trust section.

PURPOSE OF YOUR CHOSEN ACCOUNT REGISTRATION

When thinking about account registrations, what is it you want to accomplish? If the goal is to pass the asset to the intended heir, a POD/TOD registration can accomplish this.

If the goal is to have someone who can pay your bills and household expenses should you be unable to, then your options are: joint registration, designated signer, signing a limited or durable power of attorney document, or establishing and funding a trust.

Property Titles

Most items applicable to account registrations also apply to real property — meaning tangible assets like your home and car.

For your real estate assets, many states now offer the option for you to prepare and file a transfer-on-death deed. Just like a transfer-on-death account registration, this deed names your beneficiaries, but you retain ownership while alive. This form of titling avoids probate, is easier to establish than setting up a trust, and avoids the problems that come with adding an adult child as a joint tenant.

Now that you understand the importance of account registrations and asset titles, it is time to move on to beneficiary designations, which also take precedence over a will or trust.

Beneficiary Designations

Accounts such as IRAs, 401(k)s, and other company retirement accounts all pass according to a beneficiary designation. Life insurance and annuities also pass according to a beneficiary designation. If you set up a POD or TOD account registration, that is also a form of a beneficiary designation.

No matter what your will or trust says, upon your passing a financial institution must distribute these types of accounts, policies, and annuities according to the most recent beneficiary designation on file.

Mistakes I Frequently See

Many people name beneficiaries and never update them. They often incorrectly believe a current will or trust will take care of it. Here are some mistakes I have seen:

- Ex-spouse still named as primary beneficiary on old retirement accounts or life insurance

- Parent or siblings named as a primary or contingent beneficiary when the intention is to have spouse/children named

- Children named as primary beneficiaries when the intention is to have assets pass directly to the current spouse

- Current spouse named as the primary beneficiary when intention is for some assets to pass directly to children from a previous marriage

- Improperly drafted trust named as beneficiary of a retirement account

When it comes to retirement accounts, your beneficiary designations have a big impact on the options available to your heirs. If you structure these beneficiary designations thoughtfully, your heirs will be able to "stretch" out distributions over many years.

"Stretch" Characteristics of IRAs and Roth IRAs

IRAs and Roth IRAs have some pretty cool features for your loved ones. One set of rules applies if your spouse inherits the IRA; another set of rules if it is a non-spouse beneficiary.

IRAs Passing to Spouses

A spouse who inherits an IRA has two choices:

1. Treat the inherited IRA as their own IRA (by either rolling the inherited IRA into their own account, or naming themself as the account owner), or

2. Remain the beneficiary of the IRA.[172]

The two choices have different consequences.

If you treat an inherited IRA as your own, then all the rules that apply to your IRA will apply.

For example, let's assume your spouse was 75 at death, and you are 65. As your spouse was over age 70½, they were taking their required minimum distributions (RMDs). Upon their passing, you roll their IRA over to your own (after taking their RMD for their final year) - now you will not have to take RMDs again until you reach age 70½.

If you remain the beneficiary then a different set of distribution rules will apply. You must take distributions at some point - that point will depend on how old the original account owner was upon their passing.[173] For a surviving spouse who has not yet reached age 59½, this second option may be preferable as, if needed, this option would allow them to take withdrawals in any amount, at any time, without a penalty tax.[174]

IRAs Passing to a Non-Spouse Beneficiary

A non-spouse cannot treat an inherited IRA as their own or roll it over into their own account. A non-spouse beneficiary of an IRA can take all the money out immediately if they would like to, although this may not be smart from a tax perspective.

---

172 When I say "remain the beneficiary" I mean it literally. This type of account has a registration that looks like this: "Sally Sample, Inherited IRA, Beneficiary of Wally Sample". Different rules apply than if it was just "Sally Sample, IRA".

173 Additional details on Inherited IRAs can be found in my About.com MoneyOver55 article, I Inherited an IRA: Now What, at: http://moneyover55.about.com/od/iras/a/I-Inherited-An-Ira-Now-What.htm

174 Whether it is a spouse or non-spouse beneficiary, no penalty tax applies to distributions from inherited IRAs.

If they want to take money out of the inherited IRA slowly, they must at least take distributions from the IRA according to their life expectancy, as spelled out in Table I of IRS Publication 590. This ability for beneficiaries to stretch out distributions over their life expectancy is often referred to as a "stretch IRA".

When naming beneficiaries for your IRA accounts, there are several things to keep in mind if you want your heirs to have the option to stretch distributions as long as possible.

- The easiest solution is when all beneficiaries are human beings (not trusts). The younger the beneficiary, the longer their ability to stretch out the distributions and income over their lifetime.

- If you name a trust as the beneficiary of your IRA, and all beneficiaries of the trust are human, the IRA may still stretch out the distributions - but now they must be distributed over the oldest beneficiary's lifetime. This may not be ideal if some beneficiaries are younger than others. However, when properly drafted, the trust structure may afford creditor protection to the beneficiaries.

- If you name a trust as the beneficiary of your IRA and not all beneficiaries of the trust are human (for example, a charity is one of the beneficiaries), this may void the ability to stretch out distributions.

Best Practice for Beneficiary Designations

If you are married, this is your first marriage, and there are no children outside of the marriage, then ideally your spouse is named as the primary beneficiary on all IRAs and retirement accounts. Assuming your children are all functioning adults, they can be named as contingent beneficiaries.

The legal concern with this structure is that upon your passing your spouse could re-marry, leave everything to their new spouse, and bypass your children. If this is a concern you may need a more complex structure (trust) to address this.

Consider a more complex structure if any of the following apply:

- You are in a second marriage and have children from previous marriages,

- You have minor children, or

- You have an adult child with dependency issues or special health needs.

Review Process

To avoid mistakes with account registrations, property titles, and beneficiary designations, you need a process in place to review them.

Keep a list of accounts, how they are titled, who the beneficiary is, and when they were last updated. At a minimum, review designations anytime a life change occurs such as marriage, divorce, new child or grandchild, a child gets divorced, or retirement. When you do so, think about your activities over the last few years. Have you bought anything new such as a car or home? Have you transferred accounts to a new financial institution? If so, make sure these new assets and accounts are properly titled.

For many people, properly structuring - and regularly updating - account registrations, property titles, and beneficiary designations can quite effectively accomplish the goal of passing things along to the intended recipients without a lot of complexity.

What about probate and taxes? Do you need additional planning to avoid probate or taxes? Let's take a look.

Probate

Probate is the process of proving that your stuff should go, and does go, where it is supposed to go. It applies to things that pass according to your will, things that have only your name on them, or accounts with no beneficiary.

By properly structuring your account registrations, asset titles, and beneficiary designations, most things you own can pass directly to the intended heir — which means they would not go through the probate process.

Here are a few examples of what would and would not go through probate:

- An account titled jointly with your spouse (or as community property) passes directly to your spouse without going through probate.

- If you have a bank account titled only in your name, it will be subject to probate.

- If you have an account titled in the name of a trust that you have established, the successor trustee takes over, and that account does not go through probate.

- If you established a trust, but did not change your account registration to the trust, then that account will be subject to probate.

- Personal belongings (such as an art collection, jewelry, boat, ATV, or motorhome, etc.) that are titled only in your name, will go through probate.

In some states, probate is expensive and can take a long time. In other states it is relatively simple and quick.

Many states have a "small estate" affidavit form that can be used to expedite the probate process when the dollar amount of assets going through probate is under a state set limit.

Often people confuse probate with taxes. Probate is a process, and sometimes fees are involved, but probate is not a tax.

When it comes to taxes, some types will apply, and some won't.

Taxes

Many people make decisions based on outdated rules and beliefs about taxes.

As you begin to organize your affairs, it is important understand if and how the following things apply to your situation:

- Estate taxes (federal and state)

- Inheritance taxes

- Income taxes

- Gift taxes

Estate Taxes

An estate tax is a tax assessed on the value of all things a deceased person owned. Estate taxes can be assessed at both the federal and state level, but there are currently less than 20 states that still impose their own estate tax.

Federal Estate Taxes

For federal estate taxes, as of 2016, the first $5,450,000 of stuff you own can be passed along free of estate taxes.[175] This $5,450,000 is referred to as the "exemption amount", and it is indexed to inflation.

For married couples, this exemption amount is portable, so any unused exemption amount can be ported or transferred to the surviving spouse. This means a married couple can thus pass along $10,900,000 estate tax-free. As you can see, under current estate tax law, the average person will not have to worry about estate taxes.

This large estate tax exemption amount and feature of "portability" came into law in 2010. Up until 2010 many couples used a certain type of trust structure referred to as an *A/B Trust* or *Family/Marital Trust* to reduce the potential impact of estate taxes.[176] If you have a trust established prior to 2010, consider having it reviewed in light of the changed rules.

State Estate Taxes

Many states have eliminated state-level estate taxes. You will have to check the rules in your state to see if they still impose such a tax. For those states who do impose an estate tax, just as with the federal estate tax, there is an exemption amount. This amount varies from state-to-state.[177]

Inheritance Taxes

Like state-level estate taxes, inheritance taxes are on the decline and are currently only assessed in a few states.[178] An inheritance tax is not the same thing

---

175 You can always pass along an unlimited amount to your spouse (assuming they are a U.S. citizen) with no estate tax applied.
176 This type of trust structure has other purposes beyond minimizing estate taxes. We'll discuss this in the trust section.
177 See About.com's "Wills & Estate Planning State Estate Tax and Exemption Chart" for additional details: http://wills.about.com/od/stateestatetaxes/a/stateestatetaxchart.htm.
178 See About.com's "Wills & Estate Planning State Inheritance Tax Chart" for additional details: http://wills.about.com/od/stateestatetaxes/a/inheritancetaxchart.htm.

as an estate tax. Each state that has an inheritance tax does it a bit differently, but in general it is dependent on who receives the property and their relationship to the person who passed.

For example, spouses are exempt from inheritance taxes. In some states descendants are exempt, while in other states they are not. Check with your state to see if it still imposes an inheritance tax.

Income Taxes

When you inherit assets, or pass along assets to heirs, there are two types of income taxes to be aware of; *capital gains taxes* and *ordinary income taxes* (such as the tax rate imposed on interest income and traditional IRA withdrawals).

Capital Gains Taxes

On a capital asset (such as a home, a stock, or a mutual fund) you have what is called your *cost basis*; what you paid for the asset (plus improvements or reinvested dividends). Upon your death, your heirs get what is called a "step-up" in cost basis which means their cost basis for tax purposes is the value of the asset at your date of death.[179]

Let's look at an example using your home.

Assume you bought your house many years ago for $100,000. Assuming no major improvements to the home, this $100,000 is your cost basis. Today the home is worth $400,000. Upon death, your heirs inherit the house worth $400,000 and immediately sell it. How much do they pay in taxes?

Assuming they sell the home for $400,000, they pay no capital gains taxes on the $300,000 of gain because their cost basis was stepped-up to the date of death value.

This step-up in cost basis can be voided by titling your property inefficiently. This happens frequently with the common practice of adding an adult child to the title of the house.

---

179 Your estate is valued at either your date of death value or by something called the "alternative valuation date" which is the market value of all assets six months after your date of death. All assets in your estate must be valued as of the same day. There is no ability to pick date of death valuation for one asset and the six months after valuation date for a different asset.

For example, let's say after your spouse passes, you add your son to the title of your home. Technically you have gifted him half the value of your home, and instead of the home passing to him at death, he co-owns it with you now.

This means he does not get that entire step-up in cost basis upon your death; only the interest attributed to you gets a step-up. Let's look at the numbers.

Assume the same facts: you paid $100,000 for the house, upon your death it is worth $400,000, and your son (who is listed on the title as a joint tenant) sells it for that amount.

Your half of the asset gets a step-up in cost basis, so your share of the house has a basis of $200,000. Your son's share, however, would have a basis of $50,000 (half your original basis). So he owes tax on $150,000 of gain. At a potential 20% cap gains tax rate, that is $30,000 in taxes owed.[180] This could have been avoided by having the asset transfer to him on death rather than using joint ownership.

This example applies to investment accounts (stocks, mutual funds) as well as property. This situation can easily by avoided by titling accounts more efficiently.

COMMUNITY PROPERTY STATES AND STEP-UPS IN COST BASIS

Some states use "community property" law which essentially says that property acquired during marriage is owned jointly. Property held as community property receives a step-up in cost basis on the entire property at the death of the first spouse.

For couples living in a community property state, one possible tax strategy may be to hold low basis assets for as long as possible. Upon the death of the first spouse those assets can then be repositioned with no tax consequences.

---

180 For those in community property states see this fantastic example by Financial Alternatives, "Should One Hold Appreciated Assets in Community Property or Joint Tenancy", at http://financialalternatives.com/wp-content/uploads/2014/02/How-Should-One-Hold-Appreciated-Assets.pdf.

Ordinary Income Taxes

Ordinary income taxes at death depend on whether a spouse or non-spouse is inheriting the asset. If your spouse is inheriting everything, they should have no major income tax consequences, but their filing status will change from married to single, so they may end up paying taxes on future income at a higher tax rate.

Assuming a non-spouse beneficiary (with the exception of the break on capital gains tax due to a step-up in cost basis) for the most part, if you would pay income taxes on it, your non-spouse heirs will pay income tax on it.

For example, as you take withdrawals from a traditional IRA, those withdrawals are taxed as ordinary income at your current tax rate. When your heirs inherit a traditional IRA, they pay ordinary income tax on any withdrawals they take at their current tax rate.

You've seen how the tax brackets work in Chapter 4, so you can see that it may not make sense for heirs to cash in an inherited traditional IRA all in one tax year. There could be a benefit to spreading out the distributions.

NO STEP-UP IN COST BASIS ON NON-QUALIFIED ANNUITIES

When someone inherits a non-qualified annuity (meaning an annuity that is not inside an IRA or other retirement account) they always have the option of withdrawing all the money right away. Gain (any amount in excess of cost basis) is considered to be withdrawn first and is subject to ordinary income taxes. When the beneficiary takes that withdrawal they will report it on their tax return, and it will be taxed at their marginal tax rate.

Heirs do not get a step-up in cost basis on non-qualified annuities. For example, assume you put $100,000 into a deferred annuity that is worth $200,000 when you pass. Your daughter was named as the beneficiary. She cashes in the annuity and reports $100,000 of taxable income on her tax

return. As non-qualified annuities are not eligible for a step-up in cost basis this $100,000 is taxed at ordinary income tax rates, not at capital gains tax rates.

To avoid a lot of extra taxable income in one year, it does not usually make sense for a beneficiary to withdraw a large chunk of money from this type of account all at once. Most of the time they have the option to "stretch" the distributions out over longer periods of time.

Things That Pass With No Income Tax

Roth IRA withdrawals are tax-free to you, and tax-free to your heirs (but the value of your Roth IRA account(s) will be included in your estate to determine the value of your estate for estate-tax purposes.)

Non-spouse beneficiaries of Roth IRAs are required to take distributions over their life expectancy. They can withdraw the money faster if desired, but as the distributions are tax-free, stretching them as long as possible usually makes sense.

Life insurance proceeds also pay out tax-free to your heirs. (But if you were the owner of the life insurance policy, the total death benefit is included in your estate to determine the value of your estate for estate-tax purposes.)

As life insurance pays out tax-free, if you don't need to use your required minimum distributions from your IRA for income, one option would be to consider using them to purchase a life insurance policy that pays tax-free proceeds to your heirs.

I have seen such strategies proposed many times by people who sell life insurance. Some of these strategies have merit; some don't. If you are considering such a strategy, you may want to have it evaluated by an advisor who doesn't benefit financially if you purchase the insurance.

Note Although income tax consequences may be minimal, if your assets exceed the estate tax exemption amount, estate taxes may be assessed. For those with large estates that contain illiquid assets like real estate and business interests, advanced planning is needed so a surviving spouse isn't forced to fire-sale assets to pay estate taxes. Life insurance can be a good solution for these situations.

Gift Taxes

Most of you will never have to be concerned with gift taxes, but you should know that if you give away too much to any one person in any one year, a gift tax return may need to be filed.

In 2016 you can give up to $14,000 per person per year to anyone, and you need not worry about filing a gift tax return. As a couple that means you can give up to $28,000 per year to each of your children ($14,000 from each of you.)

If you give away more than that, a gift tax return should be filed.

Example: Wally and Sally want to give their son John $100,000 for the purchase of a home. The first $28,000 is excluded because of the gift tax exemption. Although they file a gift tax return, no actual gift tax is owed on the next $72,000 because it "uses up" some of the estate tax exclusion amount of $5,450,000. After this gift, Wally and Sally would each still have a remaining estate tax exclusion amount of $5,414,000.[181]

As you can see, the gift tax is not going to be of concern to the average person. However, if you plan on gifting in excess of the annual gift exclusion amount then you should file a gift tax return.

Trusts

A *trust* is a legal tool, and when it is the right tool for the job, it should be used. However, like many tools, if it sits on the shelf for years without any maintenance, it may not work properly.

---

181 In this example the $72,000 gift amount that was in excess of the annual gift limit was presumed to be made half by Sally and half by Sam. So each of their estate tax exclusion amounts were reduced by $36,000.

You may have a trust that was set up years ago, for reasons that were valid at the time, but those reasons may not exist today. In these situations, the trust can add unnecessary complexity upon your death. This is why trusts, like other parts of your plan, must be reviewed every few years.

Let's start by looking at how a trust works and what it can accomplish.

Trust Basics

A trust is a legal document that provides instructions on how the assets in the trust are to be handled, and by whom they are to be handled.

There are three main parties to a trust:

- *Grantor* – the person or people whose property is going into the trust

- *Trustee* – the person or people in control of the trust assets

- *Beneficiary* – the person or people who will benefit from the trust assets or inherit the remaining assets one day

With the most common type of trust, called a *living trust* or *revocable living trust*, the grantor, trustee, and current beneficiary are the same set of people.

For example, let's say Wally and Sally Sample set up a revocable living trust. They consult with an estate planning attorney who drafts their trust document.

The title of their trust is "The Sample Family Revocable Living Trust, dated August 9, 2016." The trustees are Wally and Sally, so they can easily sign for and make decisions about any property in the trust while they are alive.

They are also the current beneficiaries of the trust, but upon their death (or in the event they are incapacitated) the trust names the successor trustees (people who can then make decisions), and it spells out what is to happen to the property in the trust, who it is to go to, and over what time-frame.

| Tip | "Revocable" means you can change the terms of the trust any time. Contrast this with an "irrevocable" trust where you cannot change the terms. Some trusts are structured so they are revocable while you are living, but become irrevocable upon your death. |

More Than the Trust Document is Needed

Once a trust document is completed, assets must be moved into the trust by changing the account registration and/or property titles to the trust.

It is astonishing to me the number of people who set up a trust, but don't change their account registrations or property titles to the trust. In this situation the trust can become a nearly useless document. It may be sitting there, on the shelf, but if no assets are ever titled in the trust, what exactly does that document apply to? Not much.

| Tip | A pour-over will can be used to fund a trust after your death, but those assets must now go through probate. Much easier for your heirs if you move the appropriate assets into the trust before your death. |

As you have seen, most assets can be passed by using the proper account registrations, asset titles, and beneficiary designations, so why might you want or need a trust?

Why Have a Trust?

Trusts are good at accomplishing three main objectives:

1. Names someone (a successor trustee) to manage your assets that are in the trust if you are ill, incapacitated, and/or upon your death.

2. Avoids the probate process.

3. Allows you to control how assets are disbursed and used long after you are gone, and when properly structured, can offer creditor protection for heirs.

Here are a few examples of family circumstances which may lead toward a trust as an estate planning solution:

- Minor children

- Children from previous marriages

- A special needs child or relative that you want to provide for

- Future creditor protection for heirs (or to protect assets from a child's spouse)

- Heirs who are not capable of making their own wise financial decisions (such as an adult child with alcohol, drug, or gambling problems)

- Desire to protect a share of your assets upon your death so if your spouse remarries the assets still ultimately pass along to your children or to a beneficiary of your choice

If you have a situation that you think entails the use of a trust, you should seek professional legal advice.

Unfortunately, I have seen many people who were "sold" boiler-plate trusts that don't accomplish their objectives at all.

Properly drafted trusts can make your and your heirs' lives much easier during a difficult time. They can also offer valuable creditor protection for heirs. For example, assume one of your children is going through a lawsuit, and during that time inherits funds. If the funds are given to them outright, creditors can place a claim against those funds. If the funds are passed along in a trust that has the appropriate language in it, your child's inheritance will be safe from those creditors.

You want to be able to understand your trust, and your beneficiaries should understand it too. Take the time to determine what you want to accomplish, and when working with attorneys don't be shy about asking questions about any terms you don't understand.

A/B OR FAMILY/MARITAL TRUST STRUCTURES

Many revocable living trusts have provisions to divide the trust into two halves upon death of the first spouse. One half, referred to as the "A" Trust or Marital trust, is for the surviving spouse's share of the assets. The other half, referred to as the "B" Trust[182], Family Trust, or Bypass Trust, is for the decedent's share of the assets.

This type of A/B Trust structure used to be necessary to reduce potential estate taxes for married couples, but with 2010 tax law changes, for many people it is no longer needed for that particular purpose.

Another reason for this trust structure is to protect assets for the children of the marriage in case the surviving spouse remarries. The idea is that the surviving spouse should use the assets in the A trust first, then, if necessary, can use the income (and maybe principal depending on the terms of the trust) from the B trust, but any remaining assets in the B trust would pass directly to the children.

Second (or Third or Fourth) Marriage

If you are in a second marriage or there are children outside the current marriage, then you are likely going to need to spend extra time structuring your estate plan.

Here are a few options.

---

182 Although morbid, it helps to remember which is which by thinking of the "A" trust as applying to the assets or the spouse above ground, and the "B" trust as applying to the assets for the spouse below ground.

Structure Beneficiary Designations

If your surviving spouse may not need all your assets to continue a comfortable retirement, you may be able to structure your beneficiary designations so that some assets pass directly to your children.

For example, assume you have two children from a previous marriage. You have talked with your current spouse and agreed that some of your IRA will go to your two children. Your beneficiary designation might look like this:

- Spouse: 50%

- Child 1: 25%

- Child 2: 25%

Depending on the account values and ongoing family financial status, these proportions can easily be revisited and changed from time-to-time as needed.

Set Up a Trust

An estate planning attorney can help you establish a trust structure that allows your existing spouse to have use of the assets, but upon their death the remaining principal will pass directly to your children.

One way of doing this is with the A/B trust discussed earlier, where your surviving spouse may use the income from the B trust, but not the principal. The principal will eventually be passed to the children upon the surviving spouse's death.

Another option is a *QTIP* Trust. QTIP stands for qualified terminable interest property. This structure is often used for a home in situations when you want a surviving spouse to have use of the home for their life, but upon their passing, the home would pass to children.

Use Life Insurance

If you want to make sure your children receive something upon your death, one of the simplest solutions is to purchase some form of permanent life insurance.

You can structure this in one of two ways:

1. Purchase a policy that leaves a specific amount to your children and then all other assets pass to your current spouse, or

2. Purchase a policy that pays directly to your current spouse, and all other assets pass directly to your children.

As your spouse can easily inherit IRAs and other assets, I think in most situations the first option has some tax advantages over the second option, but as I don't know you and your situation, I cannot definitively tell you what the right structure for you is.

ESTATE PLANNING GONE BAD

George and Faye were married for many years and had no children in common. Faye had two children from a previous marriage. In her late 50s Faye was diagnosed with pancreatic cancer and had only a few months to live. George and Faye immediately had a trust drawn up as Faye wanted 1/3 of her assets to go to each of her two children and 1/3 to George. When Faye passed, George was upset to discover it didn't work the way they thought. It was at this point that he came into my office.

The problem was nearly all of Faye's assets were in her company retirement plan. Faye had never changed the beneficiary designation to the trust, or to her children. She thought the trust document would take care of it. Unfortunately, the trust document has no control over the retirement account unless you actually complete the paperwork to make the trust the beneficiary[183] of the retirement account. George was the primary beneficiary of the retirement plan accounts, and despite seeking legal assistance, there was no way to alter this after the fact.

---

183 As discussed, Faye could have directly named her two children and her husband on her beneficiary designation so each would receive 1/3 of her account upon her death. No trust would have been needed to accomplish this.

George wants to honor Faye's wishes, and so he plans to gift assets each year to her two children. The challenge is that each time he takes a withdrawal from the retirement account, it will be taxable income on his tax return. In addition, as he gives money to Faye's children he will have to be conscious of the gifting limits.

Other Documents

Typically, essential estate planning documents are described as the will, power of attorney, trust, and living will (or some other form of health care directive).

Will – if you have properly structured your account registrations, property titles, and beneficiary designations, this document will primarily be responsible for your personal belongings. This is the place to specify things that you want to leave to a specific person, such as "gun collection to nephew Sam" or "jewelry to daughter Alice".

Financial Power of Attorney – this type of document allows a designated person to do one or all of the following:

- Manage your assets while you are alive (called a *Durable Power of Attorney* – with this structure this person has full access to your stuff now).

- Manage your assets for a limited time (such as only until Dec. 31, 2015 – perhaps something useful if you are traveling overseas to a remote area), or with a limited scope (such as "may use any assets in XYZ accounts to pay my household bills and expenses"). This is called a *Limited Power of Attorney*.

- Manage your assets only after a triggering event (called a *Springing Durable Power* – which can be triggered by an event you determine, such as your incapacitation as certified by your physician.)

Each financial institution will have its own restrictions on how they recognize the authority granted in a financial power of attorney. I have seen many cases where a financial institution refused to recognize some types of power of attorney documents because they were signed and dated too long ago, or because the institution required additional documentation before they would accept it. The advantages and disadvantages of durable powers of attorney are aptly described in the quote below:

> "Compared to a Living Trust, a Durable Power of Attorney is cheaper and quicker. There is no need, as there is in the case of a living trust, to take the necessary legal steps to transfer your assets; the Durable Power of Attorney covers whatever you list. However, a Living Trust is more certain." – *New Times, New Challenges, Law and Advice of Savvy Seniors and Their Families*, by Kenney F. Hegland and Robert B. Fleming

Health Care Power of Attorney – you should have one of these. It names the person who can make medical decisions for you anytime you are unable to do so for yourself. The person you appoint should have a copy of this document and be able to locate it quickly should it be needed.

Living Will – the intention of a living will is that you can direct, in advance, the type of medical care you would and would not like to receive during a severe illness (usually near the end of your life). One challenge some families encounter: emotional family members may take steps to preserve your life regardless of what you put in writing. Best practice is to have a professionally drafted living will and have honest discussions with your loved ones so they hear your wishes directly from you.

There is something else that I think should be on the essential estate planning documents list; a document that provides a starting place for your heirs. After all, how will they locate your bank accounts, insurance policies, safety deposit box, retirement accounts, etc.?

With more and more people moving to online banking, it can leave heirs facing a scavenger hunt. You can help by giving them a place to start.

This could be a file folder, thumb drive, binder, bookshelf, or drawer where you keep everything. It would contain contact information, account numbers, policy numbers, and other things you think they will need. If you have a good financial advisor, you'll want to provide your heirs with that person's contact name, or better yet, introduce them.

Medicaid Planning

The basics of Medicaid planning is best explained with an example.

Suppose your mom has no long-term care insurance (or has already used up her benefits), but needs care and is spending assets to pay for this care. Is there anything you can do to protect assets? Maybe – this is a special area of law referred to as *elder-care law*.

Sometimes assets can be transferred to an irrevocable trust whereby the grantor of the asset (mom in this case) maintains use of the asset while alive, but has irrevocably assigned the asset to go to someone upon her death. The purpose of this would be to reduce mom's financial assets to the point where she qualified for Medicaid. However, states have a look-back period so if this structure is not set up far enough in advance, the asset can be pulled back into the estate to reimburse the state for medical costs.

When engaging in elder-care planning, be sure to interview attorneys and find someone reputable. I have seen situations where a senior is charged exorbitant legal fees with the only recommendation being that they buy an immediate annuity, which pays a commission, which in some cases is shared with the attorney. I'm not saying an immediate annuity is a bad solution. Sometimes it is the only good solution. I am just saying you need to be cautious.

If someone in your family needs this type of planning, it is best to have an accountant, financial advisor, and attorney work as a team on these structures - and confirm that they do not share in each other's commissions or fees. In addition, be cautious of anyone pressuring you to act quickly without consulting other advisors or family members first.

Summary

Many estate planning objectives can be accomplished by deciding how to register your accounts, title your assets, and structure your beneficiary designations. These titles and designations will supersede what you have in a will or trust, so if you change your will or trust, make sure you review all of these things.

Be wary of one-size-fits-all recommendations, such as "everyone needs a trust" or "no one needs a trust".

If you have a family structure that entails the need for a trust, don't go for a boiler plate option. Interview attorneys, and find one who is going to provide the personal care and attention needed to outline your objectives and provide a solution that will work for you and your beneficiaries.

Index